UNIVERSITY ETHICS

UNIVERSITY ETHICS

How Colleges Can Build and Benefit from a Culture of Ethics

James F. Keenan, SJ

ROWMAN & LITTLEFIELD
Lanham • Boulder • New York • London

Published by Rowman & Littlefield
A wholly owned subsidiary of
The Rowman & Littlefield Publishing Group, Inc.
4501 Forbes Boulevard, Suite 200, Lanham, Maryland 20706
www.rowman.com

Unit A, Whitacre Mews, 26-34 Stannary Street, London SE11 4AB,
United Kingdom

British Library Cataloguing in Publication Information Available

Library of Congress Cataloging-in-Publication Data Available
ISBN 978-1-4422-2372-1 (cloth : alk. paper)
ISBN 978-1-4422-2373-8 (electronic)

♾ ™ The paper used in this publication meets the minimum requirements of
American National Standard for Information Sciences Permanence of Paper
for Printed Library Materials, ANSI/NISO Z39.48-1992.

Printed in the United States of America

For Michael and Cynthia Chovan-Dalton,
with love

CONTENTS

Acknowledgments   vii

1 The Absence of Ethics at American Universities   1
2 Ethics   9
3 How the Literature on the University Is Moving Slowly but
   Surely toward University Ethics   21
4 A First Case for University Ethics: The Adjunct Faculty   37
5 The Cultural Landscape of the University without Ethics   57
6 Cheating   81
7 Undergraduates Acting Badly   97
8 Gender   125
9 Diversity and Race   149
10 Commodification   173
11 A Conclusion: Class, Athletics, and Other University Matters   201

Notes   219
Index   265
About the Author   281

ACKNOWLEDGMENTS

While any reference to colleges or universities comes from material in the public forum, I decided to omit any reference to my university, Boston College, for the simple reason that my familiarity with it is much more intimate. For the sake of avoiding any error between privileged knowledge and the public forum, I thought it better to not mention Boston College, positively or negatively. Here in these acknowledgments I must refer to it, for many here helped me write this book.

First, I want to thank Katherine Dullea, Daniel Cattolica, Tony Gallanis, Maureen McGrath, Sahil Angelo, Christopher Reynolds, and Catherine Larrabee for their fine work as my undergraduate research fellows. Their fellowships were provided by Boston College, which also granted me a semester sabbatical to finish the book. I want to thank Catherine Cornille, Pat Deleeuw, and David Quigley for that.

I want to thank the Jesuits in America House and at Xavier Jesuit Community for their hospitality and encouragement, as well as my Franciscan and Jesuit brothers at Robert's House and in the wider Jesuit community at Boston College. In particular I want to thank Ken Himes, Cathy Kaveny, John Paris, David Hollenbach, Beth Floor, and Nicole Benevenia for being on the look-out for materials for me and to Grant Gallicho, Juliet Schor, Ken Himes, David Gibson, Catherine Larrabee, and Tate Krasner for reading some of the chapters. Above all, my editor, Sarah Stanton, has been simply a wise and faithful mentor for me.

I dedicate this book to my cousin Michael who teaches in an institution of higher education in New Jersey and to his wife Cynthia who works in advancement at a New York City middle school. They are signs of the hope we have in education today.

1

THE ABSENCE OF ETHICS
AT AMERICAN UNIVERSITIES

"Education corruption is universal but the type differs from one region to another."
—Stephen Heyneman[1]

The narratives that help illustrate the lack of professional ethics at American universities occur with greater and greater frequency, though most often we fail to note them as such. Our universities are riddled with ethical compromise, but rarely, even when the press exposes something shameful about a university, do we identify the issue as a lack of ethics.[2]

Consider, for instance, the first three days of 2012. The Sunday front page of the *Boston Globe* carried the story of Harvard University's cancellation of a professor's courses because of his apparently inflammatory claims in the classroom. The article described a university debate about academic freedom and a particular professor's problematic rhetoric, but neither side made any appeal to professional ethics.[3] No questions about a professor's professional ethical responsibilities were raised even though the administration cancelled the professor's course.

Ethics, an academic discipline that routinely arbitrates competing claims, is rarely invoked as a discipline to address university problems, even though the university itself hosts multitudinous courses on ethics whether in the humanities or the professional schools of law, medicine, social work, or nursing.

Just as the *Boston Globe* covered Harvard's story, the *New York Times* ran two articles on the salaries of football coaches at forty universities; in particular, the *Times* focused on the Universities of Alabama and Louisiana who were to be playing on January 9, 2012, in the National Championship.[4] Though the ethical implications of these schools of higher learning using their resources to promote football were in the background of both stories, no one brought the ethical issues about this to the fore. Finally, on the front page of the *Times*'s science section was a disturbing article titled, "How Hard Would It Be for Avian Flu to Spread?" While it was reported that the University of Wisconsin funded a study to make avian flu more transmittable, no mention of ethics was made.[5]

If we put our minds to it, we can remember quite a number of stories about unethical practices at American universities in recent years: for example, the sex abuse case that prompted the firings of the president and the football coach at Penn State, the pepper-spraying of students at the University of California–Davis, and the tragic hazing death of marching band member Robert Champion at Florida A&M University. These are stories that happened at universities and their settings, I believe, are not incidental to the narratives.

We should not think that only American universities have ethically scandalous stories. Universities worldwide have a broad set of ethically problematic narratives that are rarely named as such. Stephen Heyneman argues in "The Corruption of Ethics in Higher Education," that "Education corruption is universal but the type differs from one region to another. In North America the problem appears to be student and faculty plagiarism and cheating on examinations." After referring to other US problems like "classroom improprieties" (a vice that covers a multitude of sins), he notes: "In Vietnam, Cambodia, South Asia, Eastern Europe, and the former Soviet Union, the main problem appears to be corruption for monetary gain—the propensity to seek bribes in exchange for higher grades, accreditation, and entrance to selective programs of study. In sub-Saharan Africa, corruption includes frequent instances of professional misconduct and sexual exploitation in the classroom."[6]

We could, therefore, explore in depth professional ethics and the university in other countries. For instance, the *Chronicle of Higher*

Education provided an in-depth essay on the caste system at universities in India. The story was very disturbing and described how:

> upper-caste students beat up Dalits for no given reason; professors ignore questions from Dalit students in class; upper-caste students, with the complicity of professors, ostracize their Dalit peers or force them out of university housing; and professors compel students to reveal their caste publicly, and then give Dalits lower grades.

The entire report portrays ethically racist and classist activities and practices throughout these universities, but no one names them as such. According to the writer, most Indian universities insist on the innocence of the university.[7]

Similarly the *Journal of Academic Ethics* reports a study of Turkish university faculty done twice, in 2003 and 2008, on their perceptions regarding ethical dilemmas related to instruction, research, and outside employment activities. According to the findings of the study, faculty members believe that there is an increase in the occurrence of unethical instruction, research, and outside employment activities in the academy, but no one identifies the activities as unethical.[8]

Though we could look beyond the United States for analogous problems, for the sake of focus, we will stay with the lack of professional ethics at universities in the United States. After all, there is so much material! For instance, any week we can turn to the *Chronicle of Higher Education* as a veritable scandal sheet on the academy. Thus I can take the most recent issue possible, the weekend of November 22, 2014, as I am finishing the editing of my manuscript. In today's online edition of the *Chronicle,* we find Jeffrey R. Young's blog "Accrediting Agency Raises Questions about Chapel Hill's Compliance," which discusses how the agency has concerns that the University of North Carolina (UNC) "isn't meeting 18 different standards, on issues including integrity and admissions policies."[9] The blogger is following reports on UNC after the initial report of widespread academic fraud at UNC.[10] On the same day, the same blogger reported on the University of Virginia, "UVA Temporarily Suspends Fraternities in Response to Rape Allegations"[11] after the original story broke in *Rolling Stone.*[12] Andy Thomason reports that the University of Colorado will pay one of its philosophy professors $185,000 as part of a settlement regarding claims of relationships with students and the department's alleged "culture of sexism."[13] Finally, Dan Berrett provides an eye-opener titled, "Colleges' Prestige Doesn't Guarantee a Top Flight Learning Experience."[14]

Are these issues sensational but isolated moments across the American academic landscape or is there something more systemic here?

I believe it is systemic. In other forms of professional life, we have long recognized a strong connection between the lack of a professional ethics in a particular institutional setting and the lack of an ethical consciousness in that culture. I believe that the absence of a professional ethics is evidence of and symptomatic of a culture disinterested in ethics. For instance, as we come out of the sexual abuse scandals that have ripped apart the churches, we saw that the disinterest in professional ethical accountability of bishops and priests was sustained by the church's clerical culture that was more attuned to advancement than it was to ethical responsibility and transparency.

A similar culture is part and parcel of the contemporary American university. Simply put, the American university does not hold its employees to professional ethical standards because it has not created a culture of ethical consciousness and accountability at the university, and this is in part both because of the nature of the contemporary university and because it does not believe that it *needs* ethics.

We can certainly acknowledge that at any university, anyone can take a course on business ethics, nursing ethics, legal ethics, medical ethics, or journalistic ethics. Ethics courses in the different professions are easily available. In fact, generally speaking, if one is looking for ethical training in a profession, the courses are found at a university. The one major professional institution about which you cannot find any ethics courses listed among the hundreds available is precisely the university. If you search for a course on university ethics, you will simply not find one.

Professors and their deans recognize the need to teach professional ethics in all the other professions, but they show no real interest in professional ethics for their own profession. I will return to this insight about the lack of work in academic or university ethics, but first, to advance my introductory claims, I want to highlight how broad the spectrum of unethical university conduct actually is. To do this, we will attend briefly to a few cases across the university in development, athletics, and research.

In an effort to generate gifts from graduating seniors, two major universities, Dartmouth College and Cornell University, publicized the names of seniors who did not contribute to their class gift. The shaming of these students effectively led to near perfect support for the university class gift.[15] Remember here, this is not a law or business firm looking for their employees to chip in for a senior partner's retirement gift; these are tuition-paying, residential students at our major universities being coerced into a "gift." While rightly acknowledging the education that they received and any grants or scholarships that they may have won, these students or their parents have paid four years of tuition, housing, and other fees. Publicizing the names of graduating seniors is not only an instance of poor taste, it is an ethical abuse of personal records.

In an essay titled "Faculty Reps Botch Sports-Oversight Role," the *Chronicle* noted that faculty athletic representatives are required to protect the academic integrity of student athletes. Still, the *Chronicle* reported that faculty reps are getting too close to the teams they are supposed to oversee. At the University of Southern California, a faculty athletics representative shared blame as sports agents purportedly transferred more than $100,000 in cash and benefits to two star athletes. A professor at Indiana University–Purdue University Indianapolis improperly and unethically certified the academic eligibility of nearly one hundred players.

By the late 1980s, when college sports in the United States faced a series of high-profile academic abuses, faculty representatives were criticized for not exerting more supervision. A 1989 report by the Knight Commission on Intercollegiate Athletics singled out faculty athletic representatives for ineffective and ethically compromised activities. More than twenty years later, the *Chronicle* reports that many still lack clarity about their role. According to a 2008 report by the Faculty Athletics Representatives Association, nearly 40 percent of its Division I members do not have a formal job description and many say they receive little training. Moreover, half of the faculty representatives were not appointed with the approval of a campus faculty-governance body, but rather by high-level university administrators. Rather than being accountable to faculty constituencies, they are largely indebted to their employers.[16]

Finally, on faculty research, the *Chronicle* posted a report from the National Science Foundation. Two years after President George W. Bush signed into law the America Competes Act (2007), designed to improve US competitiveness in mathematics and science, the National Science Foundation (NSF) announced plans for carrying out a requirement of the law that all NSF grant recipients be trained in the "responsible and ethical conduct" of research. More recently, however, the NSF has relinquished any responsibility for articulating or imposing those standards; it only requires that institutions certify that they have provided ethics training, without any submission of the actual content of the instruction.[17]

There are many other scandals, for example, the student loan subsidies scandal of 2007, the fallout from the Virginia Tech shootings, college drinking, relationships between student housing facilities and university neighbors, plagiarism, grading inflation, athletics and education, sexual harassment, and so on. This survey of brief contemporary scandals helps us to recognize that the entire university suffers in part because professional ethical standards are not constitutive of the commerce of university life and this stems from the university's lack of any serious, conscious engagement with ethics.

My complaint is not simply that faculty have no training in professional ethics, but that few university employees are subject to professional ethical standards, whether those employees are in teaching, development, admissions, athletics, student affairs, security, housekeeping, or any other sector of the university. Most of all, the administrators—in particular, those at the highest level of the university from vice-presidents and the president to the board of trustees—have not been trained in professional university ethics. Small wonder then that they do not promote a culture of ethical consciousness and accountability.

My claim that the university has no evident interest in ethics, a claim that I repeatedly make in this book, cannot be addressed by simply developing a code of conduct for professors, students, coaches, admissions officers, and the rest. Before we ever articulate a professional code of conduct for each community within the university, I think we need to develop a culture of awareness among faculty, staff, administrators, and students that for a university to flourish, it needs to recognize the integral, constitutive role of ethics in the formation of a flourishing community.

I want to be clear about the issue I am trying to engage. I am not really interested per se in the ethics we are teaching. I think that, as a matter of fact, at our professional schools as well as within the humanities areas of our undergraduate programs, we can find a healthy list of courses by faculty on ethics, whether these are courses in philosophy, theology, or religion, whether in nursing, medical, business, law, or engineering schools. These courses, their professors, and their students are alive and well in contemporary higher education.

I am interested less in what the students are learning and the professors are teaching about ethics in all the other professional fields, and more in the fact that none of these courses address university professional life, that none of the professors at the universities teach any course on university ethics, and that, as we will see in Chapter 3, until this book, not one professor has written a book on university ethics.

I am also interested in the whole university life, its entire geography, its daily conduct, and not just the students and the faculty, but also all of the employees and caretakers of the university. Moreover, I am not interested in them primarily as private, singular individuals, but rather as members of a university or college whose mission and identity has been articulated.

To understand the need for ethics for the public life of the entire university, we next consider what professional ethics looks like in other major institutions and then take a look at what other writers have been saying about the university. I then introduce a remarkably neglected issue that needs ethical consideration, the role of the adjunct faculty. Getting a glimpse of that case, I propose that an appreciation of the cultural landscape of the university helps explain the obstacles to professional ethics for the university. With these fundamental insights, we then examine a host of issues that highlights the urgent need for a culture of ethics for our universities today.

2

ETHICS

"Making morals means making community."
—Wayne Meeks[1]

The university has, it seems, an awkward relationship with ethics. It teaches ethics for all professions except its own. At the university, its own faculty instructs future lawyers, physicians, nurses, financial managers, social workers, and others in ethics. University professors implicitly and often explicitly teach these emerging professionals that they *need* ethics for their own professions. The professors' general argument is that ethics is for the good of each of the professions. What they do not teach is that ethics is good for university professionals as well.

In this chapter we focus on ethics, per se. First, we see how ethics function in a profession. In this case, we turn to the medical profession to illustrate what we mean both by *ethics* and by an "underlying culture of ethics that promotes ethical conduct." In the medical profession we find a profession that depends on ethics for its flourishing.

Second, we turn to the profession of ministry. We make this turn because, like the university, the church teaches ethics, and, until very recently, the church has had almost no professional training for its employees or its administrators in the field of church ministry ethics. Our turn to the church is rather important, because not only is it another profession that teaches ethics, it is effectively the *only* other professional institution that dedicates itself to the teaching of ethics. Like the university, however, it has not believed that it needed to practice what it taught.[2]

Finally, having looked at the church, we will be able to identify some of the obstacles the university faces if it is to attempt to develop a culture of ethics in the first place.

ETHICS AND THE MEDICAL PROFESSION

Ethics enters the professions when professionals realize that their practices need some normative guidance for right conduct and right relationships. Professionals turn to ethics because they need ethics precisely as constitutive of their professional identity.

Let us consider, for instance, the question of confidences.[3] In the medical profession, clinicians of all kinds had to "wing it" for decades about whether and to what extent a physician should inform her or his patient about the patient's actual prognosis. Similarly, physicians had to consider the questions about the risks and outcomes of medical procedures but rarely communicated their assessments to their patients. In time, however, just as patients expressed interest in understanding their prognoses, they also wanted to know what therapeutic options they might have. In light of their questions, physicians eventually wanted to rely on something more than their personal intuitions and judgments; they wanted collective wisdom to be engaged.

Physicians subsequently raised questions collectively in their guilds, in their journals, in the letters to the editor of those journals, and in their teaching institutions. In these forums they asked about whether a patient should be informed of the patient's own prognosis particularly when it was uncertain, or, worse, dubious. Other "information" questions were raised from who weighs the risks, suffering, and pain in a particular protocol to whether, when, and in what situations family members, parents, and spouses should be informed.

In time, physicians and ethicists in dialogue proposed ethical norms about informing the patient, that is, they proposed public standards, guidelines, and rules based on professional consensus of what constituted right conduct regarding the communication of information about a patient's health. In time, these proposals were presented at conferences and eventually made their way into journals; later, at grand rounds physicians and ethicists began identifying their value; in time, professional guilds soon articulated more formal procedures for establishing the proposals as norms binding on their members. In time, health care facilities developed and published these norms as policies about informing patients.

Later, matters about patient consent arose and gave the question of informing the patient greater urgency. This was another development in articulating the right norms for conduct within physician–patient relations. Now the matter was not simply informing the patient about possible courses of treatment as well as the attendant risks and probabilities of outcome; rather, now the physician was obliged to obtain the patient's consent. The development in bioethics from whether to inform a patient about his or her prognosis to the obligation to obtain patient consent for a particular course of treatment maps out the development of only one component of the ethical relationship between physicians and their patients.

These developments arose from a reflective and collective culture within the medical community that found in ethics a way of achieving a consensus about right procedures in the care of patients facing challenging health situations. Physicians intentionally cultivated this culture in their teaching schools, their health care centers, and their professional associations so as to engage more robustly the issues at hand.

At the same time, similar developments happened in the professional lives of nurses. They, too, would look at what their responsibilities in reporting information were to the patient and to the physician. They had to wrestle with at times conflicting loyalties between the physician, who may have been withholding information, and the patient whom they knew to be anxious about not knowing the matters at stake. In facing this somewhat frequent situation, nurses eventually moved not only to consider the question of disclosing information, but more importantly the question of to whom their primary loyalty was owed: the physician or the patient.[4] Nursing's professional relationships were shifting as they entertained questions about their ethical responsibilities. As they turned to greater loyalty to the patient, they came to realize that something more active and definable than loyalty was needed and in time they saw that they had an ethical responsibility to be an advocate for their patients.[5] In working out their relationships, they too saw how the different ethical forums that they entered allowed them to grow collectively as professionals.

Similarly administrators in singular health care facilities and in their sponsoring systems needed to understand what their professional responsibilities were. Again, through a variety of contexts, administrators sought to promote a culture of professional ethics. Within that culture, administrators discussed the variety of issues they faced that needed to be addressed collectively. After extensive conversations with a variety of competent stakeholders, these administrators, together with ethicists, developed and articulated the ethical norms that they needed for adjudicating the claims, rights, and responsibilities of their nurses, physicians, and patients and other stakeholders in the health care profession.[6]

In this brief survey we have only attended to ethical developments about information and consent in health care ethics. Hundreds of other issues (e.g., end-of-life issues, beginning-of-life issues, access to health care, research, etc.) arose that needed to be resolved by health care professionals collectively through the different forums of guilds, publications, grand rounds, and institutional policies all using the rubric of ethics and its language of virtues, values, and norms.

Health care professionals and their ethicists entered into dialogue about how to attain consensus about right conduct within these matters. In short, the health care professionals developed not only the norms but the forums, the contexts, and the culture of ethical reflection so as to understand how to find, articulate, and institutionalize right conduct among competing but overlapping relationships.[7]

CHURCH MINISTRY AND ETHICS

One of the first lessons that we learned from the sex abuse scandals that rocked the churches, and in particular the Roman Catholic Church, is that though the churches taught ethics to its faithful parishioners, it neither instructed its administrators nor its clergy and lay ministers in professional ethics. Though it taught ethics, it did not practice them because it did not believe that it needed ethics. It presumed that if it could teach it, it did not need it.

Before the scandals broke, the church had neither stipulated its commitment to ethics nor developed the infrastructure to engage its own ethical accountability, both professionally and communally. Rath-

er, like the academy today, the church had no internal culture of professional ethical accountability. By looking at the church, therefore, we
might understand the university's situation all the better.

During the sex abuse crisis, the absence of a culture of ethics in the
church became crystal clear. Ethics was not only obviously lacking
among the predatory priests, but it was also noticeably absent in the
decision-making by bishops and their counselors as they transferred
such priests, as they failed to notify civil authorities, as they stonewalled
and defamed the reputations of concerned and aggrieved parents, and
as they left children at profound risk.

Ethics were also not evident even after the harm was done. As the
crisis unfolded, innocent priests were not protected; due process was
often breached; financial mismanagement frequently occurred; lay initiatives were treated with scorn, derision, and suspicion; and priests
who protested Episcopal mismanagement became targeted.[8]

Why was ethics so absent? Why did those in clerical or episcopal life
so rarely ask of their decisions and their practices the simple question,
"Is this ethical?" Did they have the language, structure, and practices to
even ask, let alone answer the question, "But is this ethical?"

Unlike many other professions, religious leaders rarely turned to
ethical norms to consider what constitutes right conduct in their field of
leadership and service.

I do not mean by this that religious leaders or their decisions were or
are unethical. Rather, I mean that when religious leaders such as clergy
and bishops exercise routine decision making, they turn to a multitude
of considerations, but articulated ethical norms—their specific values,
virtues, and goods, and the type of critical thinking that estimates the
long-standing social claims that these values, goods, and virtues have on
us—were not and still are not explicitly professionally engaged. In
short, ethical norms, critical ethical reasoning, and attendant ethical
practices, which frequently aid other professionals in law, business,
medicine, counseling, nursing, engineering, and even politics, played a
much less explicit role in ecclesial leadership practices.

This question, "But is it ethical?" is absent in the churches not only
in matters about sexual boundaries, but also in matters about financial
responsibility, personal and social accountability, the claims of confidentiality, the importance of truth telling, due process, consultation,

contracts, fair wages, delations, adequate representation, appeals, conflicts of interests, and so on.

Creating and supporting a culture of professional ethical discourse, mandating ethical training, and requiring ethical accountability ought not to be seen, then, as inimical to the interests of the church or its mission, but rather constitutive of it. And today, as the church continues to emerge from its scandals, it is only beginning to learn that the professional ethics of its ministers and other employees do not inhibit or compromise the mission of the church, but rather support its credibility, its community-building activity, and its teaching and realization of the truth.

Years ago, in a major work, Yale University's Wayne Meeks stated simply "Making morals means making community."[9] This insight runs throughout this book, because promoting the issue of professional ethics does not and will not inhibit or compromise the work of the university. Rather, ethics is constitutive of human flourishing, an insight that Aristotle and Paul tried to teach time and again.

So why was there so little interest in ethics, in promoting a culture of ethics and accountability, and in pursuing ethical professional insight within the leadership practices and lives of church clergy and episcopacy?

The first and more immediate answer is that until very recently seminarians, religious men and women, lay leaders, and bishops were not and frequently are not trained in professional ethics.

Those who study at seminaries, divinity schools, or schools of theology rarely receive the type of ethical training that those at most other professional schools receive. Students admitted to business, medical, nursing, or law schools take ethics courses that address the ethical issues that are relevant to their particular profession. They are taught the responsibilities and rights specific to their profession, whether these deal with matters of representation, confidentiality, client expectations, privileges, promotions, evaluations, conflicts of interest, professional boundaries, and so on. Their ethics courses in their professional schools aim to shape if not the students' internal dispositions, then at least the students' external conduct so as to become acceptable colleagues in their particular professional field. Subsequent to this education, they join professional organizations that establish minimal codes of ethical

conduct for their members. They become part of accountability structures.

Until recently, this type of professional ethical training and accountability was not available at most seminaries, divinity schools, or schools
of theology, even though many students took two, three, or four courses
of Christian ethics.

What were the courses in ethics that they took? These students
studied courses that dealt with the sexual and reproductive lives of the
laity, the social ethics of businesses, and the medical ethics of physicians
and nurses. That is, those in ministry were taught how to teach, govern,
and make morally accountable the members of their congregations with
regard to their sexual, reproductive, and marital lives as well as the
professional lives of those in medicine and business. They were taught
how to teach ethics to others.

Generally speaking, they were not taught by what ethical reasoning,
insights, or norms they should be held morally accountable as ministers,
priests, or bishops. They had no training on the keeping of confidences,
on making assignments, on professional evaluations, on the relevance of
truth-telling, on crisis management, and so on.

Moreover, in the hierarchical structure of some of the denomina-
tions, ministerial and priestly accountability was solely to "the man upstairs." A priest's or bishop's professional accountability was singularly
vertical, but again that man upstairs had had no training in fairness or
any other professional ethical standard. Thus a priest basically has been
responsible to singularly accommodate the bishop's own expectations
and judgments.

Furthermore, while we saw that physicians, nurses, and health care
administrators sought collectively to promote a culture of corporate
wisdom about right conduct within professional relationships, most
clergy never had the experience of collectively discerning what their
responsibilities or relationships to one another or to others were. Nor
did they have anything representing professional associations. While
nurses and physicians sought collective forums for practical wisdom
about their responsibilities, clergy did not.

Similarly, most bishops had little training in ethical responsibilities.
In fact, like the clergy they did not think of meeting with other bishops
or seeking their counsel or looking to exercise collective judgment.
They did meet on committees and have the structure of the national

episcopal conference but even during the crisis itself, bishops sought to control the damages without bothering to initiate any need for a corporate culture of ethical reflection.

Quite apart from the absence of any ethical standards guiding the bishop's evaluation of his priests and religious and lay ministers, there do not seem to be any specific normative standards to guide the bishop himself in his assessment of his diocesan personnel or of his own actions.

There was and remains very little horizontal accountability in this very clerical world. The priest is not accountable to fellow priests; the pastor is not accountable to fellow pastors. There is no accountability to lay leaders, even parish council presidents, unless the pastor freely chooses to do so. In the absence of even the most minimal horizontal accountability, this so-called clericalism is simply responsive vertically to the man upstairs.[10] In such an insular environment, there is no warrant or interest in a culture of professional ethical accountability.

But just as the priests were not trained in any appreciation for collective moral assessment and ethical reflection, similarly those advanced to the episcopacy were never introduced to any other fellowship on the grounds of searching for right guidelines for conduct. Without any horizontal responsibilities, clerical and episcopal accountability has been and remains singularly vertical and unidirectional.

We can think that if the nursing profession never collectively met, then their accountability would have remained what it was, singularly vertical, in obedience to the physician. Had they not sought corporately to deliberate about their ethical responsibilities, they might never have discovered their accountability to one another and to their patients.

As we close these reflections on the church, we would be negligent if we did not note that during the crisis in the Catholic Church, groups of the laity began meeting and forming collectives that sought to corporately reflect on the state of the church, on moral accountability, and on ethical responsibilities. Rightly, they called themselves "Voice of the Faithful."[11] They began to reflectively discern, with canon lawyers, theologians, and ethicists, what right conduct and right relationships were. Many bishops explicitly thwarted the efforts of these lay people and clergy acquiesced to episcopal demands to marginalize the movement, but these lay leaders managed to bring their efforts from local parish forums to regional and diocesan levels to finally national affiliation.[12] Women in particular exercised leadership in looking for these reforms.[13]

At the same time some clergy tried to prompt their fellow priests into a more collective model of trust, reflection, and ethical account-ability.[14] Other priests imitated "Voice of the Faithful" and formed forums in their own dioceses that were attempts to find collective wis-dom in the midst of the crisis, but most of these federations were never sustained.[15]

OBSTACLES TO FORMING A CULTURE OF PROFESSIONAL ETHICS IN THE ACADEMY

We can learn much from the church's handling of the sexual abuse crisis that highlights the absence of a culture of ethics from a profes-sion. Unfortunately, there are great similarities between the church and the academy and their authoritative structures. Like those in the cleri-cal world, we in the academy teach ethics that bear on the lives of other professionals but not on our own professional lives. No one studies ethics for the academy; no one takes or offers courses on university ethics.

None of us nor our colleagues throughout the academy are really trained to be ethical in the standards we use for grading papers, for seeing students, for maintaining office hours, or for evaluating col-leagues or prospective hires. We have not been taught anything about professional confidentiality, boundaries with our students, writing eval-uative letters for or about others, or about keeping our contracts. While we are attuned to a variety of issues on campus, we have not addressed the ethics about the facts that our salaries are disproportionate or that tenure decisions sometimes lack objectivity. We do not have profession-al ethical questions about our university investments, budgets, or boards of trustees, nor do we review adequately fellow faculty after tenure or after being given endowed chairs. Matters like sustainability on campuses, faculty or staff unions, university relations with neighbors, students' rights, sexual health issues, boards of trustees' terms of office, conflict of interest laws, workers' benefits, immigration issues, racial tensions, the dorm life of students, the overemphasis on research and the failure to reward good teaching, or the harm of classism experienced by many students unable to keep up with the costs of education might occasionally garner an individual faculty member's attention, but for the most part we leave that to academic administrators, who, like the faculty, have no training in ethics.

Like the clergy, our accountability is fundamentally vertical, to our chairs and deans, but not to one another, certainly not to our students, not to the university community, nor to stipulated community standards. We should read that sentence again. Like the clergy, our accountability is fundamentally vertical, to our chairs and deans, but not to one another, certainly not to our students, not to the university community, nor to stipulated community standards. Faculty have few structures of horizontal accountability. Instead, like the clergy, we mind our own business for the most part, and make few claims and lay fewer expectations on one another.

Our administrators are like church administrators. They are rarely professionally trained as administrators and they have, generally speaking, no more training in the ethics of academic administration than those who are answerable to them. Rather many if not most academic administrators come from the faculty and often return to the faculty.

To conclude this chapter on ethics, I offer one compelling example: the cataloguing of books on professional ethics in university libraries. Here I offer what I found at my own university library.

We have over four hundred thousand books stacked in our library. There each book is assigned a subject heading. Under the subject "medical ethics," we have 1,321 books; under "business ethics," 599 books; under "nursing ethics," 234 books; under "legal ethics," 129 books; under "clergy ethics," 25 relatively new books; and, under "academic ethics," 5 brand new books. Moreover, these academic ethics books are only about the conduct of professors in their classrooms and their offices. There is no book on university ethics, that is, no book on the appropriate ethical standards across the entire university.

This lack of books on academic and university ethics is alarming inasmuch as academics, more than business people, nurses, doctors, and lawyers, develop their careers precisely by writing books! Our métier and promotional mantra is "publish or perish." While we publish books on professional ethics in other fields, we apparently have very little interest in the field of professional academic ethics. Concomitantly, just as we do not write books on the topic, we do not teach the courses either. But then, none of us seem to be aware of this.

3

HOW THE LITERATURE ON THE UNIVERSITY IS MOVING SLOWLY BUT SURELY TOWARD UNIVERSITY ETHICS

"The academic profession has traditionally enjoyed a high degree of autonomy, particularly in the classroom and in research. While most academics are only dimly aware of it, the move toward accountability affects their professional lives. This trend will intensify, not only due to fiscal constraints, but also because public institutions have come under greater scrutiny."
—Philip G. Altbach[1]

While this is the first book on university ethics that I know of, there are a variety of works about the university that are related to the question I pose, though they are primarily interested in other matters. My question simply asks whether the university as an institution is willing to develop the context, climate, and structures to promote a culture of ethics for its members' personal and corporate conduct. Is the university capable of following other institutions like medicine, law, and business in providing the incentives, forums, and guidance so as to tap into the wisdom of its members as they collectively navigate the virtues, values, and norms that they would need to be professionally, ethically responsible, accountable, and transparent in their university work?

I believe that there are four different but related categories of literature that help us today to understand the situation of the contemporary university. Though they are arranged according to their different aims and audiences, we should be able to see that they are moving in a current that inevitably leads the university to face the need for ethics. Therefore, we ought to recognize that there is a historical development implicit in this review: each category builds on the platform the previous one created.

The four categories are the classic philosophical defenses about the nature of the university; in-depth (often historical) studies about the development of the contemporary university; the public-intellectual critiques on the contemporary university; and ethical critiques on some facet of academic life, whether faculty, student, or athletics. I conclude with the work of one figure who has in many ways been the pathfinder for this project, Steven Cahn.

WHY DO WE NEED THE UNIVERSITY?

The first category comprises those classic treatises on the philosophical foundations of the university. Effectively they answer the question, "Why do we need (or have) the university?" These are usually written by university presidents and effectively convey how the author envisions the university.

The classic is John Henry Newman's *The Idea of a University*. Newman wrote it in 1854 two years before he became first rector of the newly founded Catholic University of Ireland (today, University College Dublin). Newman begins his work with these words:

> The view taken of a University in these Discourses is the following:—
> That it is a place of *teaching* universal *knowledge*. This implies that
> its object is, on the one hand, intellectual, not moral; and on the
> other, that it is the diffusion and extension of knowledge and not its
> advancement. If its object were scientific and philosophical discov-
> ery, I do not see why a University should have students; if religious
> training, I do not see how it can be a seat of literature and science.[2]

Interestingly, Newman's practical administrative capabilities were less successful than the book; he resigned his office after only four years. Still, the legacy of his work remains and were he to visit the university today, with its emphasis on faculty research, he would probably question whether it adequately serves the student. He might even wonder why the research university admits undergraduate students.

Others have taken their hand at similar projects. While serving as President of Harvard University from 1971 through 1991, Derek Bok became fairly prolific at describing the nature, purpose, and contemporary challenges of the university, covering a wide array of foundational issues related to the identity of an American university. His first book on the topic, *Beyond the Ivory Tower: Social Responsibilities of the Modern University* (1984), would later be followed by other challenging works, most notably *Universities in the Marketplace: The Commercialization of Higher Education* (2004) and *Our Underachieving Colleges: A Candid Look at How Much Students Learn and Why They Should Be Learning More* (2007). Most recently he has offered a credible but very ambitious work, *Higher Education in America* (2013).[3]

Occasionally presidents are more interested in dialogue than in their own treatises. The late President of Notre Dame University, Theodore M. Hesburgh, wrote a position paper on the Catholic university and invited thirty members of his faculty to contribute to a volume he edited called *The Challenge and Promise of a Catholic University*.[4]

As we will see, these foundational works in many ways provide some of the background for understanding why we need professional ethics at the university today. Moreover, many seem that they would be sympathetic to our interest in ethics. For example, in Bok's most recent work, we find his concern about the actual ethical training of various professional disciplines and the lack of ethical conduct among graduates of American universities as well.

Echoing these treatises, one could say, as Laurence R. Veysey did in *The Emergence of the American University,* that the university originated as "a remedy for the important problems which the society faced." Veysey's claim might be a reason for its genesis, but then again we will inevitably see other reasons as well. Nonetheless, one thing is certain: if a university president attempts to articulate the goal of her or his university, invariably senior faculty will take the reasons to task. One such instance is the conflict between what Harvard University President Charles Eliot thought his university offered the university student and what William James thought it offered. James certainly raised doubts about the malleability of the Harvard undergraduate to be formed according to Eliot's idea of virtue, but his most intrepid stance was his critique of the doctoral degree.[5]

In 1903, William James wrote "The Ph.D. Octopus" in which he contends that the doctorate exerts an illusory stranglehold on the American imagination. He writes, "[I]n the minds of Presidents and Trustees the Ph.D. degree is in point of fact already looked upon as a mere advertising resource, a manner of throwing dust in the Public's eyes." Later he remarks,

> Will any one pretend for a moment that the doctor's degree is a guarantee that its possessor will be successful as a teacher? Notoriously his moral, social and personal characteristics may utterly disqualify him for success in the classroom; and of these characteristics his doctor's examination is unable to take any account whatever. Certain bare human beings will always be better candidates for a given place than all the doctor-applicants on hand.[6]

While James's critique of the doctorate continues to entertain many, more than one hundred years later, it highlights that the university occasionally promotes debate about its way of proceeding. His doubts lead to our question: "How does the university proceed?"

HOW DID WE GET THIS WAY? HISTORY BOOKS

The second category contains measured works that give an account of our genesis: how we came to be where we are.

In 1962, Frederick Rudolph wrote *The American College and University: A History* and explained the question for his book: "How and why and with what consequences have the American colleges and universities developed as they have?"[7] Looking back fifty years, this work is remarkably prescient in naming some of the key concerns for the university then and today: its finances, its admission of women, and even its decision to play football. As a history, it provides an important narrative dealing with perennial questions that face each and every university from one generation to the next.

If the first category gave us general foundational background, these books give us detail: Why was football taken up? How did student affairs develop? How did the university first face matters of gender? Knowing the history means that we can learn from it, though not be confined to it. Still, history is not without interpretation and therefore historians do not only report what happened or how we got where we are, but occasionally contend against the claims of earlier historians.

John Thelin, who wrote a tribute to Rudolph in "Rudolph Rediscovered," later wrote his own *A History of American Higher Education*.[8] Thelin's story echoes many of Rudolph's concerns about financing, sports, and gender.

Other histories of education can be much more specific. A rather noteworthy one, Helen Lefkowitz Horowitz's *Campus Life: Undergraduate Cultures from the End of the Eighteenth Century to the Present* tells, among other alarming accounts, some stories of violence on college campuses that are unimaginable today, for instance, the killing of tutors, bombings, rioting, and so on. In describing American college life from 1830 to the end of the nineteenth century, Horowitz simply writes, "This male world was violent."[9] Certainly these details from history should help us understand why today the university still encounters a rather privileged male hooliganism, an unfortunately long-lasting trait of the American university.

One historical concern is not simply about behavior but also about the university's own engagement of religious and moral formation. Veysey in *The Emergence of the American University* attempted to explain that after the Civil War, the American university began to entertain a variety of philosophical tracts that defined specific trajectories of purpose for the university and that eventually led, by the turn of the century, to the abandonment of religious and moral formation of the student as a university purpose. By the twentieth century, a more secular vision of education became institutionalized.[10]

Julie Reuben's *The Making of the Modern University: Intellectual Transformation and the Marginalization of Morality* stands as a worthy alternative to Veysey.[11] She helps us understand how we came to the insight that the contemporary university is dedicated to free inquiry and the advancement of knowledge, though the earliest conceptions of the American university were deeply rooted in matters of moral and religious education. Reuben looks at nineteenth-century reformers to see how they pursued an agenda that promoted a "value-neutral" scientific standard of truth that inevitably was incompatible with the aims of value-based religious and moral education. But her explanation was not that there was a lack of interest or effort.

According to Reuben, the reformers wanted modern notions of truth to coalesce with religious and moral formation. Their attempts failed. As she writes, "University reformers tried to modernize religion to make it compatible with their conception of science. Religion disappeared from the university because these efforts failed, not because university education neglected religion."[12]

While the stories of history do not lead us to remain stuck in the decisions that our predecessors made, they shed light on the fruitlessness of pursuing some leads among others. Knowing history keeps us, in part, from repeating the same mistakes yet again.

Reuben helps us to see that our present situation is not necessarily good news. At the end of her study, she invites us to reconsider history if only to construct a better future. She concludes her astute study with these challenging considerations.

> Scholars hoped that the distinction between fact and value would lead to more reliable knowledge as measured by general agreement. The subsequent history of academic disciplines in the twentieth century indicates that this hope was illusory. We should then reevaluate whether agreement is the proper standard by which to identify "truth." If universities can learn to tolerate more conflict, we might be able to define cognitive standards by which we can address moral questions. Since it has proved impossible to completely separate fact and value, we should begin to explore ways to reintegrate them.[13]

As inviting and important as Reuben's closing words are, however, her concerns are more narrow than ours. She is concerned with the educational and moral formation of our students as integral to the work of the university.

I am not looking at the university as a historian of education. My competency is in ethics, not in the history or philosophy of education, per se. I am not primarily asking about what we should do with our students; I am more concerned with the institution first.

As an ethicist, I am concerned with the corporate identity and structure of the university. I believe that those structures, its purpose, and its culture affect not only the students but also the faculty, the administration, the staff, the fundraisers and boards, the coaches and the adjuncts, and of course, the alumni and the communities in which the university finds itself.

I certainly believe that if we have failed the student at the university, then we have probably failed all others there as well. So the concern we have with the complex teaching mission that Veysey and Reuben describe strikes me as a pretty firm indicator that we "have a problem here," as the saying goes. That being said, I am not addressing only the question of how we should reenter the moral formation question into the students' curriculum. I am more interested in a prior question about the relationship between the university itself and ethics: does it embrace ethics because it itself needs ethics?

In fact, I believe that the questions that Reuben and Veysey raise cannot be effectively answered until we look at the actual structure and culture of the university to ask whether ethics is constitutive of the nature of the university in the first place. If it isn't, and I do not think it is, we cannot possibly ask our students to see why our teaching ethics for their personal appropriation and development is a credible act.

I want to return to an insight I shared with you in the first chapter. I believe that my attentiveness to this question arises in part from my experience as a priest living through the revelations of sexual abuse within the Catholic church in Boston. I did not think that the sexual abuse crisis was primarily about predatory priests, or even about unaccountable bishops and their minions. I thought it was more about a basic disinterest in ethics in the ordinary commerce of church life from rectories and parish houses to episcopal chanceries and diocesan facilities.

From the scandal, we learned that we were mistaken in our unexamined presupposition about the church being ethical. The absence of a culture of ethics became apparent when we found no ethical accountability structures that considered or reviewed an array of misguided and unethical decisions that affected children, parents, families, parishes, local communities, and many others.

We do not simply presume that other institutions are ethical; other institutions are routinely scrutinized as to whether they are ethical or not. We want to be sure that other institutions are acting ethically. Whether they are hospitals and other health care centers or law firms and houses of government, both local and national, we have set expectations regarding ethics and we check to be sure that those standards are observed. We believe that other institutions should be monitored.

We are less inclined to monitor the university. Questions about ethics in the university are rather rare. As it once was with the church, the university is still today presumed to be ethical because it teaches ethics. In fact, as we will see in this book, in most instances when university personnel do something incredibly wrong, identifying that activity as unethical rarely occurs. Why is that? Why don't we identify unethical activity by university personnel as unethical?

I believe we simply presume that university employees would do the ethical thing because, after all, they are competent to be at a university. If they are smart enough to be at a university, certainly they must know right from wrong.

For example, an interesting article in the *New York Times* examined the resistance of so many to the idea that Amy Bishop was unjustified in using a nine-millimeter handgun to shoot fellow faculty members in the biology department at the University of Alabama. Even after three were killed and three others were wounded, the *Times* wanted to know why so many people presumed that convicted murderer Amy Bishop must have had a legitimate grievance to murder the faculty members who denied her tenure.

One person interviewed gave his response. A professor of medical ethics at the University of Pennsylvania, Jonathan Moreno, thought that these presuppositions have to do with a long tradition that goes back to Plato: "The idea . . . is that someone who is very intelligent is assumed to be 'morally wise.' And that makes it hard to reconcile the actions of Amy Bishop, with her Harvard Ph.D., her mantle of scientific brilliance. . . . There's a common-folk psychology," Dr. Moreno added. "If you are that smart, you know the difference between right and wrong. . . . In cases like hers that contradict the framework, we look for excuses."[14]

ISN'T IT TIME TO REFORM THE UNIVERSITY? PUBLIC INTELLECTUAL BOOKS

The third category is about the public intellectual's critiques of the contemporary university. We saw previously Derek Bok's concerns about the university's mission and the commercialization of its identity. We consider these issues in Chapter 10, "Commodification." But here we look at public intellectuals who critique the academy. These authors follow a particular format: they usually consider the state of the university, name certain areas that need reform, offer some examples of colleges and universities that have what are commonly known as "best practices," and present a list of relevant guidelines for reform.

In *Higher Education? How Colleges Are Wasting Our Money and Failing Our Kids: What We Can Do about It*, Andrew Hacker, who writes regularly for the *New York Review of Books*, and Claudia Dreifus, who writes for the *New York Times*, introduce three compelling contemporary challenges to the university: the teaching versus research role of the professor, the agenda of the administrators, and the plight of adjuncts. Through a variety of anecdotes, they effectively give us a glimpse of a set of university trajectories that have to be rerouted. At the end they provide a list of schools that seem to have some facet of worthiness in something they do; they also provide a coda of reform guidelines: educate all, do away with tenure, stop depending on loans, watch presidential salaries, and so on. It basically is a diatribe against the present state of the American university.[15]

Another author, Mark C. Taylor, proposes *A Bold Plan for Reforming Our Colleges and Universities*. Taylor offers four projects: end tenure, restructure departments to encourage greater cooperation among existing disciplines, emphasize teaching rather than increasingly rarefied research, and bring teaching into new domains using emergent online networks to connect students worldwide.[16]

Neither manifesto invokes any ethical context or standards, but they do urge the reader to understand that the time to reform the university is now.

Finally Andrew Delbanco writes *College: What It Was, Is and Should Be*. This book looks again at the student and what the intentions of the college ought to be. He suggests five qualities germane to the type of educational formation that students should receive: a critical view of the present, an ability to recognize connections, an appreciation of the world, an ability to imagine beyond one's context, and a sense of ethical responsibility. His concern for the formation of a student's character is in evidence, and, much like Veysey and Reuben, this public intellectual looks at reform through the historical genesis of the educational formation of the student.[17]

Above all, Delbanco is interested in promoting the influence of a well-taught liberal arts education for the student and by extension for society, but he sees two daunting challenges, one from within the university and the other from without. First, the university itself has made a preferential option for the research university that gives less recognition and financial support for teaching excellence. Second, the growing cost of education and the lack of adequate available funding make access to such well-taught liberal arts courses limited to a student's ability to pay. In a fairly compelling review, Anthony Grafton acknowledges that Delbanco successfully delivers on two-thirds of his book's subtitle: Delbanco tells us what college was and is, but not what it should be.[18]

None of these authors, however, talk about the university as, or as needing to be, an ethical institution. They do believe that the university today needs to be reformed; they proffer different remedies and different principles for that reform. My work then is analogous to theirs: I, too, believe there is need for urgent reform, but mine is by way of promoting the constitutive role of ethics in the contemporary university.

DON'T WE NEED TO LOOK AT ETHICS IN THIS OR THAT DEPARTMENT? BOOKS

In my years of researching this project, I have yet to find a book or essay that addresses the need for ethics at the university and does not compartmentalize and subsequently focus on one particular need. Inevitably these books address cheating students, overly ambitious coaches, foolish administrators, or self-protecting faculty. Rather than asking whether the university is a social structure that promotes ethics, these authors investigate a particular type of university member (faculty, administrator, coach, student, etc.) or a particular department.

These works merit our attention, for they give us hope that the field of university professional ethics is struggling to emerge. Rather than descend into every particular text or topic, to highlight these contributions, we will focus on the works concerning two members of the university community: academic administrators and faculty.

The editors of *The Ethical Challenges of Academic Administration* introduce their collection noting that it is groundbreaking and is "intended as a first word, not the final word on the subject. This is the case," they write, "in part, because the practical activity of academic administration has not been the subject of much sustained ethical reflection."[19]

Inasmuch as many academic administrators are first academic faculty, the authors claim that there is no profession of academic administrators. As a result, they conclude their introduction with two remarkable questions: What prepares a faculty member for the ethical challenges that come with these career changes? What are the sorts of ethical challenges one is likely to face?

The answer to the first question, they write, "seems to be that there is no special preparation. The answer to the second question is typically learned the hard way, by finding oneself entangled in ethical problems, often taken by surprise. This seems to be so whether we are talking about chairs, deans, vice-presidents, or even presidents."[20]

One essay, "On the Dark Side: Lessons Learned as Interim Dean," captures the experience of an interim dean. The author, Donna Werner writes:

> An interim dean will learn the sad fact that there are faculty members who are not as interested in student learning as they are in their own personal commitments. These faculty members may be consistently late to class, or refuse to make any contribution in terms of service to the department. They may fail to keep current in their disciplines, or neglect to update their course materials. Even worse they may have inappropriate relationships with their students or otherwise violate student rights.[21]

In another essay, Randall Curren enunciates the cardinal virtues of academic administration: the commitment to the good of the institution, good administrative judgment, and conscientiousness in discharging those duties. In light of these virtues, he names the corresponding vices or kinds of failure of integrity in academic administration: failures in personal integrity in carrying out the duties of one's office, abuses and misuses of the powers of one's office, and failures to protect and promote the integrity of the institution.[22]

Turning to faculty, in *Crisis on Campus: Confronting Academic Misconduct*, Wilfried Decoo takes a case of plagiarism in a dissertation and completely unfolds the case: detection, analysis, assessment, reporting and handling, and prevention.[23] It is a fine treatment of a frequent infraction by students and faculty, though rarely reported. It highlights one simple case that academic administrators often face. We return to Decoo in the next chapter on cheating.

Neil Hamilton writes *Academic Ethics: Problems and Materials on Professional Conduct and Shared Governance* to prompt faculty organizations to develop professional codes of ethics, noting that "the only organization attempting to define a code of ethics that cuts across the disciplines is the American Association of University Professors."[24] His work is concerned with ethical claims within the context of academic freedom.

Essays on the topic tend to emerge at a moment when a writer as a faculty member gets a view of ethics and the academy and sees an especially problematic ethical wilderness within the university. For instance, the philosopher John Kekes writes a compelling essay in *The Monist* called "Academic Corruption," in which he reflects on a variety of matters in which practices that are not terribly truthful undermine fundamental claims that the university proposes to uphold.[25]

Thirty years ago, another philosopher, Michael Scriven lamented, "Professorial ethics has for too long been part of the invisible environment of the academy."[26] In a relatively recent essay, Jacqueline Klein echoed a similar sentiment in "A Collegiate Dilemma: The Lack of Formal Training in Ethics for Professors," in which she writes, "Despite the importance of ethical decisions in teaching, ethics is a difficult area for college instructors to gain knowledge of since resources about ethics are not readily visible." Furthermore, she adds, "when ethics are considered in higher education institutions, they are examined in only negative terms."[27] Finally, Candace De Russy has raised occasional concerns about the lack of ethics among professors.[28]

Elsewhere, Philip G. Altbach forecasts the professoriate in the twenty-first century and sees greater accountability on the horizon, even though university members themselves are not even aware of it. He writes: "The academic profession has traditionally enjoyed a high degree of autonomy, particularly in the classroom and in research. While most academics are only dimly aware of it, the move toward accountability affects their professional lives. This trend will intensify, not only due to fiscal constraints, but also because public institutions have come under greater scrutiny."[29]

Finally, there is the *Journal of Academic Ethics,* a biannual, which casts the net very broadly, with a particular inclination to educational and sociological studies. Started in 2003, in its inaugural issues it offered to "provide a venue for dialogue for ethical issues facing the university in the 21st century."[30] The first issue raised matters from academic freedom to tenure and faculty strikes. Since then, the journal has published articles on ethics and grade inflation, the modes of conducting human research, monitoring academic journals for unethical practices, and similar issues. A recent issue of the journal published an essay that studies what approaches to ethics have more impact on students in terms of dissuading them from cheating.[31]

These writings then focus significantly on one silo or area of life on the university campus. For the most part, they focus on the academic, that is, faculty and administrators. In that light they are studies in academic ethics. They do not move beyond the silo of tenure-line faculty or the silo of administrators. For instance, neither consider the plight of adjunct faculty, in part because they do not see them as colleagues. The books by public intellectuals do raise the challenges of the adjunct faculty because their tirade is against the university as it is today. But these more polished academic works really stay close to the faculty, to their classrooms and their offices, and never really ask the question: If these spaces have unaddressed ethical issues, what about the silos of student affairs, athletics, or development? And what about issues that cut across the university and are not limited to the faculty terrain, issues like profound gender inequity, the classist structure of the university, the unsustainable tuition-driven university, or the whiteness of the American university? These are not usually found in academic ethics.

CONCLUSION: FROM ACADEMIC ETHICS TO UNIVERSITY ETHICS

In my research, one figure alone established academic ethics as an agenda to be pursued. Stephen Cahn's groundbreaking work, originally published in 1986, has been reedited for its twenty-fifth anniversary. In *Saints and Scamps: Ethics in the Academy,* Cahn considers teaching, including the art of instruction, examinations, grades, and evaluating teaching; the morality of scholarship and departmental obligations; per-

sonnel decisions, such as faculty appointments, tenure, voting procedures, and faculty dismissals; and graduate education. It highlights how
many ethical issues face university professors. [32]

Cahn goes beyond the professoriate to involve other university personnel in his Appendixes. There he mentions graduate students, administrators, and university policies regarding affirmative action. It is the
only book that I know on ethics and the academy that goes beyond one
group of university members, the faculty.

He has also edited two excellent collections that address a variety of
ethical issues university wide. Though he never makes the case that the
university lacks a culture of ethics, he presumes that the university has a
host of ethical challenges and provides effectively two volumes of edited
essays on several topics. In 1992, in *Morality, Responsibility, and the
University: Studies in Academic Ethics,* Cahn focuses mostly on professors' rights and responsibilities, from academic freedom and sexual harassment to appointments and tenure, though he introduces a few other
issues related to students (parietal) and administrators (business schools
and partnerships). [33] In *Moral Problems in Higher Education,* Cahn
again edits a collection of essays on a variety of topics from truth telling
in writing letters of recommendation to intercollegiate athletics. [34]

In *Moral Problems,* he tells us that in the early 1990s, he arranged
with Rowman & Littlefield to publish a series, *Issues in Academic Ethics.* The series ran from 1994 to 2006, with fifteen contributions ranging
from tenure, free speech, and sexual harassment to questions about
sports, development, unions, and college presidencies. As series editor,
he easily defined the field of academic ethics.

In the light of this substantive legacy, I believe that my book builds
on Cahn's and others' contributions. Just as Cahn went beyond the
faculty to a few related university issues, I believe that we should go
beyond academic ethics to collegiate and university ethics, because the
only way we can address academic ethics adequately and comprehensively is if we attend to university ethics first.

We need to be more interested in the broader area of university
ethics than in academic ethics. While many articles on academic ethics
and students written by professors usually focus on cheating, grade
inflation, or sexual harassment, many matters of student conduct that
affect student life today do not occur in the classroom. Questions of
hooliganism, racism, classism, violence, and drunkenness, to say noth-

ing of town/gown issues remain problems for the university police and student affairs, but rarely are engaged by faculty, staff, or other stakeholders at the university. In a similar way, matters of class, gender, and race are not adequately addressed by academic ethics because they are not primarily academic issues, but university-wide matters. In point of fact, these issues on campus are rarely brought into the classroom anyway.

For instance, we see time and again troubling studies about how women fare at the university. These are not questions about women solely in the classroom, but also about women in university sports, housing, and social settings, as well as whether women exercise leadership roles at universities within their faculties, management, senior administration, and trustees. Thus in this book, rather than stay in the tight network of academic (philosophical) ethics, I am interested in the ethics found across the university and promoted by the university.

Moreover, I think of the contemporary university as connected silos or fiefdoms. I address this phenomenon later, but suffice it to say that these structures keep the university fragmented when there is no underlying structure or foundation that relates one fiefdom or silo to another. For this reason, I continually ask whether institutionally a culture of ethics underlies and fortifies a university and its multitudinous constituents.

I am asking a question that I believe is broader and more fundamental than Cahn's significant agenda. In fact, as I said, I intend to build mine on his.

I also think that this book could offer a contribution to all the efforts that I have herein acknowledged. To the apologiae for universities, I hope this book will make those apologiae more credible. To the historical accounts, this work proposes a more inclusive and fundamental approach for investigating ways of promoting the moral formation of the student. To the public intellectuals, this work outlines a more focused, yet also comprehensive standard based on ethics that future critiques could employ. To the ethicists, this work provides a social foundation for their contributions.

4

A FIRST CASE FOR UNIVERSITY ETHICS: THE ADJUNCT FACULTY

"The army of part-time professors teaching at the region's colleges are merely working stiffs at the bottom of an enormous and lucrative enterprise."
—Lisa Liberty Becker[1]

In this chapter we look at the first group of persons for whom ethical questions about the university need to be asked: the adjunct faculty. It is worth remembering that in books on academic ethics, matters about adjunct faculty are rarely raised. Those books are aimed at the tasks of the academic: her or his classroom and office responsibilities.

Stephen Cahn, the veritable trailblazer of academic ethics, makes little reference to them in his own book, *Saints and Scamps*, where he focuses on teaching, scholarship, and personnel decisions. In even the last section on personnel decisions, he focuses on questions of fairness, honesty, and transparency regarding interviewing, receiving, evaluating, promoting, and tenuring faculty. Adjunct or contingent faculty are really not tenure faculty's business, or so the culture has us believe.

In Cahn's edited books, *Morality, Responsibility and the University* and *Moral Problems in Higher Education*, adjunct faculty do not appear either. There are essays on hiring, on affirmative action, and on the experience of faculty, but again the presupposition is tenured or tenure-track faculty. The academic ethics issues are about academic freedom, tenure, research, office responsibilities, committee work, letters of recommendation, and relations and responsibilities with students; adjunct or contingent faculty do not appear in studies in academic ethics. Nonetheless, in his later collection we can see how academic ethics begins to look beyond the professor's classroom or office.

It is typical of Cahn's genius that he deepens, develops, and expands his enquiry. He has, for instance, essays on university policies like admissions and merit- versus need-based scholarships, the neutrality of a university, and even athletics. But still, interestingly, fellow faculty, albeit adjunct or contingent, are not on Cahn's horizons of academic ethics.

In fact, several of the populations we consider in this book are not in those or other works on academic ethics. For instance, in academic ethics, staff, women, and hooligans are no more mentioned than adjunct or contingent faculty. Academic ethical challenges tend to be more about both debatable issues directly affecting the professors' profession (tenure, academic freedom, affirmative action) as well as faculties' responsibilities (teaching, researching, serving, promoting) rather than persons and relationships. The only relationships that academic ethics occasionally raises are between faculty and students, which includes everything from favoritism to dating to sexual harassment.

By starting with adjunct faculty, we lay a new groundwork that gives us access to ethical issues often overlooked and not considered "material" for academics. By looking at this population, and the others, we can see the context and the predicaments of these members of the so-called university community.

Yet looking at adjunct faculty is not easy for one basic reason: They are, in their university employment, basically and constitutively ignored. As we will see, they understand themselves as outsiders, as not being colleagues to faculty, but not because they do not want to be colleagues. They have no permanency, few benefits, often no office or even a mailbox, and certainly few relationships with "fellow" tenured or tenure-track faculty. We will see their own narratives about their experience of isolation and alienation, and these narratives, I think, are basically true.

They not only feel ignored; they are ignored, even by those raising ethical issues for faculty. Yet what is most curious about this is that they can no longer be ignored. Even if human decency, ethical responsibility, or moral alertness did not wake us up to the situation of adjunct faculty, their sheer numbers do. As Derek Bok noted, "By 2012, a large majority of college instructors are not on tenure track."[2] Andrew Delbanco writes, "In 1975, nearly 60 percent of college professors were full-time faculty with tenure or on the 'tenure track.' Today that fraction has declined to around 35 percent, which means that most students are being taught by part-time contingent employees who have limited stake in the institution where they work."[3] In other words, at many universities, the majority of the faculty are adjuncts. You might want to ask yourself, "Who are the faculty that books on academic ethics actually engage?"

As we approach adjunct faculty, I want to deal with three significant preliminaries. First, I need to come clean about the way I have totally ignored adjunct faculty. As you will see later, I think many readers who are tenured or tenure-track faculty could see themselves much as I see myself. Second, I look to the question of teaching and how it is prioritized by both the tenured and adjunct faculties. Finally, I turn to the historical development of the emphasis on research over teaching for the professional advancement of tenured faculty. After these introductory comments, we will descend into the plight of adjunct faculty at the contemporary American university.

COMING CLEAN

In my ten years at my university, I have been working on faculty development, mentoring junior tenure-track faculty, and developing programs for graduate students from advising and mentoring to developing a culture of teaching formation in our doctoral program. Still, in my university and in my department there are adjuncts. I know next to nothing about them and as I researched more and more, I realized that the gulf between tenured faculty and adjunct faculty has few secure ways of passage connecting us. I know little about the terms of their employment. Like other tenured faculty, I have consciously and unconsciously, and conveniently, worn blinders about their work and their context.[4]

I have managed to tell myself they do not concern me. (They do, but I managed to tell myself otherwise.) Recently, an adjunct who is also a journalist, Lisa Liberty Becker, asked to interview me because she is writing on adjunct faculty and heard that I was writing this book on university ethics. In the course of the interview, she concurred that I had a pretty good handle on the issues that adjuncts face. But before we descended into the details, she asked me an important question: "What do you know about adjuncts at your own institution?" "Next to nothing," I replied. "I have managed to tell myself they do not concern me." Then I added, "I'm acting chair next semester; assuredly I will find out."

I say this simply to let the tenure-line faculty get some space to acknowledge that they probably conveniently do not care about adjuncts. As we will see in the next chapter, there is within the university structure a cultural myopia that allows us to not think about the adjuncts. It is the fault of the structure of the university, but it is our fault, too.

Take this test. Imagine for a moment, as a tenured faculty member, you learn that your university president is about to declare an end to sabbaticals, tenure, and academic freedom. I imagine that the tenured faculty would be up in arms and would argue, rightly, that these changes would threaten the nature of the university, the pivotal role of critical inquiry in the classroom, and the fundamental need to protect intellectual rigor and investigation. They would also expect one another to stand in solidarity together as fellow teachers, committed to the very vocation of serving the university community. Eventually we would think of those more vulnerable than us, the junior tenure-track faculty: just imagine the impassioned claims we would hear from one another about our interest in protecting the futures of our junior tenure-track faculty. That self-understanding and sense of solidarity that could galvanize tenured faculty to think of one another and to think of junior tenure-track faculty does not make it to our minds as we learn about the many threats to the adjunct faculty. They may be threatened, but we are not. Surely, we are both faculty, but our understanding of our ethical responsibilities somehow conveniently ends with those tenured and those following us on the tenure track. Our solidarity rarely extends to the adjuncts.

TEACHING

Contrary to reports otherwise, both tenured and adjunct faculty love teaching. At the end of his study on the reformers of American higher education from the late 1890s to the mid-1920s, Laurence R. Veysey tells us that faculty were, generally speaking, very satisfied with their work: "[T]he great majority of university professors expressed contentment with academic life as it then existed."[5] In 1897, for instance, the American literary critic at Williams College, Bliss Perry, wrote, "I know a few who would gladly change their calling, but only a few. . . . I find college teachers peculiarly happy."[6] More than twenty years later, former Yale University President Timothy Dwight wrote, "[I]t is, I think—at heart, for those who have the inclination towards it—the most desirable of all kinds of life." These are not random or simply anecdotal remarks. These are, as Veysey acknowledges, the "dominant picture."[7]

To appreciate the matter of adjunct faculty, we have to remember that adjuncts work as they do not because the work is lucrative but because it is a rewarding profession. Still, some lament that as teachers they may not be the best for students. This is, I think, not at all accurate. For instance, Andrew Hacker and Claudia Dreifus refer to studies that suggest "a strong relationship between dropout rates and having contingent faculty teaching basic freshmen courses" and that when students were taught at community colleges by adjuncts that "their odds of going on to four year colleges decreased." Like me, they follow these reports with anecdotal remarks about their experiences of asking students the names of their favorite professors at the schools they visited and remark that "the students frequently mentioned a contingent."[8] Former Harvard President Derek Bok refers, too, to those studies,[9] but also notes that another study disproves the claim.[10] Wisely, Bok concludes, "Student course evaluations find that part-time and adjunct professors are usually rated at least as highly as the regular tenure-track faculty, while the few studies that attempt to measure directly the effects of part-time instructors have come to mixed conclusions."[11]

More recently, however, a study from Northwestern University found "consistent evidence that students learn relatively more from non-tenure line professors in their introductory courses." Studying data on fifteen thousand students from 2001 through 2008 at Northwestern University, the authors noted: "These differences are present across a wide variety of subject areas, and are particularly pronounced for Northwestern's average students and less-qualified students."[12] The study prompted quick responses from tenured faculty who noted that a study of one university hardly makes for general applicability. Anita

Levy, a senior program officer at the American Association of University Professors, retorted:

> I am not surprised that introductory classes might be better taught by contingent faculty members simply because most tenured faculty more often teach advanced courses. My worry is that a study like this can be used to justify hiring more contingent faculty who won't have due-process protections or job security and might not even have offices. It's part of the just-in-time, Walmartization of higher education. [13]

Quite aside from who makes the better teacher, Bok notes that "it is often said by critics that the quality of teaching is not as good as it should be." He believes that the critics misconceive the problem: "The usual explanation is that universities and their faculties are so preoccupied with research that the professors neglect their teaching in order to spend more time in the library or laboratory." But the fact is, "By more than 2-1, they consider teaching more interesting and important."[14] In another study it was found that American professors enjoy their teaching more than their counterparts in other countries. Furthermore they were least likely to report that they were more interested in research than teaching.[15]

Nonetheless, because of university expectations regarding merit for research, more tenured faculty are estimated for promotion and merit increment by research standings rather than teaching achievements. Still, Bok notes that whether adjunct or tenure track, "a remarkable 99.6 percent of college professors agree that developing students' ability to think critically is either 'essential' or 'very important.'"[16] He adds, "More than 90 percent believe that it is *the most important* aim of undergraduate education."[17]

FACULTY RESEARCH

Since 1992, the average amount of time for tenured professors' teaching has diminished. Bok writes, "[T]he decline appears to have resulted from a reduction in the number of classroom hours required of the faculty." This reduction results from increased demands for publishing as well as more administrative tasks that senior faculty assume.

Bok also notes that the emphasis on research has made faculty much more specialized and that therefore "most faculty members prefer to teach the kinds of specialized courses and seminars that are aligned with their scholarly interests. Not surprisingly, teaching what professors know best does not always coincide with what undergraduates most need." As a result, core courses, "Great Books" programs, and other generally classical liberal arts–type courses are assumed by adjunct and part-time faculty.[18]

Of course, this is completely contrary to the original design of making research constitutive of university professors' profiles. Being better researched, faculty, it was presumed, would be more resourceful mentors. Julie Reuben notes that the university reformers at the end of the nineteenth century saw research as "an important extension of the new teaching objectives." Reuben notes, "Faculty took the lead in promoting university-sponsored research" to teach students how to investigate. By supporting these faculty initiatives, universities could claim that they were graduating students with the "highest forms of mental reasoning" and that through the research they were offering to society pathways to social progress.[19] The synthesis was complete by the turn of the century. In 1906, The American Association of Universities sponsored a conference session called "To What Extent Should the University Investigator Be Relieved from Teaching?" The first speaker opened the discussion: "Teaching without research is not university teaching." The closing speaker echoed the unanimous sentiments, "We do not want the two things separated, we want them combined."[20]

By the 1920s, the mutual relationship between research and teaching was challenged. Critics complained that researching faculty were out of touch with their students; scientists replied that research itself was an important mission of the university and pointed to their contributions in the recent war. Reuben notes that first scientists, receiving funding from outside sources, sought to carve out "an independent realm for research." Scientists were followed by social scientists, but the latter attracted large numbers of undergraduate majors and their teaching responsibilities were much more apparent than the scientists who had in the 1920s far fewer majors. Nonetheless, foundations like Carnegie and Rockefeller began funding social scientific research and, in time, the social scientist also carved out a separate role for research. By the end of the decade, the scientists and social scientists developed criteria for professional university advancement as fundamentally depending on the quality of their research. [21]

Nonetheless, the proposal that a faculty that researches more teaches better remains unproven. As Bok notes, whether a faculty member does research or not seems to impact little the effectiveness of one's teaching. After assessing extensive comparable studies, Bok writes, "[T]he soundest conclusion to draw from the existing studies is that engaging in research has no significant, demonstrable effect, either positive or negative, on the quality of undergraduate teaching." [22]

ADJUNCT FACULTY: THE AMERICAN FEDERATION OF TEACHERS SURVEY

In 2010, the American Federation of Teachers (AFT) produced the first survey of part-time adjunct faculty. It provides some of the fundamental data that we need to understand the situation. The report begins with these words:

> Most Americans would be surprised to learn that almost three-quarters of the people employed today to teach undergraduate courses in the nation's colleges and universities are not full-time permanent professors but, rather, are instructors employed on limited-term contracts to teach anything from one course to a full course load. These instructors, most of whom work on a part-time/adjunct basis, now teach the majority of undergraduate courses in U.S. public colleges and universities. Altogether, part-time/adjunct faculty members account for 47 percent of all faculty, not including graduate employees. The percentage is even higher in community colleges, with part-time/adjunct faculty representing nearly 70 percent of the instructional workforce in those institutions. [23]

The survey came to three summary insights:

First, "part-time/adjunct instructors are generally pleased to have teaching jobs and enjoy teaching."
Second, "part-time/adjunct faculty members vary considerably in the extent of their participation in the institution as well as their ambitions to teach on a full-time basis."

Third, "the survey highlights serious shortcomings in the financial and professional support received by part-time/adjunct instructors."

Regarding the second point, the survey notes that the part-time/adjunct faculty members are "about evenly split" between "those who prefer part-time teaching (50 percent) and those who would like to have full-time teaching jobs (47 percent). About 46 percent of the respondents have previously sought full-time college teaching employment. . . . Differences surface repeatedly in the survey between those who aspire to full-time teaching jobs and those who do not."

In other words, half of the part-time/adjunct faculty are content with their present positions; half are not. Still, the report continues "job satisfaction among part-time/adjunct faculty is fairly high, but there are distinct variations. . . . Satisfaction varies considerably between those seeking full-time teaching employment (49 percent of whom are very or mainly satisfied) and those who prefer to work part time (75 percent very or mainly satisfied.) Satisfaction is lower among part-time/adjunct faculty members at four-year public universities."

There is widespread concern among part-time/adjunct faculty about bread-and-butter conditions:

About 57 percent of the survey respondents say their salaries are falling short.

Just 28 percent indicate that they receive health insurance on the job.

Only 39 percent say they have retirement benefits through their employment.

Even among those who receive health or retirement benefits, however, there are significant gaps in coverage. Unionized part-time/adjunct faculty members earn significantly more than their nonunion counterparts and are more likely to have some health and pension coverage.[24]

Regarding their futures, "Fully 62 percent believe full-time opportunities are falling short of expectations, a number that rises to 74 percent among those who have sought full-time employment. About 44 percent of all those surveyed believe they are not given a fair opportunity to obtain a full-time position, rising to 55 percent among those who have pursued a full-time position."[25]

UNDERSTANDING THE SITUATION OF
ADJUNCT FACULTY

The story regarding adjuncts gets bleaker, however, as we look to the details. The AFT instituted a second survey under the aegis of the Coalition on the Academic Workforce (CAW). It had three summary insights:

The median pay per course, standardized to a three-credit course, was $2,700 in fall 2010, and ranged from a low of $2,235 at two-year colleges to a high of $3,400 at four-year doctoral or research universities.

Part-time faculty respondents saw little, if any, wage premium based on their credentials. [26]

Professional support was minimal for part-time faculty members' work outside the classroom and for their inclusion in academic decision-making. [27]

For the most part, the study of part-time adjuncts who are satisfied with their positions are often persons in other careers providing course instruction based on their own career competency or who find that the course or courses they teach are, as one writer said, "adjunct to my life."[28] Part-time adjuncts looking for full employment tend to be younger persons often with a doctorate accepting last-minute offers to teach one or two courses at one school, and other courses elsewhere. Their lives are often adjunct to their teaching.

As another study shows, this majority is hired within three weeks of the beginning of a semester, are rarely given any orientation to the university, and have little access to educational resources, from photocopy machines to offices. The study also found that the management that hires these faculty does not have any appreciative understanding of the lack of resources afforded the adjuncts. [29]

Sarah Kendzior provocatively refers to them as "indentured servants," fulfilling piece-labor work for the university. She asks why so many professors who study injustice ignore the plight of their peers. "They don't consider us their peers," the adjuncts wrote back. She then outlined that many academics think of the meritocracy of the academy and that those with tenure-track jobs deserve them and the others do not. [30]

Besides their alienation and isolation resulting from inadequate salaries, benefits, and institutional support, four other noteworthy considerations help us to understand the predicament of adjunct faculty.

First, tenure-track and tenured faculty as well as departmental
chairs simply take for granted the secondary status of adjunct faculty.
Like Kendzior, Janet Casey in a soul-searching essay tries to fathom
how tenure-line faculty who engendered a variety of political movements concerning race and gender are unable to significantly raise their
own voices of concern for colleagues who are adjuncts, especially when
tenure-line faculty have been identified repeatedly as the participants
most needed for real, potential game-changing. She writes:

> I believe that the failure of most [tenure-track] faculty members to
> attend seriously to [non–tenure track] issues has far less to do with
> self-absorption than with a tendency to see contingent labor use/
> abuse as merely an employment (i.e., market economics) issue rather
> than a problem framed by questions of social justice and academic
> freedom. Viewing contingency hiring purely as a market issue, of
> course, allows us to dismiss it as something largely beyond our con-
> trol; viewing it in reference to social justice and academic freedom,
> however, makes it continuous with earlier struggles in the academy,
> and suggests that the problem must be resolved by those within the
> system.[31]

We will see later in Chapter 10, "Commodification," how adjunct faculty are justified as a "market issue," but Casey rightly raises the matters
of social justice and academic freedom that make adjunct faculty not
only related to the administrators who hire them, but also to the tenure-
track faculty who share the same vocation. She offers four basic strategies for tenure-line faculty: Learn the facts and find out the actual
statistics about the circumstances of adjunct faculty; commit to exploring change and imagine the university faculty five, ten, or fifteen years
from now; enter into collegiality with all faculty regardless of their status (she writes, "It is more difficult to ignore the circumstances of those
you know on a personal level"[32]); and prepare to make sacrifices because that is the only way that a fair faculty will develop.

Second, absurd as it may seem, inasmuch as cost-cutting led to adjunct faculty, further cost-cutting procedures at universities often run
right to the adjunct faculty line. A clear indication of this has been that

universities, which are faced with implementing the Affordable Care Act and recognize that thirty hours of work constitutes full-time employment and therefore requires provision of health care benefits, have quickly lowered the number of hours for part-time adjunct faculty.[33]

Third, the civil liberties of adjunct faculty are unclear. Inasmuch as tenure and academic freedom go hand in hand, academic protection for adjunct faculty is not in evidence. Just as recruiting and hiring of adjunct faculty often happens on the spot, suspending, firing, or refusing to renew a contract also happens without much scrutiny or transparency.[34] As Maria Maisto, president of the New Faculty Majority (NFM), recently wrote: "Considering that only about 22 percent of adjuncts are unionized and that unionization is often (though definitely not always) the best way to get due process, I think it's very safe to say that the vast majority have few to no due process rights."[35]

In her essay, "Class Warfare," Lisa Liberty Becker explains that "union organizers have targeted adjuncts, advocating for higher pay (including a pay scale in some cases), a guaranteed number of courses per semester, continued employment, benefits, and representation in the faculty governance." But she adds, "Here in Boston, unions claim that local universities are ruthless in blocking SEIU's [Service Employees International Union] efforts to organize."[36]

Fourth, the construction of adjunct faculty is simply not sustainable as "Harvest Moon" well describes what led to her decision to leave her adjunct career.

> I took a hard look at the facts: $2,500 per course, no health coverage, no job security, no unemployment insurance. And then I considered the likelihood that my circumstances would ever improve. It was difficult to admit to myself that, if anything, my real earnings would likely continue to decline even as my expenses increased. The word that came to mind was "unsustainable." It was an epiphanal moment.[37]

The plight of the adjunct faculty is very disturbing and the effective role they play in "augmenting" the faculty is even more problematic when we turn to state schools. Alan Finder in the *New York Times* noted:

> Many state university presidents say tight budgets have made it inevitable that they turn to adjuncts to save money. "We have to contend

with increasing public demands for accountability, increased financial scrutiny and declining state support," said Charles F. Harrington, provost of the University of North Carolina, Pembroke. "One of the easiest, most convenient ways of dealing with these pressures is using part-time faculty," he said, though he cautioned that colleges that rely too heavily on such faculty "are playing a really dangerous game."[38]

REAL PERSONS

The *New York Times* provides the narrative of Barbara Lynch who teaches nine courses in communications and public speaking at five different colleges. She teaches twenty-seven hours a week at Hofstra University in Hempstead; Polytechnic University in Farmingdale; and the three community colleges of Nassau County, Suffolk County, and Queensborough. Her commute is about two hundred miles a week. She is looking for full-time employment. She either shares an office with sixteen other adjuncts or has no office at all.[39]

The stories of the impoverishment of adjuncts like Barbara Lynch are embarrassingly common. They tell stories of food stamps, welfare, and Medicaid.[40] CNN refers to them as "the working poor."[41] The Democratic Staff Report of the House Committee on Education and the Workforce concluded their report in January 2014 by writing: "In short, adjuncts and other contingent faculty likely make up the most highly educated and experienced workers on food stamps and other public assistance in the country."[42]

More recently, the death on September 1, 2013, of an adjunct, Margaret Mary Vojtko, formerly employed at Duquesne University, has helped to make better known the often challenging situation of adjuncts. Signing tweets with the hashtag #iammargaretmary, many adjuncts see in her sad death some of their own narrative.

The life and death of Margaret Mary Vojtko became known when Daniel Kovalik, senior associate general counsel of the United Steelworkers Union, which was attempting to unionize the university's adjunct faculty, wrote an op-ed essay in the *Pittsburgh Gazette* that highlighted the remarkably unstable and decrepit situation in which Vojtko lived. Kovalik wrote that she worked on a contract basis from semester to semester, with no job security, no benefits, and with a salary of between $3,000 and just over $3,500 per three-credit course over the course of twenty-five years. "Even during the best of times, when she was teaching three classes a semester and two during the summer, she was not even clearing $25,000 a year, and she received absolutely no health care benefits."[43]

His essay went viral, though attempts were subsequently made by Duquesne to offer their side of the story. Later, L. V. Anderson of *Slate* provided an investigative narrative that argued that events leading to the death of Vojtko were the result of some of her own choices. Still, Anderson is clear to say that Duquesne, like most universities, does not have an equitable arrangement with its adjuncts.[44]

Rightly, Gary Rhoades notes that the issue is not solely the university's relationship with this one adjunct: "The larger issues are not about individual responsibility or culpability for actions toward Vojtko, but rather, about collective responsibility for the structural conditions of work that contributed to her circumstances, and that leave significant segments of the academic workforce with no benefits and low pay."[45]

Finally, Margaret Mary Vojtko had been one of the university's adjuncts urging the unionization of the university's adjuncts. But Duquesne University, having earlier acknowledged the adjuncts' right to unionize, now argues that to protect its religious values, it should be exempt from federal labor laws allowing unionization.[46] There is irony here in that, while asserting its Catholic identity, the university implicitly ignores the Catholic tradition's deeply committed support for the right of workers to unionize.[47] The Catholic Scholars for Worker Justice, for instance, provides a fundamental objection to them and other Catholic universities that make the claim of exceptionalism in the face of unions. On their site they post both a petition to allow unions to organize adjunct workers at Catholic colleges and universities as well as a working paper arguing for adjunct rights to unionize at such colleges.[48]

INNOVATIVE RESPONSES TO THE ADJUNCTS' SITUATION

There are three major innovations designed to respond to the conditions of these adjuncts: The Adjunct Project, The Delphi Project, and the New Faculty Majority (NFM). The approach of each is fairly distinctive and they each complement one another well.

The development of adjunct faculty at any university is so related to supplementing the tenure-track faculty that university policies regarding adjunct faculty are in many instances *sui generis*. Whatever contractual relationships, job responsibilities, security, and personnel benefits an adjunct has with one university will differ with the next university. Certainly this is also true of tenure-track faculty at a university; trying to understand their salaries, benefits, and responsibilities depends upon a variety of concerns at the given university. The university's decision is based on its perception of the "market" as well as its own interest or support of a particular area of a particular department. Thus, inasmuch as adjuncts are supplemental to the tenure-track faculty, all the more are a particular university's contracts with its adjuncts that particular university's construction.

The Adjunct Project is a listing of the salaries of individual courses according to the departments and schools at each of the listed 3,852 colleges.[49] Inasmuch as the universities are not truly transparent entities, gathering that information has not been easy, but it has been very supportive of adjuncts in their search for some sense of equity.

The Delphi Project is a wide array of interested parties seeking to better communication among interested parties while advancing the narrative of the adjunct faculty's situation so as to remedy their lack of equity, their exclusion from the university campus, and their impediments to educational resources. On October 2, 2012, Adrianna Kezar, Susan Albertine, and Dan Maxey presented "The Delphi Project on the Changing Faculty and Student Success" in a notable essay in *Inside Higher Ed.*[50] In light of the fact that universities are not taking any real initiatives to remedy the unsustainable adjunct status of contingent faculty, these scholars proposed five guidelines to prompt change.

The first is a call for collective action to address the situation of adjunct faculty. The second urges the incorporation of multiple perspectives so that a more sustainable solution is found. Shared perspectives lead to the third guideline, an appreciation for the common ground by which consensus is formed, community develops, and more effective policies emerge of incorporating those previously marginalized.

Their fourth guideline articulates a vision of a future professoriate. In the place of the present three-tiered system (tenure track, full-time non–tenure track, and part-time non–tenure track)—that is, a difference of three kinds of professoriate—the authors present one professoriate that is differentiated by varying degrees of shared responsibilities. In their drafting of the project with an array of stakeholders, they came to agree on many common principles of this one professoriate: "academic freedom, shared governance, a livable wage, and greater job security for non–tenure-track faculty (in the form of multiyear contracts). There was also agreement that teaching and scholarship cannot be fully unbundled, that institutional roles should differ by institutional type, and that above all other goals, student success should be the primary focus of any faculty work."[51]

They conclude their guidelines recognizing the "need to learn to trust each other in order to address this problem." But they add that "trust in higher education has worn thin following the decline of shared governance, the rise in unilateral decision-making, and the apparent protectionism of narrow interests among the various stakeholders."[52]

Like the writers of the Delphi Project essay, Maria Maisto, president of the NFM, wrote her manifesto in *Inside Higher Ed*, "The Adjunct's Moment of Truth."[53]

The impressive and resourceful website for NFM is first and foremost designed to advocate for the rights of the adjuncts. The mission statement of NFM is quite clear. It:

> is dedicated to improving the quality of higher education by advancing professional equity and securing academic freedom for all adjunct and contingent faculty. For this purpose, NFM engages in education and advocacy to provide economic justice and academic equity for all college faculty. NFM is committed to creating stable, equitable, sustainable, non-exploitative academic environments that promote more effective teaching, learning, and research.[54]

Four verbs dominate the site: *educate, advocate, litigate,* and *legislate.* The "rights" of the adjunct is the object of each verb. The cooperative, multiperspectival philosophy of the Delphi Project very much animates the NFM strategy. Tabs on the different constituencies are on the home page: adjuncts, tenure-line faculty, administration, parents, students, policy makers, media. Each is addressed with very specific approaches and insights, yet all converge on the mission statement.

In one way, the toughest constituents are the adjuncts themselves, caught between wanting to get a university appointment and frustrated by the experience that so frequently occurs. With the number of tenure-track appointments drying up, many adjuncts try to convince their colleagues to join them in advocacy whether in union organization movements or something more comprehensive like NFM.

But adjuncts are vulnerable and "throwing their lot" with other adjuncts is considered a risky move by many such vulnerable people. But that is the NFM message: The "time is now" to join forces.[55] Maria Maisto's very sympathetic manifesto captures her own experience, in which she wonders how she can manage to not avoid "The Adjunct's Moment of Truth."[56]

Josh Boldt addresses the adjuncts even more directly: "Stop Looking for the Treasure Map, and Start Laying Bricks."[57] NFM is, therefore, an attempt to gather adjuncts together and to help them see that, by being united and not disenfranchised, they have the possibility of reform. But as Boldt reminds them, so long as each goes looking for some unfulfillable dream, each fails to work with one's colleagues to address the overriding problems common to all adjuncts.

As the public face of NFM, Maria Maisto has been indomitable, bringing the adjunct's message to a wide variety of audiences.[58] After testifying to the House Education and the Workforce Committee, one congressman asked for more comprehensive narratives about the plight of adjuncts. Maisto responded, "Of course we have volumes and volumes of stories and research, as well, and we will be happy to share that with the committee."[59]

AN ETHICAL PROPOSAL

It should be obvious at this point that the plight of the adjunct needs a variety of approaches and clearly the initiatives ought not be reduced to one. That being said, adjuncts are alienated at a place called the "university," a place that the *Encyclopedia Britannica* refers to as a "community of teachers and scholars."[60] Not only that, but these alienated individuals are the new faculty majority. Something deeply unsettling about the university appears when we turn to the adjunct's situation, but when we turn to them in light of an ethical inquiry into the university, their situation is even more striking.

I hope to suggest in the next chapter that there is something about the university's very structure that makes the phenomenon of the adjunct today possible, but here I want to conclude by offering my own ethical proposal to my colleagues so that we expand our own circle of who deserves that meritorious title of *colleague*.

Besides the adjunct's own individual reluctance to throw his or her own lot in with others, there is the tenure-line faculty's refusal to throw their lot in with adjuncts. Indeed, that reluctance, I believe, underlies the disinterest of tenure-line faculty in adjunct faculty. Adjuncts work singularly with the departmental chair and have few pathways to the department as such. They are assiduously ignored despite their commitment to teaching. If adjuncts were to identify conceptually their natural ally, it should be the tenure-line faculty, but that is not the case. Deborah Foreman's "We're Not Your Colleagues" is a fairly revealing account from the perspective of the adjunct of the tenure-line's implicit position toward hard-working, dedicated faculty.[61]

The foundations of most ethical systems are based on the shoring up of particular relationships. For Aristotle the virtue of friendship is a mainstay for the common good, "not only a necessary thing but a splendid one."[62] He writes: "Friendship is the bond that holds the community together, and lawmakers seem to attach more significance to it than justice, because concord seems to be something like friendship, and concord is their primary object—that and eliminating faction, which is enmity."[63] He identifies *friendship* not only as a feeling but as "a state, as an activity."[64] For Aristotle, without friendship the community cannot hold together; the absence of friendship is similarly the great barrier to the flourishing of a community.

Analogous to Aristotle's idea of friendship, contemporary ethicists write that the virtue of solidarity manifests itself, time and again, as constitutive for human progress. Solidarity is the appeal to forge interpersonal relationships between and among diverse constituencies who recognize the need for one another. The call to solidarity is born out of the awareness that certain social structures impede the relatedness among dependent groups of persons. It is therefore a summons to cross existing divides and to enter the framework of others who enjoy or suffer a markedly different worldview.[65]

Over the years, many American universities have notably tried to raise consciousness of its students by supporting them in their trips to Appalachia, Haiti, and a wide variety of other outposts so that students can enter into solidarity with an entirely other constituency. Students learn from these endeavors that such solidarity is not a one-way street. They learn in these settings how to work with others on the same project, as is the case for instance of Habitat for Humanity. As they participate in a project, they become aware of very differing presuppositions that animate the other's worldview. Yet as they engage in such work, they find that they not only give, but that they receive and in fact they often return to the university from immersion experiences with the witness, "I received more than I gave."

In a similar way, the practice of solidarity is not based on any anonymous one-way act of charity. Rather solidarity is constitutively able to function only where the differing constituencies are participative in the same projects and enter into a relationship of commitment for achieving the same end or purpose. As I was doing my research for this chapter, Janet Casey gave me a fuller idea of how the tenure-line faculty must enter into interpersonal relationships of concern and commitment if the university is ever to resolve its unsustainable present policy of part-time adjunct faculty.

If solidarity is more than a feeling, but a state and what today we might call a *practice,* we could see a fairly broad range of practices that tenure-line faculty could pursue in order to develop a relation of solidarity with their adjunct colleagues. Casey suggested four overarching strategies, which we can identify now as being practices of solidarity: Learn the facts, commit to exploring change, enter into collegiality with all faculty regardless of their status, and prepare to make sacrifices. The third practice, collegiality, is the heart of academic solidarity. Entering into collegiality requires a host of actions beginning with the lifting of the veil of ignorance and finding a way of recognizing the adjunct faculty not as outsiders, but rather as one of us. Certainly, tenured faculty should advocate for true substantive changes in the contractual relations between the university and adjunct faculty, but the tenured faculty need to be first collegial with their colleagues, all of them.

CONCLUSION

The rise of adjunct faculty at the university is in part due to the decline of available positions in tenure-track lines as well as the reduction of class loads for tenured faculty. The reduction of tenure-track lines is not simply the result of faculty costs. Questions about the decisions regarding the allocation of university funds are exactly the reason why the Delphi Project and the NFM realize that more comprehensive investigations into the adjunct situation are needed. Like them, I, too, intend to raise ethical questions about the investment the university makes in the teaching of its students in Chapter 10, "Commodification."

The case of the adjunct faculty situation is preeminently an ethical issue. In most instances, their employment is simply not based on any evident principles of justice or fairness. Remedying that situation, however, requires that they, as both vulnerable and alienated—that is, as oppressed—need to have partners who recognize the injustice of their situation. Without a doubt, their partners should be the tenure-line faculty, and their response ought to be, I think, first and foremost solidarity. In standing in solidarity, adjunct faculty too may begin to ask for greater accountability and transparency from the university in the way employees are hired and treated and in the way finances are allocated.

5

THE CULTURAL LANDSCAPE OF THE UNIVERSITY WITHOUT ETHICS

"Generally speaking, a million-dollar president could be kidnapped by space aliens and it would be weeks or even months before his or her absence from campus was noticed."
—Benjamin Ginsberg[1]

In this chapter, we look at the world of the contemporary university and discover three foundational insights. First, the faculty (whether adjunct or tenure-line) are especially individualistic in their professional work and are not as prone as other professionals to work in tandem or as partners with other colleagues. Second, the university is not a professionally relational world at all, but rather a series of fiefdoms, with hierarchical classes running across the entire university structure. Third, nature abhors a vacuum: absent a culture of ethics, other cultures inevitably move into a university. The cultures described here could not happen if a culture of ethics were in place. Without ethics and its own vigilance, what do we have?

THE ISOLATING INDIVIDUALISTIC WORLD OF THE FACULTY

In 2008, I was invited to deliver a plenary presentation at the 2009 annual convention of the Catholic Theological Society of America. The title was "Impasse and Theological Ethics" and if anyone knows anything about the field of Catholic theological ethics, they would have presumed that the impasse I intended to address was that between bishops and theological ethicists.

When I received the invitation, I was at the beginning of a fourteen month cancer therapy for a stage III melanoma that included major surgery, two significant infections, and twelve months at the maximum dosage of interferon. In the light of this experience, I decided, contrary to expectations, to reflect on my experience of encountering impasse in my illness and how that impasse taught me to embrace solidarity with others.[2] During the talk, I reflected for a moment on whether where we teach and work, the university itself, promotes solidarity.

I went in this direction because a colleague of mine, M. Shawn Copeland, had awakened in me a suspicion about the university and its culture. Ten years earlier, while editing with the Mennonite ethicist Joseph Kotva a collection of essays on church ministerial ethics, we received from Copeland an essay not about the church but about the academy. Titled "Collegiality as a Moral and Ethical Practice," she wrote about a young black woman theologian who finds that her white colleagues are as strikingly naïve about their privilege as they are about her own challenges.[3] Copeland focused not only on their self-understanding, but also on the isolating character of our training and our working in the academy.

I had never seen an essay on university culture and ethical issues before, nor thought about the isolationist culture of our workplace. While the essay remained in the back of my mind for years, it came fully forward as I was preparing my talk on impasse and solidarity. The more I considered the university, the more I recognized how right Copeland was.

Unlike most professionals and civil servants, we function very much as individuals in the academy. Aside from department meetings, we study alone, work alone, teach alone, write alone, and lecture alone; we also grade students individually and write their singular letters of recommendation.

We cannot underestimate the individualism of our scholarly formation and our professional lifestyle. While almost every contemporary professional works in some form of partnership or team work—police officers with their partners, firefighters with their ladder companies, health care workers with their team, and lawyers with their firm—we faculty train alone and then work virtually alone.

Think of the dissertation! What other field of work requires its professional formation to be at least five years of working alone on one's own project with the last two years spent effectively in solitary confinement? Why is this, the highest expression of academic wisdom, so individualistic and so isolationist?

Someone might say yes, but there is mentoring. However, even the relationality in mentoring is not terribly thick. How many hours, during those four, five, or six years (35,040, 43,800, or 52,560 hours) do the advisor and mentee actually see and sit with one another? Is it at all analogous to other professional relationships where juniors literally shadow their mentor?

I began to see that the isolationism and the attendant lack of solidarity makes us dull in our sensitivity to matters within the academy that we should be critiquing. Nowhere is this more clear than in our lack of knowledge about the working conditions of our colleagues, the adjunct faculty, who, as we will see later, function almost as indentured servants at our universities.

One interesting corollary to the highly individualistic world we work in is found in the university's prescription that we write with a detached, inaccessible, frigid, dense style. An emotionally detached place like the academy trains us to be wary of writing anything accessible to others outside our field because it could compromise the style of a professorial reputation.

Martin Anderson describes well academic publishing: "An academic book or a scholarly article is not expected to sell many copies, nor appeal to many people outside a select intellectual circle. Thus isolated, the typical academic intellectual operates freely, uninhibited by the judgment of outsiders, subject only to the verdict of colleagues who themselves are judged by the same narrow criteria." He added, "And that is one of the major reasons why, paradoxically, the level of ethical behavior is substantially higher in the commercial world of the professional intellectuals than it is in academe. Most people will do the right thing if they have to."[4]

Robert Zemsky sees that inevitably faculty have to become connected and that this will be a formidable challenge to the isolated individualism of the faculty. He proposes, "As individuals we will have to abandon that sense of ourselves as independent actors and agents." He suggests that solidarity among faculty could develop by looking not to shared governance, but to shared responsibilities. But, he adds, "In a world in which faculty members have become independent contractors in all but name," the challenge is considerable.[5]

At his inauguration, Samuel O. Thier, president of Brandeis University (1991–1994), saw the culture of isolationism within the university as a pervasive challenge:

> [T]he collegial community of scholars finds itself in disarray largely because of the growth and specialization of scholarship and the competitive funding system. The excessive separation of disciplines has been stabilized and perpetuated by external professional societies. Teaching has been devalued in comparison to research, further dividing the faculty.

He concluded:

> Issues such as political correctness seem to me much less threatening to the future of the university than the intellectual isolation of its scholars, the separation of the humanities from the sciences, and even of one science from another. Add to these concerns tensions between graduate and undergraduate education, as well as between scholarly isolation and responsiveness to the external community, and one has the basis of a fundamental challenge to the modern university.[6]

I could not agree more.

There is a deep disconnect between what faculty teach and how we live. In a recent essay reflecting on how tenure-line faculty are responding to the rise of adjuncts, Robin Wilson reports on how many tenured faculty are fighting to retain their control: solidarity with adjuncts is far from their minds. Wilson writes: "Tenured professors frequently want it both ways." As one faculty member explained, these faculty bemoan contingent professors' poor pay, lack of job security, and the meager respect they get on campuses. But at the same time, they are "circling the wagons," refusing to put their non-tenure-track colleagues on equal footing by giving them full seats on the faculty senate. "It's the whole 'We are elite and privileged and yet we want to talk about the downtrodden.'"

Wilson quotes another faculty member, this time an adjunct: "The great hypocrisy of higher education right now, especially in English departments, is that many professors who teach Marxist theory turn around and just perpetuate this tiered labor structure that theoretically they'd be completely against."[7]

Of course, the same disconnect between one's published ideas and one's personal practices is not a vice only for faculty. The most frequently cited disconnect between what one teaches and what one practices comes from University of Virginia president Teresa Sullivan. In 2012, University of Virginia students striking and engaging in hunger strikes so that university employees would be paid a minimum living wage of $13 an hour cited a page of her own textbook, *The Social Organization of Work,* in their own campaign against her.[8] Sullivan wrote that "being paid a living wage for one's work is a necessary condition for self-actualization."[9] If there is a disconnect between what academics teach in the classroom and how they act outside them, it is usually caught by those wanting some semblance of ethics in university life.

Certainly many faculty have great relationships with a variety of members of the university. My argument, however, is that, professionally speaking, there is not a structure that promotes those relationships. Teaching, grading, and mentoring is measured against singular professionals. It is not just in those areas of university work that we are standalone individuals. Think, for instance, of office hours. What other professional corporate life lets their employees come to work whenever they want to? Other than the classes we teach and the occasional (monthly?) department meetings we may have to attend, most faculty can choose to arrive for any office hours we want. Not only are we free to name our office hours, but there is rarely any expectation to host office hours during any specific time that would be convenient to others. By office hours, we are required to be available to another person, presumably a student in need, yet we can set those hours whenever we want and rarely are we required to be there in the office for more than four or five hours a week. What other professional has such autonomy?

Note, I am not suggesting that faculty have only four hours of work. With teaching, letters of recommendations, publishing, and other academic demands, many faculty have a full week of work, but that work is on our time, our place, and again usually alone. Hardly any other modern professional works this way.

If we should want to teach with another colleague, then what? What machinery does the university have to accommodate such a design? What "credit" do we get for teaching with another? What credit do we get if we teach with another from another department, or worse, another school? What if we write with another? Will we receive full credit for the authorship? Certainly all these matters can be rectified, but for now, as it has been historically for the past eight hundred years, one's teaching, writing, and mentoring, and one's evaluation as faculty has usually defaulted to being a singularly accountable agent.

Still, we should be able to see that if individual faculty took the initiative to enter into practices of solidarity with others, this could lead to the possibility of developing and sustaining an ethical community within the university. When faculty elect to join a seminar, volunteer to be on a university committee, offer to be the faculty advisor of a student club, or host their class at home with a meal, they enter into relationships that make community possible. But these turns to the practices of solidarity are themselves turns to ethical practices. With ethics, community can flourish. Without ethics, the community breaks down.

THE UNIVERSITY'S LANDSCAPE

When we ask how tenure-line faculty who know that there are adjunct faculty at the university can actually not think about their colleagues' "piecework" existence, we should not only turn to the faculty's individualism and their own myopia as an explanation; we need to also consider the social landscape of the university.

In fact asking faculty questions about why they don't know about the conditions of the adjuncts is like asking faculty if they know where their students live, whether their students have received merit- or need-based scholarships, or which students might have been hospitalized or arrested over the weekend. Most faculty only know about such issues incidentally. As Julie Reuben explains (and as we will see in Chapter 7, "Undergraduates Behaving Badly"), with the reforms of the 1890s, faculty effectively withdrew institutionally from concerns about their students' private lives.

The faculty's ignorance in either instance is explained by their own individual way of working and by the blinders they wear as they go from their office to their classes. It is explained also by the social contours of the university that do not foster community, friendship, or solidarity, but rather departmentalize personnel groupings routinely.

Faculty are not only in the dark about their adjunct colleagues and their own students, they also do not know much about faculty salaries, either those in their department or those in other departments. And unless they read the *Chronicle of Higher Education,* they do not know salaries that one makes at other universities in comparable departments doing comparable work. [10]

Just as faculty do not know much about students, adjunct faculty, or others' salaries, neither do other university employees know much about others at the so-called university. Plant managers, cafeteria workers, student affairs' deans, financial aid officers, admissions boards, custodial workers, trustee members, campus ministers, university police, and librarians each have their own definable domain and their members know mostly what happens within that domain. Rarely are there occasions to go beyond one's domain (except when they go to university sporting events). The university might think of itself as a community, but it's a thin one at best.

Any reading of the literature on the life of the university tells us that the university's structure is very clear in its *vertical* direction; each cluster knows without a doubt who answers to whom in the upwardly oriented structure of unilateral accountability.

The geography of the American university horizontally is not terribly clear, however, because its terrain is defined by clusters or domains unto themselves. [11] I think that the university horizontal structure is best understood as fiefdoms, a perfect description of the university, inasmuch as both are deeply rooted in the medieval world. Moreover, structural fiefdoms, like universities, are not related horizontally, except at the top.

The more I looked to see who else was writing about fiefdoms at the university, the more I found other metaphors used to describe the on-the-ground culture of the university: private business corporations, organized anarchies, caste system, and drug gangs. After I turn to fiefdoms, we will consider these other metaphors that help capture the social contours of the university that lacks a culture of ethics.

FIEFDOMS

Happily, I am not the only one who uses the term fiefdom when looking at university culture. One medieval studies doctoral student uses the concept of fiefdom as a key to define, compare, and contrast the four-year university with the community college.[12] Elsewhere a Canadian professor of social and political theory has written about the feudal university thwarting any attempts at interdisciplinarity.[13] A journalist similarly sees the obstacles to collaboration at his own university and blames the obstacles on fiefdoms.[14] Charles Hugh Smith, who blogs on matters of finance, uses the term fiefdom frequently and applies it to universities among other entities.[15] In *The Independent,* Michael Day attributes the decline of the Italian university to family fiefdoms. He writes: "In Rome's La Sapienza University, for example, a third of the teaching staff have close family members as fellow lecturers. Overall, the country's higher institutions are 10 times more likely than other places of work to employ two or more members of the same family."[16]

I believe that the university, stemming as it does from the medieval era, is affected structurally by its roots. Not only does its hierarchical structure make its accountability flow unilaterally and singularly vertically, but it also inherits the geography of fiefdoms that hinder matters not only of accountability and transparency but also of relationality, distributive justice, and the common good.

Fiefdoms are a university trademark evident in two ways. First, as we have seen, its major employees, the faculty, work alone. Teaching remains, even in the twenty-first century, a fairly singular affair.[17] The academy's vocational or professional structure is a fairly medieval identity, much like Abelard's, though it is hard to find anyone else in most other contemporary corporate professions interested in emulating his individualist existence.

Second, universities are organized by departments, a structure that gives the suggestion that each department shares something in common with another, but given the hierarchical structures of the university, such a shared identity functions less in the operations and more in the purported mission design.

Departments are part of the fiefdom structure, in part because higher level administrators can treat departments differently without others in other departments knowing any differently. In fact, in many ways these administrators function as feudal lords. Life within the department is determined much less by what happens in other departments as by what happens between senior administrators and that department. At universities, at least the administrators know that knowledge is power.

In fact, the *Chronicle of Higher Education* recently published a compelling essay about how much departments differ from each other precisely because the make-or-break element for each department is the chair. Despite the fact that more managerial expertise is required of the chair, again like their own administrative superiors, academics believe they can assume leadership positions without any managerial training. Moreover, more department chairs are being asked to do fundraising and in this new development, they tend to represent more and more the dean they serve. Their responsibilities become less and less connected with other chairs and more with the dean of the school in which their specific department is housed.[18]

Fiefdoms are not only seen in the academic sector, but in the student affairs life as well. Just as faculty might not know the student's personal conduct, neither does student affairs know the student's academic life. Similarly health and counseling services, development, alumni relations, athletics, dining services, and many other departments function separately and are accountable to the different university managers who make their own assessments according to their specific domain's criteria. In short, the standards, communications, and information of each domain are not set across the university itself, but are particular to and remain within the domain of the particular fiefdom. It is for this reason that the only two constituencies who know what occurs across the university are the clients—that is, the students—and the president.

At the university, other than the president, only the students know what they can get from whom. This is a knowledge set that neither faculty, counselors, librarians, nor development officers enjoy or show an interest in. Still, though they know what is available, the students do not know anything about the actual effectiveness of any particular domain except anecdotally.

Vice presidents, in their cabinet meetings with the president, share their information with one another. The hermeneutics of their own domain's standards are explained and understood. Reports across the domains are gathered, shared, and assessed. With the president, the vice presidents have an overall sense of the corporate community, but the sharing of information across the university has not happened anywhere near the ground where most university employees work, for there is no such transparency or accountability at the university, at least horizontally.

In short, aside from meetings of the president's cabinet and some general reporting at trustees' meetings, the university does not promote the sharing of standards, information, or goals particular to any department or domain. Similarly there are few structures, policies, or practices that are in any way designed to fortify any relationality among any of the providers of any of the services at the university.

In terms of ethics, this is fairly problematic because, as we know from Aristotle, there is some relationship between the *polis*, or the actual community, and the common good that makes possible human flourishment. That is, to the extent that members of the *polis* as a society participate in and contribute to the common good, there is human flourishment. But at the university the players on the ground do not see a coherency in the community nor an operative notion of the common good.

The bureaucracy of the university does not have an internal horizontal structure of engagement, nor are there any in-built structures of horizontal accountability within the university. Worse still, the bureaucracy of the university shows no sign of checking itself, continues expanding, and eventually is no longer sustainable.[19] All these challenges prompt us to ask how we can overcome the obstacles to good community and provide a sharing of the common good.

When we hear the hardships of adjunct faculty and when we see rising tuition (another unsustainable solution), coupled at the same time with expanding bureaucracies and their attendant appointments and competitive salaries, we realize that the university's fiefdoms are very much the most compelling of all challenges. While the Delphi Project believes that they need to engage other stakeholders at the university to talk about redressing the adjunct situation, there is very little groundwork at any existing university that could sustain that conversation.

Inasmuch as the university shows little interest in forging a culture of ethics, it similarly shows little interest in facing the real challenges of building community, a good that depends on honesty, trust, and human sympathy.

Benjamin Ginsberg's *The Fall of the Faculty: The Rise of the All Administrative University and Why it Matters* serves as a wake-up call to the development of the cadre of senior administrators across the university. It also helps us to appreciate the evolution of fiefdoms at the university. If one were to ask which came first, the fiefdoms or their feudal lords, then the latter is clearly the creator of the former. Though I did not see Ginsberg using the word *fiefdoms,* his book certainly helps strengthen the validity of the metaphor: with the rise of the "all-administrative university" came the feudal lord administrators setting up their own domains.

We cannot underestimate their rise: Whereas there were about 250,000 administrators and professional staff members in 1975, about half the number of professors, by 2005 there were over 750,000, easily outnumbering tenure-track professors.[20] While noting that universities always had administrators, Ginsberg also notes their contemporary rise even at a time of fiscal restrictions: "Every year, hosts of administrators and staffers are added to college and university payrolls, even as schools claim to be battling budget crises that are forcing them to reduce the size of their faculties. As a result, universities are filled with armies of their functionaries . . . who more and more direct the operations of every school."[21]

Ginsberg peppers his text with a variety of quotes to highlight his warning: from former Harvard dean Henry Rosovsky's observation that the quality of a school is likely to be "negatively correlated with the unrestrained power of the administrators"[22] to the National Labor Relations Board referring to faculty participation in shared governance as little more than a "sophisticated version of the familiar suggestion box."[23]

Ginsberg's claim about the expanding presence of the administration notes not only how large their salaries and governing powers are, but also how sizable their staffs are.[24] After all, they have to govern a domain or fiefdom.

Ginsberg reflects on their rise and concomitantly the decline of the faculty's involvement in university decision making. "At most, though perhaps not all of America's thousands of colleges and universities, the faculty has been shunted to the sidelines. Faculty members will learn about major new programs and initiatives from official announcements or from the campus newspaper. Power on campus is wielded mainly by administrators whose names and faces are seldom even recognized by students or recalled by alumni."[25]

He does not deny that faculty have some control at the university, but he locates exactly the boundaries of their control.

> At most schools to be sure, faculty members control the content of their own classes and, for the most part, their own research agendas. The faculty, collectively, plays a recognized though not exclusive role in the hiring and promotion of its members. Outside these two areas, though, administrators seldom bother to consult the faculty. And, should faculty members have the temerity to offer unsolicited views, these will be more or less politely ignored. Thus, there are few schools whose faculty members have a voice in business or investment decisions. Hardly any faculties are consulted about the renovation or construction of buildings and other aspects of the school's physical plant. Virtually everywhere, student issues, including the size of the student body, tuition, financial aid and admissions policies are controlled by administrators.[26]

I think that now we can understand another reason for faculty writing on academic rather than university ethics. Academic ethics is about the study of right and wrong behavior, practices and structures within the faculty fiefdom. Faculty, outside the control of any other fiefdom, implicitly heeds Ginsberg's advice and stays out of those other fiefdoms and only focuses on their own. Until now.

"ORGANIZED ANARCHIES" AND OTHER METAPHORS

Years ago, given the ambiguity of American university presidential leadership and governance, Michael Cohen and James March proposed thinking of universities as "organized anarchies."[27] Rather than ignore the ambiguity of the metaphor, Cohen and March urged presidents to embrace it. "Organized anarchies" was developed in an article, provocatively called "A Garbage Can Model of Organizational Choice."[28]

Since then, two other metaphors developed. One is tightly linked to the issue of adjunct faculty and their predictably constant supply of labor. The metaphor is of the faculty as a drug gang; it has just recently surfaced but has been eloquently and clearly proposed and defended. More sprawling and very frequently proposed is "the caste system" with its "untouchables," applied both to the adjunct faculty and, by one scholar, to the university staff personnel.

I know of no one else who has reviewed these metaphors, and I suggest these are not competitive with one another but rather quite complementary: fiefdoms capture the context or the lay of the land of the university, the caste system covers the culture, and within these are a faculty resembling drug gangs. Let's see how nicely they fit together on the contemporary university.

DRUG GANGS

On November 12, 2013, Alexandre Afonso, a lecturer in political economy at King's College London, caused a stir with a blog post titled "How Academia Resembles a Drug Gang."[29] The blog at the *London School of Economics* also published it a month later[30] and as Scott Jaschik notes at *Inside Higher Ed,* the post is getting favorable reactions elsewhere online.[31]

Referring to an article on the internal wage structure of a Chicago drug gang, Afonso found "that the income distribution within gangs was extremely skewed in favor of those at the top, while the rank-and-file street sellers earned even less than employees in legitimate low-skilled activities, let's say at McDonald's. They calculated 3.30 dollars as the hourly rate, that is, well below a living wage."[32] Afonso puts these facts into perspective:

> If you take into account the risk of being shot by rival gangs, ending up in jail or being beaten up by your own hierarchy, you might wonder why anybody would work for such a low wage and at such dreadful working conditions instead of seeking employment at McDonalds. Yet, gangs have no real difficulty in recruiting new members. The reason for this is that the prospect of future wealth, rather than current income and working conditions, is the main driver for people to stay in the business: low-level drug sellers forgo current income for (uncertain) future wealth.[33]

Afonso notes how these over-eager new members are so easy to recruit, especially when their predecessors are shot, arrested, or finally leave the system for something more stable, though less attractive. He writes: "With a constant supply of new low-level drug sellers entering the market and ready to be exploited, drug lords can become increasingly rich without needing to distribute their wealth towards the bottom. You have an expanding mass of rank-and-file 'outsiders' ready to forgo income for future wealth, and a small core of 'insiders' securing incomes largely at the expense of the mass. We can call it a winner-take-all market."

Afonso sees that the academic job market is like a drug gang with its "expanding mass of outsiders and a shrinking core of insiders." Though he acknowledges that this trend affects labor markets everywhere, the academy is "a somewhat extreme example of this trend. . . . Academic systems more or less everywhere rely at least to some extent on the existence of a supply of 'outsiders' ready to forgo wages and employment security in exchange for the prospect of uncertain security, prestige, freedom and reasonably high salaries that tenured positions entail."

What Afonso's hypothesis does then is challenge the claims that the present supply of adjuncts is not sustainable. Afonso writes:

> So what you have is an increasing number of brilliant PhD graduates arriving every year into the market hoping to secure a permanent position as a professor and enjoying freedom and high salaries, a bit like the rank-and-file drug dealer hoping to become a drug lord. . . . Because of the increasing inflow of potential outsiders ready to accept [these kinds] of working conditions, this allows insiders to outsource a number of their tasks onto them, especially teaching, in a context where there are increasing pressures for research and publishing. The result is that the core is shrinking, the periphery is expanding, and the core is increasingly dependent on the periphery.[34]

Afonso seems pretty right. In *The Atlantic Monthly*, Jordan Weissmann writes that the Council of Graduate Schools reported that from 2011 through 2012 the number of first-time students enrolled in PhD programs rose by 7.7 percent. In light of fewer tenure-track positions, to say nothing of the shameful prospects of adjunct teaching, Jordan asked readers to propose an explanation.

Interestingly, again proving Afonso's point, readers' responses repeatedly referred to the "Special Snowflake Syndrome." As one reader, "Flightless Pigeon," wrote:

> When you're the best in your department as an undergrad and all of your professors are acting as though you're the Chosen One to carry on the field, even if statistics tell you there are 200 applications for every tenure-track job opening, you're the best in your department; of course you'll be the best of those applications. It isn't until you're a full-fledged grad student that you realize that EVERY ONE of those 200 applications comes from someone who was once the best in their department.[35]

Chris Blattman, an assistant professor of Political Science and International and Public Affairs at Columbia University, concurs:

> When I was a PhD student myself at Berkeley, and heard how just a third of history PhDs get academic jobs (despite Berkeley arguably having the best program in the world), my first thought was not "this is unfair" but "what the hell are these PhD students doing?"
>
> It's a little hard to say the wool is pulled over their eyes when at the same time they are being trained to be critical and well-informed scientists of social systems.[36]

Fiefdoms and drug gangs are vivid metaphors that help us appreciate the social culture and landscape of the contemporary university that does not promote the culture of ethics; the worst of them is the next one, the one that highlights how well the organized fiefdoms are managed, not in providing community but in promoting caste structures.

THE CASTE SYSTEM

In 2010, Pablo Eisenberg, a senior fellow at the Georgetown Public Policy Institute, proposed the caste system metaphor: "American universities and colleges are riddled with a caste system that violates our societal sense of fairness, justice, and decency." He immediately described how no one outside of university employees knows this, but those within do:

Neither the general public, nor parents, nor the large majority of students are even aware of its existence. College administrators and tenured faculty, who are acutely aware of the system, have done little or nothing to remedy the problem. It is a festering sore that threatens not only the quality of higher education but the system's ability to recruit and retain good teachers.

In that context, he describes adjuncts as the university's "untouchables": "*Contingent teachers,* as adjuncts are officially called, are the 'untouchables' of our college system."[37]

Eisenberg then asks, do we really need a caste system to survive? He answers by pitting the salaries of the universities' CEOs against the needs of the adjuncts:

> According to the *Chronicle of Higher Education*, at least 24 CEOs earned over $1 million in 2008. Many more will surpass the $1 million mark in a couple of years. High-level administrators—and there appear to be more and more every year—are also receiving huge increases. Yet these CEOs and their highly paid administrators can't seem to find the money from their endowments, operating budgets or slush funds to give a measure of financial justice to their academic "untouchables."[38]

Eisenberg makes his message clear: The people who could make the changes do not have the desire or appreciate the need to make them. They certainly do not have the personal incentive.

Two years later, Eisenberg writes again and refers to the report on adjunct faculty that the New Faculty Majority conducted the preceding year. Summarizing many of the points seen in Chapter 4, he writes, "They remain the 'untouchables' of our education caste system. College presidents and administrators seem to be looking the other way."[39] Then Eisenberg turns to the CEOs' salaries again, but notes that the university CEOs making more than $1 million are a lot more numerous than the twenty-four CEOs two years earlier: "CEO compensation has grown enormously in recent years; some 40 CEOs currently receive over $1 million. The number of administrators, many of them superfluous, has also increased significantly as has their salaries and benefit packages."[40]

In "The Deepening Caste System in Higher Education," Martin Kitch also uses the metaphor of caste system to talk about adjunct faculty, but he warns tenured faculty (who are saddled with more and more obligations from publishing to administrative and bureaucratic tasks) and adjunct faculty (whose salaries, benefits, and futures are drying up) against fighting against one another. "In the deepening 'caste system' in higher education, the only 'faculty' who are prospering are those who are so atypical as to demand the creation of a different classification altogether."[41] Like Ginsberg and Eisenberg, Kitch sees the expanding role of overpaid university administrators as the problem.

Kitch makes a number of comparisons to the way that universities make fairly expensive decisions that are not subject to accountability. In "The Deepening Caste System," he complains about wealthy peers of presidents and trustees being brought in to teach courses at extraordinary salaries. Elsewhere, in an essay on "Gilded Goodbyes," he discusses at length the sizable corporate packages that retiring presidents receive from trustees who come with the same corporate mentality of rewarding persons exorbitantly upon retirement.[42]

Kitch relies on the caste system metaphor, but he occasionally turns to the corporate metaphor as well, and makes I think an astute observation about the academy and its imitation of the corporate model. After discussing cases that illustrate how "a sense of privilege and a sense of entitlement have trumped even the business standards to which our increasingly corporatized institutions are ostensibly being held," he writes that these and other cases:

> demonstrate that universities aren't really comparable to corporations, and most administrators are not professional managers. The closest business model is, in practice, not the publicly owned and publicly accountable corporation but, instead, the privately owned business in which the owners can, without repercussion, periodically reward their favorites and indulge their more eccentric whims.

He notes that the model is all the more offensive when speaking of the publicly funded university "that should be more strictly accountable both to the students paying ever-higher tuition and to the taxpayers providing public subsidies."[43] The privately owned business model is not far from its own origins, the fiefdom that worked with no real transparency or accountability, but basically followed the directives of its feudal lord.

In the *Georgetown Public Policy Review,* three authors look at the caste system that merges by extension in the way universities hire faculty. Their "research suggests that the current system remains mired in a prestige-based caste system that diminishes the importance of individual merit in favor of affiliated honor, or institutional pedigree, when hiring." Using political science departments as a case-study, they argue "that the de facto academic hiring policy is to focus on candidates from elite universities and that this policy is harmful to the vast majority of PhD-granting programs." They note, "Chasing prestige stratifies academic programs (and their PhD-graduates) into 'born' winners and losers, with the biggest winners of meritless prestige being the Ivy League."[44]

The economist Niall Ferguson, in "College Becoming the New Caste System," turns to the metaphor for another reason, suggesting that by the university's recruitment system and by its successful launching of its graduates, the American university is creating a Brahmin class, assuring the United States of a rigid caste system: "The real problem is not that our college system is failing. The problem is that it is succeeding all too well—at ranking and sorting each cohort of school-leavers by academic performance."[45]

Ferguson is taken with Charles Murray from the American Enterprise Institute and his recent book, *Coming Apart,* where Murray argues, among other issues, that the top universities are creating these "cognitive elites."[46] Quite apart from Murray's own read on the matter, what is interesting is to see how on either side of the ideological divide, a few educators are concerned by the way universities are participating in and perpetuating class distinctions in education.[47] We will see more on classism at the university later.

Ferguson writes, "In 1997, just over a hundred elite colleges, which admitted fewer than a fifth of all freshmen, also accounted for three quarters of the ones with SAT or ACT scores in the top 5 percent." He asks whether this is meritocracy in action. "The problem is that this cognitive elite has become self-perpetuating: they marry one another, live in close proximity to one another, and use every means, fair or foul, to ensure that their kids follow in their academic footsteps (even when Junior is innately less smart than Mom and Dad)."[48]

What Ferguson and the Georgetown authors highlight is the enormous stratification within the American academy, which we will reconsider in Chapter 10. The term *cognitive elite* does not seem an unfair attribution for the students we recruit or graduate or the tenure-track faculty we hire. In all cases, however, the caste system metaphor gives us something of a context to appreciate how this intellectual stratification that happens in American university life merits ethical assessment.

The caste system metaphor has received a fair amount of traction. The New American Foundation and the *Washington Monthly* held in late 2013 a forum on "Higher Education's New Caste System." The forum looked at how those from racial minority and low-income groups are affected by the stratification prompted by American university recruitments,[49] but it also heard and discussed President Obama's plan to rate colleges on their affordability, accessibility, and outcomes.[50]

For the most part, the metaphor functions either to describe adjunct faculty as the untouchables and administrators (and for some, senior faculty) as implicitly the Brahmin leadership or the rising Brahmin being admitted into and graduating from the top schools in the United States and elsewhere.

Pablo Eisenberg introduces us to another use of the metaphor so as to discover another group of "untouchables," the university staff.

Pablo Eisenberg returns to the caste system metaphor in two essays to focus on the university staff, that is, its secretaries, custodians, food service workers, and others. The issues of the staff are raised only by Eisenberg and no other writer. The only other place one finds any written, published concern about the conditions of the staff are in reports about student strikers who fight for a livable wage for staff.[51]

As I said earlier, other than the university president, the only constituency who knows the services of all the fiefdoms are the students. That the faculty and others in counseling, athletics, development, or security do not know about the conditions of other university employees highlights again how deep the fiefdom geography is alive within the university's caste-system culture.

Protesting students have tried to raise consciousness about the conditions of other workers, especially custodians and food service employees, at their universities. For instance, from the early Harvard protest in 2001 for a livable wage for some of the custodians there[52] to the hunger strike at Georgetown[53] and more recently the student strikes at the University of Miami, Stanford University, and several Texas universities,[54] we have seen a new consciousness-raising "solidarity" between students and workers arising as a countersign to the fiefdoms that house the so-named caste system.[55]

Eisenberg takes note of this solidarity in two essays: one in early September 2012 in the *Chronicle of Higher Education*[56] and then an expanded one two months later in *The Huffington Post.*[57] He began his first critique: "More than 700,000 employees at American colleges— gardeners, security guards, cleaning crews, janitors, food-service personnel, etc.—do not earn a living wage, the bare-bones amount sufficient to provide a minimally decent standard of living for their families. This is a disgrace to our system of higher education and a sad reflection on the moral leadership of our colleges."[58]

Eisenberg explains: "For a wage earner with a family of four to meet the federal poverty line of just over $23,000 a year, he or she would have to net about $13 an hour, seven hours a day, five days a week, for all 52 weeks of the year." Then he described the campus worker: "Very few low-wage workers on American campuses even earn a poverty-level income, let alone receive health benefits. Many work only nine or 10 months a year and are often barred from receiving unemployment benefits during the few summer months they are unemployed. Yet their work is an essential ingredient of college life; without them, campuses couldn't function."

He asks: "Why are they so poorly valued and treated? Why have they become the 'untouchables' of our higher-education caste system?"

Eisenberg first identifies "our growing class divide, in which blue-collar and low-level service workers are granted little or no respect and are treated accordingly. The fact that so many of these workers are members of minority groups taps into lingering negative attitudes about immigrant workers and people of color."

He then turns to the fact that "many colleges have become big businesses, reflecting corporate values." Then he adds, "Like corporate executives who want to cut budgets and maximize profits, college administrators say there is no money in their budgets to raise the wages of their low-income employees. Yet they find plenty of money for athletics, new buildings, and additional highly paid administrators."

Eisenberg notes the student protests with university employees conducting living-wage campaigns, but comments how little ground they have gained: "The opposition of college administrations in general has been surprisingly fierce, often led by chancellors and presidents otherwise known for their liberal perspectives and moderate views."

After narrating a bit the campaigns at Georgetown and Miami, Eisenberg comments on how no one but students recognized the plight of the campus worker. "The treatment of low-wage workers on campus is an issue that flies below the public radar, is ignored by public-policy officials and college trustees, and is dismissed by college administrators as little more than a nuisance. The insouciance and apathy of faculty members throughout academe has permitted administrators to avoid taking any action to remedy these inequities. Professional associations like the American Association of University Professors seem to have ignored the matter."

Citing Georgetown, Eisenberg argues against the claim that "institutions don't have the money to grant additional funds to their blue-collar staff." He writes: "[T]he cost of providing such increases is often a tiny percentage of the institutions' budgets. For example, Georgetown's cost of providing a living wage to its approximately 500 campus workers amounted to only a little over $2 million a year. Georgetown's annual budget in 2010 was more than $900 million."

Eisenberg concludes by taking aim at the overseers: "Public officials responsible for overseeing state colleges are clearly not doing their jobs in ensuring decent working conditions at their institutions. Trustees of private colleges seem to have washed their hands of their obligation to monitor and, where necessary, change the policies and practices of the institutions for which they are ultimately responsible."

Eisenberg summons faculty and others to solidarity with these workers as well as with contingent faculty. Knowing that student activism alone is insufficient, he writes: "Until public officials, administrators, faculty members, students, and the general public are sufficiently aroused to demand major changes, it is unlikely that we will see a major transformation in the way colleges in this country are run."[59]

CONCLUSION

In a recent article in the *Chronicle of Higher Education,* Jeffrey Williams, a professor at Carnegie Mellon University, writes about the "Great Stratification" at the contemporary university: "[I]nstead of the traditional idea of a community of scholars, all roughly equivalent, we now have a distended pyramid, with a huge base of people whose primary job is teaching, often entry-level courses; a layer of specialists in particular fields and researchers who may hardly even teach above them; and a thin spire of administrators commanding the peak."[60]

Williams wants to be clear: this is no ordinary pyramid. He acknowledges other such structures, like those in the health care profession, but he notes how harsh the economic differences are at the university.

> Rather than a horizontal community of scholars, or even a pyramid with reasonable steps of rank, the American university has adopted its own harsh class structure: the mass of the contingent (and other workers) struggling at the bottom, tenure-stream professors in the middle class speaking for the university's intellectual values and productions, and superstar faculty and administrators in the upper class setting its direction and taking the greatest rewards.

Struggling to find a better picture to depict the inequity, Williams writes: "Graphically, it is not really a pyramid any longer, but a large, pancake-shaped bottom tier barely above level, a visible middle layer above it, and finally a barely visible aerie rising above them." And then Williams concludes, "The shape of academic labor is profoundly unbalanced."[61]

Our universities are not fair to many of their employees. There is something deeply disturbing about these inequities at our highest education institutions. Like the church, the university needs to be exposed for its pervasive disinterest in ethics. Inasmuch as these are our culture's two long-standing institutions that teach ethics, we should not miss how disturbing it is that their "lapses" are fundamental ones about justice and the treatment of persons. In short, their lapses are *precisely* about ethics.

If the lapses at these institutions are both ethical, then we need to ask, how can we change the situation? The change must be structural. We must acknowledge, as I have shown here, that the possibility of communicating, knowing, and learning about our institutions is not easy because of the very structure of the university: its fiefdoms and its caste or class stratifications.

We must find ways of knowing more about our own universities, their practices, and their policies. The first step is assuredly to move beyond our own fiefdoms and our castes so as to learn about how others are faring in our so-called university community and to work in solidarity with them for greater equity and true community.

But then we must take aim at our overall structures and look to ensure structures of horizontal accountability as well as opening the pathway of accountability in our vertical structures that until now have functioned in only one direction.

But in order to build those structures we need first to have an ethical culture that inspires and initiates those structures. We will need to create a culture that expects accountability and transparency from the top and from the horizons. We need to recognize that employees should be able to know whether women in all departments at the university, from faculty to staff, from athletics to libraries and dining services, receive the same wages as their male colleagues. We need to see the reports that finally moved a president to accept one candidate for the provost's appointment over another. We need to know how much of the university's budget and revenues come from its athletic program and whether these numbers reflect the claims of the university's mission statement. We need to know how the poorest paid adjuncts survive and what the university is doing about responding to their situation. We have to ask how many prospective students from Asia, Africa, and Latin America will be recruited by our admissions personnel and what plans the university has to assist the university faculty and student body to know how to welcome and support these students.

In short, we need a culture to level the ossified structures of our fiefdoms that keep privileges about information and decision making as the operative defaults at our universities. As we do this, we cannot simply stay with our own cohorts. Just as faculty need, too, to know better the situation of the fellow adjuncts, faculty and student affairs personnel must build bridges between each other.

If we are really interested in running universities where students learn the collaborative work of critical thinking collectively and of attending to the needs of the common good, then we must take ownership of our universities and learn those lessons as well. When we learn those lessons, we will build the university to represent the future we are seeking rather than the past where we are presently entrapped.

6

CHEATING

"I love honor codes, but honor codes are about a culture, and I'm not
sure how you get that going."
—Trevor Brandt-Sarif, a Harvard University junior from California[1]

Since the university exists for the study, understanding, and teaching of
truth, cheating and other compromises of intellectual integrity are the
most inimical and vicious of university practices. If we want clear evidence that our universities lack ethics, then cheating stories are good
indicators. I am looking at cheating not because of its role in either the
classroom or in a student's life; rather, because of our interest in university ethics, I want to look at cheating, the most evident form of a moral
lapse, against the backdrop of a university's culture.

Two insights about cheating today are especially alarming: it is on
the increase and involves those who are already ahead of the curve just
as much as anyone else.

In a definitive essay on cheating at university campuses, Donald
McCabe and Linda Klebe Trevino write that cheating at universities is
"frequent and growing." Their argument comes in three stages: cheating is getting worse and worse, it can be diminished by an honor code,
and one needs an underlying culture of integrity to accompany the
honor code.

The evidence to make their three-fold claim consists of "a decade of
research in which we have surveyed over 14,000 students on 58 different campuses, from small liberal arts colleges to large comprehensive
universities."[2]

HOW PERVASIVE IS CHEATING

McCabe and Trevino begin their data on cheating with the 1965 doctoral dissertation of William Bowers who surveyed over five thousand students on ninety-nine campuses and found that at least half of those responding engaged in some form of cheating since coming to college. McCabe and Trevino note that Bowers believed his estimate was conservative.

Bowers found that students' college peers had probably the most influence on fellow students and argued that campuses that disapprove of cheating prompt their students to cheat less. In short, he believed peer pressure best explains which campuses have more or less cheating.[3]

In their own studies, McCabe and Trevino found that, while Bowers's insight on peer pressure was right, matters have worsened:

> In a 1993 survey of students on nine campuses included in the Bowers study, we found disturbing increases in the level of serious cheating on tests and exams. In 1963, 26 percent of the students on the nine campuses, none of which had honor codes, acknowledged copying from another student on a test or exam; by 1993, the percentage had grown to 52. In addition, we observed a fourfold increase in the use of crib notes, from 6 to 27 percent.

Elsewhere Jon Marcus adds to the bad news; he conjectures that the more education a person has, the more likely one is to cheat:

> If anything, academic misconduct is more prevalent among elite students than others, at least according to research based on a survey of 2,000 students at the University of Arizona that was released in March [2012]. Cheating was reported least among low-income students receiving financial aid and students who were the first in their families to go to university; it was most common among students from well-educated families. The more educated a student's parents, the more likely [the student] was to cheat.[4]

The New York Times found somewhat similar insights: There is more cheating, including among high achievers. In the wake of scandals at the Air Force Academy, Stuyvesant High School, and Harvard University, Richard Pérez-Peña writes in "Studies Find More Students Cheating, With High Achievers No Exception," that experts say the reasons are relatively simple: "Cheating has become easier and more widely tolerated, and both schools and parents have failed to give students strong, repetitive messages about what is allowed and what is prohibited."[5]

Pérez-Peña interviewed Donald McCabe, who said, "I don't think there's any question that students have become more competitive, under more pressure, and, as a result, tend to excuse more from themselves and other students, and that's abetted by the adults around them." McCabe added, "There have always been struggling students who cheat to survive. But more and more, there are students at the top who cheat to thrive."

Pérez-Peña quotes another expert who observes that "the ethical muscles have 'atrophied,' in part because of a culture that exalts success, however it is attained." Referring to elite colleges, he describes the type of thinking alive and well in that culture: "We want to be famous and successful, we think our colleagues are cutting corners, we'll be damned if we'll lose out to them, and some day, when we've made it, we'll be role models. But until then, give us a pass."

To cap off the prevalence of cheating at universities today we can turn to the *Harvard Crimson*, the university's student newspaper, which interviewed their incoming freshmen and found that 10 percent admitted to cheating on an exam before coming to the school. They also reported that 42 percent admitted cheating on homework or a problem set. This figure reminds us not to think of cheating as occurring first or foremost in the classroom.[6]

WHERE ARE THE FACULTY?

The problem of cheating is not a student problem primarily; it is a university problem. As Pérez-Peña notes,[7] not only do the students influence their classmates, but faculty also could promote intellectual integrity at the university.

In a fascinating essay in the *Chronicle of Higher Education*, Alison Schneider did not look at the more fundamental question—What type of culture would promote a more honest set of practices among students?—but rather the more immediate one: "Why Professors Don't

Do More to Stop Students Who Cheat." Her answer inevitably turned to the lack of a university culture that tangibly supported faculty who tried to enforce more integrity. In a word, as cheating increases, a few faculty are heroic martyrs; otherwise they are less and less inclined to be bothered.

Like others writing on cheating, Schneider asked McCabe for his assessment of faculty actions in the face of cheating. "In the majority of cases of trivial cheating, I think most professors turn a blind eye. The number who do nothing is very small, but the number who do very little is very large."[8]

Referring to his 1993 study, McCabe asked eight hundred professors at sixteen institutions whether they ever reported cheating: 40 percent responded "never," 54 percent said "seldom," and 6 percent said often.

Schneider also interviewed Jon Kerkvliet, who has done his own study and found that it was not the type of test that changed cheating rates in a classroom but the faculty member's actual involvement with warning students and acting on the warnings. Kerkvliet found, however, that whenever he presented his results, he was confronted with questions from faculty asking, "Why should we care when administrators don't seem to?"[9]

Schneider received a benign account of administrators' indifference to cheating from a professor at a major research university who said that faculty at his university "can't be bothered. They're not rewarded for teaching; they're rewarded for research. There's no future in pursuing cheating from the standpoint of a professor's self-interest." But most of Schneider's accounts were not so benign: "Those professors who do pursue cheating allegations often complained that they feel victimized by the process." Later in the essay, after referring to some incredible stories of professors trying to report cheating, she writes, "Professors who push to penalize cheaters somehow find themselves tied to the whipping post."[10]

Still, these unfortunate heroes know their counterparts, who are not students, but fellow faculty. After discussing how rampant plagiarism is, and how sites like CheatHouse.com provide term papers for sale,[11] Andrew Delbanco remarks, "I know two faculty friends at a prestigious college who entertain themselves each spring at the commencement ceremony by going through the printed program checking off names of seniors whom they know to have submitted at least one plagiarized paper. It's not uncommon for these students to be graduating with honors."[12]

Subsequent to Schneider's essay, the *Chronicle* hosted a colloquium of published letters, which effectively agreed with her findings, supporting them with even more stunning examples from other universities. One professor wrote differently, trying to reflect on a bigger cause, a larger issue, commodification. He wrote:

> The increasing casualness with which students seem to be cheating and committing plagiarism is, in my opinion, just another symptom of the paradigm shift from education as the enhancement of a person's character and abilities—something that an individual has to work to attain—to education as a consumer product—something that must be handed over on demand to all who pay their tuition.

He added:

> If education is a product to be bought and sold, and each of us involved in the educational process—teachers and students alike—is construed simply as an atomistic individual following his or her own self-interest, then on this economic model cheating may indeed be an efficient way for the student to attain the best payoff—the highest grade—on his or her investment, while an instructor's making waves serves no one's interest and is counterproductive to maximizing the institution's profits.[13]

Clearly the question of cheating is not about a singular student's actions. Students at some universities and colleges give other students the support to cheat; students at other universities live in a different culture where honesty is promoted and cheating is inhibited. Similarly at some universities some faculty who oppose cheating find that cheating is an insurmountable problem; at others, cheating is a rare incidence. The difference, as we will see, depends on the underlying culture at the university. And, of course, commodification *does* have something to do with it, though it is not the only matter.

HONOR CODES AND UNIVERSITY CULTURE

Since Bowers's study, almost all evidence shows that honor codes can make a significant contribution in reducing the incidence of cheating. As a result of these studies, more universities have begun appropriating honor codes, while others have become more convinced of their already existing codes. Nonetheless, the much quoted essay by McCabe was precipitated by an editorial in the University of Virginia's student newspaper, *The Cavalier Daily*, which called for abolishing that university's famous honor code in the wake of a cheating scandal in an introductory physics course.

In reply, McCabe musters evidence from coded schools like Mount Holyoke, Smith, Kansas State, Vanderbilt, Washington and Lee, and Wellesley. Traditional codes at these schools work.[14] However, he begins his argument by acknowledging that a code must be supported by an underlying "culture of integrity." He writes:

> Simply having an honor code means little if students don't know about it. It must be introduced to new students and made a topic of ongoing campus dialogue. The level of trust placed in students on honor-code campuses establishes academic integrity as a clear institutional priority. The high value attached to honesty and, perhaps more important, the privileges accorded to students under traditional honor-code systems creates a culture that makes cheating socially unacceptable among most students—Bowers's concept of peer disapproval.[15]

McCabe is sympathetic to large campuses with commuting students where implementing an honor code and developing a shared culture is very challenging. But he finds that even at those campuses where a modified code went into place, cheating decreased especially in comparison with noncoded schools.

He describes one recent study in which he surveyed 2,200 students at twenty-one different schools. Nine had traditional honor codes (though one was a "hybrid"), nine were noncoded, and three large public universities had modified codes.

McCabe expected that the large public universities would be in the worst straits, but found:

Self-reported cheating was actually lower at these three schools compared with the nine noncode campuses surveyed. One-third of the students at the large universities acknowledged one or more instances of serious cheating compared with almost half of the students at the noncode schools. One in ten students at the universities acknowledged repetitive serious test cheating versus one in six at the noncode schools.

He concludes, "We believe such data suggest that most schools can develop strategies to reduce the level of student cheating."

McCabe adds that modified codes only work if two critical elements are in place: the university must "communicate to its students that academic integrity is a major institutional priority" and students must participate in campus judicial reviews of any violations of the code and "should play a major role in its (the code's) development and implementation."[16] In other words, the university must promote a culture of integrity and students must participate in its practices.

Regardless of debate about the utility of a code, more and more universities rely on them and give testimony to their usefulness. Writing from Hamden-Sydney College, two professors write in the *Chronicle of Higher Education* that their "honor code is strictly enforced, and the enforcement is handled by an all-student court. Students convicted of lying or cheating can expect to receive punishments ranging from suspension to expulsion." Like others before them, they add, "However, honor codes don't always work. Mr. McCabe says that their success depends on a 'culture of academic integrity' that leads students to take enforcement of the rules seriously. . . . When it works, the culture makes for a successful honor code as much as the honor code makes for a successful culture."[17]

A CULTURE WITHOUT A CODE?

The 2012 Harvard University cheating scandal generated much media coverage. Rather than rehash the details of the scandal, we might wonder aloud at a possible solution. We could follow the *Boston Globe*'s editorial where they suggest that commodification has a lot to do with the scandal. They argued that the scandal was "perhaps . . . an inevitable result of today's educational marketplace, in which a college education has become a transaction: a means of earning a degree for your resume, rather than a place to explore the life of the mind." It concluded with ironic darkness, suggesting, "At the least, the students who didn't cheat in the class might deserve a partial refund."[18]

But surely there are more immediate matters that need to be addressed than the broadcloth of commodification. Besides honor codes, there must be other ways of reducing cheating. After all, what happens when a culture of integrity is purportedly promoted, but an honor code is not adopted? In that instance, what does one offer to give the culture its practices? All of the authors cited previously noted that you cannot have an honor code without an underlying culture of integrity, because each supports and better realizes the other. They work in tandem. If not an honor code, then what practice?

A year after the cheating scandal was uncovered at Harvard, the university seemed to find itself in a difficult position—wanting to have a culture of ethics, but resisting a code of honor. "I do think more understanding [of academic ethics] would be helpful," said Michael Mitzenmacher, a Harvard computer science professor who has served on the college's Administrative Board, the body that oversees disciplinary issues. "But I don't think a stated honor code necessarily would be."[19]

Harvard has had a long engagement with trying to find practices to discourage cheating, but it has until now consistently resisted an honor code. In a witty *New York Times* op-ed piece titled "Song of the Cheaters," Rebecca Harrington offers an eye on Harvard culture as it wrestles over time with occasional difficulties with cheating. She narrates from the *Crimson* several episodes from the nineteenth century until relatively recently about the presence of proctors at exams, and then introduces the notion of an honor code and reports that in 1994, a *Crimson* journalist wondered whether "the absence of an honor code or a clear set of rules regarding cheating at Harvard has left undergraduate students wondering about what does and what doesn't constitute cheating." Reflecting on that comment, she begins her conclusion asking, "Is Harvard clear enough about what 'cheating' means?"

The 2008 Harvard graduate offers this reply:

> Perhaps the best answer can be found in the writings of the Harvard philosopher William James, who, in 1888, much concerned with cheating, invoked the idea of establishing little honor clubs, kind of like fraternities to keep people honest. The proposition, he recalled,

was rather scornfully shut down. He turned to *The Crimson* in his discomfort, saying: "The impression this episode gave me of the debilitated tone of social responsibility here was startling. By *social responsibility* I mean the willingness to act for the social ideal, no matter how much obstructive individuals have to suffer . . . why it should be so lacking here I do not know."[20]

Jon Marcus at the *Times Higher Education* also asked what practices Harvard will put in place to express the culture of integrity that Harvard wants to realize. Marcus noted that while Harvard does not have an honor code, its president, Drew Gilpin Faust, has said she is entertaining the possibility of implementing one. Marcus noted that last year, the university added a voluntary pledge for first-year students to uphold "integrity, respect, and industry." Is that enough, he wondered.

He reported that a survey by the *Yale Daily News*, the university's student newspaper, "found that the majority of the 1,037 respondents had not read the policies on academic honesty in the student handbook and did not know the rules about sharing or copying work. Like Harvard, Yale has no honor code and both seem to have student populations confused about what constitutes cheating."[21]

Marcus added a question. If there is an epidemic in cheating, as the *Chronicle* suggests, what credibility is there in enforcing any rule against it? If accountability is not a regular practice, can accountability be randomly enforced?

The contention by many students caught cheating in the "Intro to Congress" course at Harvard was that the professor was unclear as to what was acceptable for the exam. (This is, of course, an embarrassing claim, whether those who use it know it or not.) Marcus reported that the excuse is a standard response. "When 200 business students on a strategic management course at the University of Central Florida were accused of cheating in an exam in autumn 2010, they also blamed the professor for being unclear in his instructions." He added that "when 17 former nursing students at Maricopa Community Colleges in Arizona were accused of cheating last year, they sued, too—again contending that the instructions were unclear."

Marcus returned to the question of commodification again as he interviewed Teddi Fishman at the International Center for Academic Integrity at Clemson University: "We have substituted the credential as a goal instead of education as a goal. It's as if you were going on a round-the-world trip but all you really wanted was the passport stamps."

"One of the reasons students give for cheating is that they would be disadvantaged if they don't cheat because so many other people are cheating," Fishman says. "That's what executives who get arrested for fraud say, too."

These discussions reveal to us the inevitable connections needing to be made between creating a culture of ethics and stipulating the right practices that sustain that culture. Happily, after all its discussions, the Faculty of Arts and Sciences at Harvard University on May 6, 2014, voted overwhelmingly to adopt an undergraduate honor code to be put into effect in the fall of 2015.[22]

THE THRILL OF CHEATING, SINCE NO ONE GETS HURT

In a 2013 study in the *Journal of Personality and Social Psychology*, "The Cheater's High: The Unexpected Affective Benefits of Unethical Behavior," the lead author Nicole Ruedy reported a "high" after effectively cheating. This contradicts the common opinion in moral behavior that one feels badly after one acts wrongly. In a nutshell the researchers found the following:

> Many theories of moral behavior assume that unethical behavior triggers negative affect. In this article, we challenge this assumption and demonstrate that unethical behavior can trigger positive affect, which we term a "cheater's high."
>
> Across 6 studies, we find that even though individuals predict they will feel guilty and have increased levels of negative affect after engaging in unethical behavior (Studies 1a and 1b), individuals who cheat on different problem-solving tasks consistently experience more positive affect than those who do not (Studies 2–5).
>
> We find that this heightened positive affect does not depend on self-selection (Studies 3 and 4), and it is not due to the accrual of undeserved financial rewards (Study 4).
>
> Cheating is associated with feelings of self-satisfaction, and the boost in positive affect from cheating persists even when prospects for self-deception about unethical behavior are reduced (Study 5).[23]

At the end of their study, they note, "The type of unethical behavior we examine involves actions that are clearly understood as unethical (as our pre-test findings show), but they do not involve direct harm to a salient victim."[24]

They suggest that the impact of peer pressure ought to be investigated. This is an interesting development that ironically furthers the case for promoting a culture of integrity. That is, if students are getting a high from cheating, a practice promoted by group pressure, then that group pressure has actually created a cheating culture. Since, as we saw, nature abhors a vacuum, it ought not come as a surprise that a vicious culture occupies the place a virtuous one could have been. This, I think, is what caused William James's consternation.

Not only do the researchers suggest that the group promotes the cheating but it also dissipates considerably any individual's guilt that may result. "Future research should investigate how the cheater's high scales to groups. Quite possibly, when groups of people coordinate an effort to cheat the system, it could exacerbate the cheater's high by diffusing responsibility for negative outcomes and building a sense of camaraderie from cheating together."[25]

Jan Hoffman at the *New York Times* interviewed Nicole Ruedy. There she notes: "The fact that people feel happier is disturbing, because there is emotional reinforcement of the behavior, meaning they are more likely to do it again." But Dr. Ruedy noted that the study's cheaters believed that no one was hurt by their actions. Here she believed there was a place for teaching people that cheating does have its victims. "Perhaps people could be made aware of the costs that others actually bear," she said. "Identify victims of their behavior." It seems an easy enough discussion, though with an eye to the long reach of peer pressure, one wonders how many students would convince others to dismiss the argument.

Hoffman found another way of diminishing the high: Aim at the self-satisfaction. "Companies could send a message that 'a monkey could game our system,' undercutting cheating as clever and emphasizing how much employee integrity is valued."[26]

The studies reinforce exactly what we have been reading. Cheating is culturally promoted and peer-driven. It depends on ignorance and ambiguity and does best for one who wears blinders: One who cheats proverbially does not know the entire situation. The one who cheats does not see the intrinsic wrongness of cheating, does not know what cheating exactly is, does not recognize any ill effect of cheating on oneself, and does not believe that his or her actions hurt anyone. In short, there is a convenience to the cheater's ignorance that keeps him or her protected, all the more so when accompanied by the validation of his or her own classmates.

Dan Ariely calls this environment the "fudge factor," which captures in many ways the inconvenient ignorance named previously, coupled with ambiguous remarks by faculty regarding actual classroom expectations and faculty's general disinterest in matters of reporting.[27]

In light of all this ignorance, there seems a need for clearly taught experiential lessons that instruct students otherwise. For this reason in his book, *Cheating Lessons: Learning from Academic Dishonesty*, James M. Lang, after describing the fudge factor, acknowledges that cheating is deeply rooted in ignorance and therefore its remedies must be brought to the classroom where foundational lessons can be taught, learned, and practiced. He offers a fourfold constructive plan to promote an understanding of academic integrity: fostering intrinsic motivation, learning for mastery, lowering stakes, and instilling self-efficacy.[28]

I find his lessons are not as much to address cheating as to address the vacuum in student personal and collective formation that makes cheating so attractive. In other words, Lang proposes that students discover in what he calls "an instructive learning environment" what it means to be appropriately a student. As he writes in his conclusion, cheating happens "for understandable reasons, in response to a specific environment and can best be addressed through thinking hard about that environment and making modifications that will better motivate students to learn and give them the tools they need to do so."[29]

THINKING HARD AND BROADLY ABOUT LESSONS FOR ACADEMIC INTEGRITY

In *Campus Life*, Helen Lefkowitz Horowitz observes how fraternities were able to promote cheating. She notes that though they did not initiate cheating or any other acts that defy university standards, they did "link them in a coherent culture which passed it on to successive generations of college men."[30]

We know now that a culture that promotes academic integrity must have attendant practices that realize deeply and broadly the necessity of academic integrity on a campus.

We know too that faculty are needed as classroom teachers to effectively use the practices and explicitly support the culture. Faculty need to read, discuss, and share a good set of lessons, like those from Lang, that promote a proper learning environment and a fresh understanding of the meaning of university study and the vocation of the student. In turn, this will require administrators and boards to rethink their promotion of research without attendant value and concern for university teaching and hopefully prompt them to aim for a better balance that offers teaching some parity with research for faculty tenure and promotion.

We also know that implicit messages that arise from commodification, like justified worry about getting good grades, having the well-graded transcript, and paying to get ahead, are formidable and only become more influential and effective when left unchallenged. This too needs to be taken into account.

In entering competitively for their much-needed tuitions, universities are the first to promote a commodification model of education. It is the university and not parents and their children who first developed the idea that university education was a purchasable commodity.

Promoting academic integrity is, therefore, a rigorous project and in some instances, a countercultural one. It is more than an honor code and more than an administration articulating a cultural claim into its mission statements. The practices for combatting cheating and promoting academic integrity are considerable.

A survey of the literature shows us then how formative structures can help faculty to engage students more creatively. Still, some other material helps us in discovering and appreciating how broadly and deeply we must work to develop the practices and culture necessary for academic integrity. Along the way, we might find the daunting project of talking about not just classroom academic integrity but university-wide academic integrity.

For instance, Wilfred Decoo's lengthy work on plagiarism is a model of thoroughness of appreciating how competent on plagiarism one ought to be to assess the proper penalties and solutions. Using a case of plagiarism in a doctoral dissertation, Decoo covers in seven chapters such topics as detection, analysis, assessment, reporting and handling, and prevention.[31] But the book is exhausting and when one looks at it, one might feel so inexpert that one would put back on the blinders and look for the friends of Delbanco! Surely we must develop ways of being trained to better estimate and address plagiarism.

But students are not the only ones on campus who cheat and plagiarize. Faculty and administrators do as well, with the same supportive cultures, the same comforting blinders, and the same belief in the innocent consequences of their actions.

In "The Truth, the Whole Truth and Nothing but the Truth," Paul D. Eisenberg begins his noteworthy essay, "Whatever may be true of them in other aspects of their lives, academics in their professional work and lives face some particularly knotty problems about truth telling." Eisenberg does not address faculty research though he does refer to ways that faculty may suppress data so as to highlight their own claims, but he believes that faculty are already able to determine right from wrong in these types of matters. Rather, he wants to address other cases less frequently found in the classroom and more often in the office. He attends to writing comments on students' papers and exams; adjudicating a right, not overinflated grade; recommending (or not) fellow faculty to inquiring students; telling a student whether their decision to go onto graduate school is a good one; and writing a letter of recommendation. Any faculty reading the essay would easily acknowledge that they would have liked knowing that an article like this was written by a colleague, because most of us make the judgments we do about ambiguous situations with little genuine clarity and even less shared common wisdom.[32]

In another model essay, George Sher takes one simple matter, a letter of recommendation for a student or a colleague.[33] While all letters of recommendation are essentially designed to help a student or colleague get accepted into a position of some sort, Sher offers insights about how some letters can be grossly exaggerated or even lack truthfulness and suggests ways that faculty can achieve a balance in the letters they write. His essay should be tucked into every new faculty member's welcome orientation.

In another set of essays, we find faculty and truth-telling moving into gray areas, especially as some professional matters are discussed. While looking at a host of academic personnel decisions, Rudolph H. Weingartner considers using a simple tenure case to highlight how university personnel decisions have particular problems of their own.[34] David Lewis asks about how we assess the truthfulness of candidates, of what they teach, and of the philosophical doctrines they may hold.[35]

Of essays on administrators and truth-telling, there are, as we saw in Chapter 5, unfortunately very few. But two are worthy of note. First, Bruce Kimball's essay concerns evaluating when one is both prejudicial and objective, a too common paradox.[36] In the second, an essay that provides us with an appropriate closing thought, David Kline discusses how, as a faculty chair, a faculty might find a "white lie" compelling as an administrator of faculty, but might not find the same case compelling if taught in class. Kline invites the reader to consider our professional dilemmas as eminently teachable ones.[37]

CONCLUSION

Throughout this chapter, then, we begin, I hope, to see formidable influences that cannot be simply "policed" away. True, the university is in trouble. Cheating is an obvious indicator of how problematically compromised university education is; cheating needs to be addressed and the ethical formation of the university needs it now more than ever. Cheating is hardly the only ethical problem at the university and so it should be clear that developing a culture of ethics at the university can help not only combat the vices and their attendant practices of cheating, but it can also begin to subdue the commodification culture that tries to reduce all of education to a transaction of commodities. A culture of ethics helps cultivate, wherever it exists, an appreciation for the common good and all the goods that it needs including the value of an education that teaches us to develop the skills of critical thinking that must be put to use if we seek a future where humanity may flourish.

Cultures need practices to keep them alive and a culture of integrity needs its practices, like an honor code, if it is going to be credible in expressing its collective belief that wisdom is only found in the true pursuit of truth.

7

UNDERGRADUATES ACTING BADLY

"Precisely because its community is so diverse, set in a society so divided and confused over its values, a university that pays little attention to moral development may find that many of its students grow bewildered, convinced that ethical dilemmas are simply matters of personal opinion beyond external judgment or careful analysis. Nothing could be more unfortunate or more unnecessary."
—Derek Bok[1]

In this chapter we look at undergraduates behaving badly, a phenomenon that is only worsening. If you think that racially themed parties at universities are nastier and more frequent than ever, you are right. If you think hazing is more pervasive, more dangerous, and more brutal than ever, you are not mistaken. If you think fraternities have more dangerous accidents, more parties, and more alcoholic binges than ever, you are unfortunately correct. If you think that sexual violence is up and that rape is a much more common campus event, you are right.

Whether a university has a fraternity or not, undergraduates behaving badly is a progressively worsening reality. As Michael Sperber told us more than ten years ago, in *Beer and Circus: How Big-Time College Sports Is Crippling Undergraduate Education*, when universities bought into football and other sports, they bought into partying, big time.[2] Come to college, come to party. Fraternities make it easier to party, but if there are no fraternities, heck what are hockey matches for?

As the party scene envelops the campus, most faculty are silent, at best passive witnesses to these events. Make no mistake about it: Faculty have become the beneficiaries of big-time sports, of wealthier fraternities, and of higher tuitions guaranteeing their salaries.

As the online video company that promotes the worst of hooliganism and college partying, *I'm Shmacked,* advertises so well,[3] videos of students partying is a great recruiting device today. School partying attracts prospective students, especially those paying full fare. As we will see, many of those who can pay their way have been what Helen Lefkowitz Horowitz calls the "college men and women," that is, the people most inclined to go clubbing and partying.

Today, who addresses the excesses of undergraduates behaving badly? Student affairs does. We already saw that Julie Reuben explains well the reasons why university faculty relegated student moral formation to student affairs.[4] Today student affairs takes care of students' living situations, their extracurriculars, their meal plans, and their personal successes and failures. But where are the faculty?

Most faculty only know their students as they are in their classes and not elsewhere on campus. Faculty know students as recipients of the wisdom faculty impart according to the syllabi that they develop. Those syllabi set the parameters for the expected exchanges between faculty and students. Most faculty don't engage students about the very decisions they are making today: about friendships, about living situations, about family, and about helping make ends meet.

Rightly, faculty have no oversight over students. But faculty do have a formative role, albeit an intellectual one. They could enter into debates about campus events and offer their opinions. They could bring the matter of campus activities into their classes. But many avoid this. They say, "That's not what I'm paid to do." "The administration doesn't want my interference." "Why bother, the students will do what they want." "I tried, and no one stood with me."

Take for instance ethics: Those teaching ethics in any of the different professions prepare students to make a panoply of complicated decisions in the business, medical, nursing, or legal world. Why cannot faculty help students to realize that the ability to make decisions professionally arises from the capacity to make personal ethical decisions? Faculty who teach ethics in the professions rarely turn more immediately to preparing students to face their weekends, their friends, or their constant moral dilemmas. Who are we teaching? Are we not teaching people whose personal capacity to make decisions today will enable them to make the professional ones tomorrow? Do we not need to help our students understand that they cannot isolate their personal lives from their professional lives, that the virtues they develop now on campus are the virtues that they will have in the future?

This chapter tries to show the compelling need for faculty to enter university ethics. Faculty need to engage their students today in the decisions they face and need to make. As we will see, when faculty get involved in university matters and even write as academics about undergraduate students behaving badly (or well), they make an enormous contribution. But the number of faculty doing this are few.

One exception that I found when I taught my course "Sex, Gender, and Body" is *Sex and the Soul: Juggling Sexuality, Spirituality, Romance, and Religion on American College Campuses,* a book by Boston University's Donna Freitas that speaks to many contemporary students' experiences of the hook-up culture, a culture that promotes sexual activity but one that rarely gets critically engaged by faculty on campus.[5]

Freitas acknowledges that she's a bit of a lone voice and acknowledges that students don't know how to navigate these issues, not only personally but intellectually as well. She understands that every student has a very social face, caught up in a very public, very collective identity, but she also encounters even in class a private self, one who wrestles beneath the social mask to work out more clearly her or his own identity. Freitas complains that other faculty are not writing material that she can use and makes the exception, citing *Just Love* by Yale's Margaret Farley, which offers a normative framework for sexual ethics shaped by justice in sexual desire, love, and action.[6]

Like these two faculty members, we too can offer our perspectives from the social sciences, the humanities, and the professional schools. We can enter into the messiness of university ethics.

A BIT OF HISTORY

Before the American Revolution, universities were started for the most part to train evangelical clergy to teach and preach.[7] These students went on to become ministers and among them, some entered the professoriate.

Until the end of the eighteenth century, the American university had this fundamental mission and structure. As attractive as the early roots of American university life might seem to the parents of prospective students at today's Ivies, the reality would not have been terribly attractive to their children. The plight of the eighteenth-century undergraduate was to be virtually at the mercy of faculty who not only controlled the school but who also ran the accommodations.[8] The undergraduate was kept in his place by a social structure with little freedom and even less recourse. That social structure ran deep and a world of deference marked the relationship between faculty and students. As Helen Lefkowitz Horowitz describes in *Campus Life: Undergraduate Cultures from the End of the Eighteenth Century to the Present,* "The prescribed student role was to pay, pray, study and accept. If they found their instructor vindictive or their food rotten, they had no legitimate recourse other than withdrawal."[9]

The American Revolution changed that. As the Republic emerged, only 2 percent of Americans were enrolled in university, either as sons of the wealthy, who tried to learn the social graces that went along with their class or the poor who sought ministry. As the Republic grew, however, others arrived who saw university as a pathway to the professional life.[10]

These sons of patriots were not only not given to ministry, they were not given to deference. They arrived more inclined to expressing their demands and to taking advantage of what the university offered. In particular, wealthy students who "did not depend upon college for a position in the world" led the way.[11] Unfortunately, the faculty and administration, still accustomed to deference and still believing that their evangelical rhetoric would persuade even the most rebellious in their classes, did not see any need to respond.

Horowitz tells the story that the faculty and administration's failure to give any hearing to their students' complaints inevitably led to protest and riot. And while university presidents successfully put down these demonstrations, often with the local support of neighbors fearing disorder, they did nothing to diminish the growing resentment that students harbored toward their elite instructors.

Eventually, by the beginning of the nineteenth century many students saw themselves as "college men" at war with their faculty. Of course, not every student was an aggressive college man. Horowitz writes: "By the late eighteenth century American youth in college divided into two basic paths. Undergraduates might become college men or remain outsiders."[12]

"College men" were club-oriented guys. They went to college to escape their parents' and neighbors' moral order. They disdained college teachers and administrators who dared to become their parental surrogates. Horowitz writes:

> College men saw the four years as a staging ground for their adult lives; they insisted, however, that it was not merely a time of preparation. For them life was now. Thus their eager pursuit of the pleasures of the table and the flesh and their high tolerance for the excesses that accompanied indulgence. They refused to judge each other as they were judged and offered mutual aid to those threatened with being caught and sympathy to the convicted.[13]

By their mutual aid, college males became united with one another "against their faculty." Though they boasted democracy, their society had a clear hierarchy among the ranks of the college males where "athletic prowess, social grace, and a sense of fair play weighed significantly." Horowitz adds: "Male college life proved both stable and adaptable. It remained constant in its belief in the war between students and faculty, its devaluation of academic work, its willingness to cheat, and its disdain for those outside its circle."[14]

Horowitz tells of the deep and abiding loyalty of students for one another in ignoring any academic claims: the real measure of success was not grades but rather the judgment of one's peers.[15]

Throughout the nineteenth century, the world of the university was a man's world. "Implicitly, collegiate codes taught undergraduates that only men were important, and thereby strengthened the masculine hegemony of the late nineteenth century."[16]

In describing American college life from 1830 to the end of the nineteenth century, Horowitz tells us that campus life for college men was somewhat violent: "College men battled each other in interclass rivalries and outsiders in town-gown conflicts." Most notably, they engaged in "rushes," violent free-for-alls that pitted sophomores against freshmen. Stories about "rushes" can be found all over the Internet. Across the country, university sophomores over extended periods brutally initiated freshmen into university life. Many universities have records from 1850 to 1910 depicting bloody "rushes" between freshmen and sophomores.[17] These rushes were not only the bloody, fallowed fields from which fraternities were born; collegiate football also emerged from these violent clashes.[18]

The birth of fraternities occurs in this context and these societies simply emerged from the reckless, newly minted practices of brutally initiating neophytes. Hierarchy and exclusion would accompany these practices. It is important for us to realize that fraternities did not arrive at campuses as if coming from some other context: on their worst days, fraternities were a natural, evolutionary development of the practices that early American college men collectively engaged.

Of course, university presidents were opposed to fraternities from their inception. From the early 1830s, whether at Amherst, Williams, or the University of Michigan, presidents routinely opposed them, ineffectively. Fraternities claimed the American right of free association and university presidents realized that they lacked the authority to gain the upper hand. In the war between faculty and students, the fraternity was and, as we shall see, remains an indefatigable outgrowth of early American collegiate life. The authority of fraternities is rooted in their being a natural development of the protected male collegiate world of the nineteenth century.[19]

Understanding campus life helps us to see that universities never had ethical cultures, not at least among the college men. Rather, in many ways they were the world of adolescent men using force and abusive rhetoric to assert leadership and order. Think of the adolescents as a little older and, on occasion, more mature than those in *Lord of the Flies*. While many may think that *Animal House* gives us the quintessential view of campus hooliganism, William Golding is better than Harold Ramis in capturing all that's disturbing about the collective of adolescent schoolboys when they take control. *Lord of the Flies* is like nineteenth-century university life; it's a much more brutal *Animal House* without the humor.

Violence was coupled with moral abandon. Horowitz writes: "Freshmen learned early in their college course that they could openly enjoy pleasures frowned on by parents and hometown gossips. Male college culture was assertively hedonistic." She reports one student writing about the "wholly delightful irresponsibility" he encountered as a freshman at Yale: "We kicked up our heels in that pleasant college town like colts in a pasture."[20]

There were also the outsiders. The first of the outsiders were those studying for ministry who took courses, studied, and worked with professors, but never became insiders of student life. Though originally they predated the arrival of the college male, as extracurricular activities became part of college life and the war between faculty and students developed, later ministry students went to the sidelines, uninterested in the emerging campus culture. Horowitz notes, "Either by inclination or out of fear, the future ministers avoided the hedonism and violence of their rowdy classmates." These sought the approval of their faculty, not their peers. She adds, "When the fraternities formed, these students stood outside."[21]

By the beginning of the mid-nineteenth century, others entered the university but only its academic life and not the university campus culture. Horowitz writes: "[O]ther outsiders took the pastors' places: ambitious youth from all over rural America; the first college women; immigrants, especially Jews; blacks; veterans after World War II; commuters; and, beginning in the 1960s, women continuing their education."[22]

Not surprisingly, the first women who went to college were outsiders. "Those who entered Oberlin in 1837 differed little from the men (outsiders). All shared in the life of pauper scholars. When women entered the University of Michigan in 1870 and Cornell in 1872, the college men on campus put them in outsiders' mold."[23] Co-educational institutions forced their male students to sit beside female students in class, "but they allowed the men to dominate the all-important life outside the classroom. Insisting that the extra-curriculum be for men only, the organized male students moved to exclude women completely from their organizations."[24] Horowitz concludes, "Thus for many men in coeducational institutions, as in all male ones, college life offered full immersion into the group life of male peers. If American boys needed a period of separate trial and initiation before entering adult society, this was it."[25]

The first women to attend college were "as serious and aspiring as any male outsider." The pioneer women students "saw themselves cast in the role of outsiders."[26] These women "defied feminine conventions to take their minds and aspirations seriously" so as "to become teachers, doctors, or scholars."[27] "Where they penetrated into formerly all male preserves, such as the University of Michigan or Cornell, they were as unwelcome as any uninvited guest. College men organized in fraternities rejected them as outsiders."[28] Horowitz narrates the different ways that women at both schools were excluded, but notes that, "[r]ejected by the college men, the early coeds found companionship and occasionally love in the ranks of male outsiders."[29]

Women in all-women colleges had the same strong-minded character traits as the first women at co-educational institutions and in many ways resembled the "outsiders." By the 1890s things changed. When women first arrived at male universities, they lived in boarding houses. To recruit more women, co-educational institutions began developing residence halls and soon more middle-class families began sending their daughters as well to live at the universities. "Unlike their pioneering predecessors, these daughters of the middle class brought more conventional notions of womenhood into the college world and the belief that they, like college men, had come for fun. They did not see college as a steppingstone to a career but as a way station to a proper marriage."[30] Simply put, these women became the partners of college men.

As a parallel universe to the college man, these women eventually formed female fraternities, later known as *sororities*. From there the "college women" emerged. College men and women both embodied the "hedonism and recklessness of the genteel."[31]

Horowitz sees a third path develop in the twentieth century that she calls "the rebel." The rebels "rejected parental ways and questioned the broader society."[32] They believed that they had original solutions to contemporary problems. With regard to gender, the rebels broke two university codes: "the absolute distinction between men and women on campus and male presumptions about the place of women in college life."[33] So women were also rebels but, like the outsiders, they were noticeably different from the rowdy college men and women.

I find these categories helpful, not as actual typologies but as heuristic ones, pointing us, generally speaking, to differing groups and helping us to appreciate the different stances of men and women on campus. As such, I think they help us understand something about the challenges that women have at the university, a point that I develop in Chapter 8. College men and women continue to inhabit contemporary American universities. The outsiders and rebels do as well. The man's world that outsider women encountered in the nineteenth century is just as apparent at the contemporary university.

FRATERNITIES AND OTHER COLLECTIVES

In her compelling essay in *Atlantic Monthly*, "The Dark Power of Fraternities," Caitlin Flanagan acknowledges that fraternities "raise millions of dollars for worthy causes, contribute millions of hours in community service, and seek to steer young men toward lives of service and honorable action." But she adds, "They also have a long, dark history of violence against their own members and visitors to their houses, which makes them in many respects at odds with the core mission of college itself."[34]

While noting that hazing causes but a small fraction of the harm that fraternities bring, Flanagan reports in her year-long investigation that "lawsuits against fraternities are becoming a growing matter of public interest, in part because they record such lurid events, some of them ludicrous, many more of them horrendous. For every butt bomb, there's a complaint of manslaughter, rape, sexual torture, psychological trauma." While she notes that most of these suits are settled somehow and never make it to trial, still, "the material facts of these complaints are rarely in dispute; what is contested, most often, is only liability."[35]

Referring to a series of articles on fraternities by *Bloomberg News*'s David Glovin and John Hechinger who noted that since 2005, more than sixty people have died in incidents linked to fraternities, twenty-four of them freshmen,[36] Flanagan adds that the figure is "dwarfed by the numbers of serious injuries, assaults, and sexual crimes that regularly take place in these houses."[37]

When I started this project in the spring of 2012, I remember reading the following article about police responding to a noise complaint in the Boston neighborhood of Allston. The story helped me to see the human face of those affected by fraternities' hazing.

> Police sought criminal complaints Tuesday against 14 suspects accused of beating and binding five Boston University students and then covering them in hot sauce and honey as part of a fraternity hazing scheme.

Early Monday morning, police responded to a noise complaint in what could have been another loud, late-night house party, on an Allston street notorious for them.

Police found a circle of students shivering in the cellar, bound, in their underwear and doused in honey, hot sauce, chili sauce, and coffee grounds.

"All five were shivering and horrified and fearful looks on their faces," police officers wrote in a report.

When an officer asked the students if they were ok, one shook his head no as tears fell down his face.

When the condiments were washed off, police could see that welts covered their backs.[38]

I realized that these young men who were beaten, humiliated, and frightened beyond belief were no different than the students in my own classes. I wondered how many faculty in the Boston area, for instance, would refer to the local incident in their classes. For instance, of those teaching ethics in the greater Boston area (there have to be easily a hundred courses in ethics taught in any semester at Boston-area universities), would there have been even one professor who thought this local scandal about twenty-year-old students being brutalized by fellow students merited even a minute of comment?

If any faculty do mention it, they don't write about it. For all those who have written on hazing, I found only five who wrote as faculty. The first was Winton Solberg, a historian who wrote an essay on hazing at his university, "Harmless Pranks or Brutal Practices? Hazing at the University of Illinois, 1868–1913."[39] There he compares the styles and decisions by two very different presidents and notes that by 1913 the practice had run its course thanks to the president "who demonstrated that educational leadership made a difference. He was responsible for the policy that participation in hazing of any kind would lead to dismissal from the university."[40] While suggesting that those who haze are bullies, Solberg notes that though "hazing was long a serious problem in higher education," "college and university histories rarely do more than make fleeting reference to the subject."[41] When it comes to brutal campus practices, administrators, like their faculty, brush aside such events affecting their campus.[42]

Four other faculty members highlight the significance of faculty contributions when addressing the ethics of university life. In 1990, Hank

Nuwer, an associate professor at Franklin College in Indiana, published *Broken Pledges: The Deadly Rite of Hazing,* a study that begins with the death of a pledge, Chuck Stenzel, at Alfred University in 1978 but then covers so many instances of hazing that we begin to appreciate the practice's pervasiveness.[43] Eleven years later he wrote *Wrongs of Passage: Fraternities, Sororities, Hazing and Binge Drinking,* where he focused on the historical roots of hazing in the United States and both the Greek system and non-Greek organizations that have coercive drinking as a constitutive part of their hazing.[44]

In *The Hazing Reader,* Nuwer provides, through a collection of fifteen essays, many foundational insights and concepts for better understanding the ethical issues of hazing.[45] Several essays merit our attention.

First, Nuwer reproduces Irving Janis's essay "Groupthink" in order to help us understand the effectiveness of a collective and how it thwarts the concerns of individuals. Janis explains:

> I use the term "groupthink" as a quick and easy way to refer to the mode of thinking that persons engage in when they are deeply involved in a cohesive in-group, when the members' striving for unanimity overrides their motivation to realistically appraise alternative courses of action. "Groupthink" is a term of the same order as the words in the newspeak vocabulary George Orwell used in his dismaying *1984*—a vocabulary with terms such as "double think" and "crimethink." By putting groupthink with those Orwellian words, I realize that groupthink takes on an invidious connotation. The invidiousness is intentional: Groupthink refers to a deterioration of mental efficiency, reality testing and moral judgment that results from group pressures.[46]

In the introduction to the Janis essay, Nuwer appropriates the term and applies it to university fraternities and therein mints a new word, *Greekthink.* Nuwer writes:

> I adapted the term "groupthink" to become "Greekthink," a reference to the less common, but more dangerous, fraternal groups that engage in reckless behaviors and pledging rituals, display near-delusional feelings of invincibility, fail to heed individual member's or their national executive's moral qualms in the interest of group unanimity, put a newcomer in harm's way, and demonstrate post-

incident denial in the face of clear-cut evidence that they have erred. Likewise, the theory helps explain why pledges will risk death for esteem, backslapping and bonding with a fraternity chapter.[47]

Nuwer reports too that when he explained to Janis the connection that he made, Janis remarked, "All of us are very hungry for that sort of thing. None of us can get enough of it."[48]

Nuwer's use of *Greekthink* helps us to appreciate the effectiveness of group identity on college campuses. Horowitz comes close to it when she describes the abiding loyalty of college men when they are at war with the faculty. But Nuwer goes further in describing how Greekthink suppresses the moral instinct and the ethical judgment. Certainly, as Nuwer himself acknowledges, Greekthink occurs not only in fraternity houses; it belongs to any campus collective (think sports, even residential college, or any other student group) that seeks to reduce itself to an identity, that is to a unanimous group, and therein pledges loyalty to one another above any other moral claim. It is the culture of the college male.

In a lengthy essay, "Hazing and Alcohol in a College Fraternity," James Arnold tells the story of studying for four years (1991–1995) the use of alcohol by a local chapter of a fraternity (INS, a pseudonym) at a midwestern public university.[49] He sums up how the perpetual use of alcohol at the fraternity wove into the hazing rituals, destroying any semblance of a moral order or a capacity for ethical judgment:

> If one accepts the hypothesis that INS (and groups like them) can be accurately described by an addictive organization model, then perhaps the ingrained, dysfunctional behaviors of the group can be better understood. The continuing central importance of alcohol to the group can be compared to an individual alcoholic/addict seeking the next "fix." And the perpetuation of hazing practices and rituals—which go on, as does alcohol use after many educational and intervention attempts—fit into the "ethical deterioration" characteristic of an addictive organization. It is my belief that hazing is abusive and wrong—and only an organization whose ethical and moral foundation had significantly eroded could permit such activity to exist.[50]

In the face of the collapse of any moral order, Arnold concludes: "This all comes down to the moral question: How ought we (as campus administrators, fraternity executives, and others) to be in relationship to a fraternity? It stands to reason we should not continue our roles as codependents and maintain this addictive system; instead we need to change this unhealthy relationship."[51]

Arnold's work is disturbing; it helps us to see that the fraternity itself, coupled with its collective dependence on alcohol, leads to an eroding of any moral impulse to change. It has a strong spiraling downward effect. Not only that, but he believes that universities are often complicit in their implicit tolerance of their practices. We could add that the faculty's disinclination to address any of the ethical issues of these practices on their own campuses places them as at best passive witnesses to these collective actions. The downward spiral happens on their watch.

Nuwer has developed a website and there lists videos of hazings, narratives of accounts of the deaths of pledges, grieving parents testifying against hazing, and strategies for banning hazing. There he offers his own definition of hazing: "an activity that a high-status member orders other members to engage in or suggests that they engage in that in some way humbles a newcomer who lacks the power to resist because he or she wants to gain admission into a group."[52]

Along with this, he records student deaths related to hazing. Beginning with Franklin Seminary, Kentucky, in 1838, Amherst College in 1847, and Cornell University in 1873, he names 182 student deaths, with 57 having occurred since 2000. While many of those in the twentieth century were related to "rushes," we can see as we enter the twenty-first century the spiraling downward effect suggested by Arnold.[53]

Two other faculty authors merit our attention. Elizabeth Allan read *Broken Pledges* and was so profoundly motivated by Nuwer's account of Chuck Stenzel's death and his mother's grief that she dedicated herself to dismantling hazing practices. She was the lead investigator of "Hazing in View: College Students at Risk: Initial Findings from the National Study of Student Hazing."[54] In this study of more than eleven thousand responses to surveys at fifty-three colleges and universities, Allan defined hazing as "any activity expected of someone joining or participating in a group that humiliates, degrades, abuses, or endangers them regardless of a person's willingness to participate." Her study found the following:

[Fifty-five percent] of college students involved in clubs, teams, and organizations experience hazing.

Hazing occurs in, but extends beyond, varsity athletics and Greek-letter organizations and includes behaviors that are abusive, dangerous, and potentially illegal.

Alcohol consumption, humiliation, isolation, sleep-deprivation, and sex acts are hazing practices common across types of student groups.

There are public aspects to student hazing including: 25% of coaches or organization advisors were aware of the group's hazing behaviors; 25% of the behaviors occurred on-campus in a public space; in 25% of hazing experiences, alumni were present; and students talk with peers (48%, 41%) or family (26%) about their hazing experiences.

In more than half of the hazing incidents, a member of the offending group posts pictures on a public web space.[55]

Today, besides teaching at the University of Maine, she is one of the founders of *StopHazing.org*, which has the mission to eliminate hazing through education. The website claims, "StopHazing now serves as a resource for accurate, up-to-date information about hazing for students, parents, and educators and helps to educate more than 30,000 visitors/month."[56]

Allan also contributed two notable essays to Nuwer's collection. In "Initiating Change: Transforming a Hazing Culture," Allan writes with Susan Van Deventer Iverson at Kent State about the successes that they had on other campuses in working against a hazing culture. As we saw in Chapter 6, "Cheating," these authors are concerned with the underlying cultures that promote students to act wrongly collectively. Significantly, they do not think of hazing as an event as much as a culture that promotes practices that lead to catastrophic events. Describing cultures "loosely defined as the shared assumptions, beliefs and 'normal behaviors' (norms) of a group,"[57] they examine how students exist in these cultures.

They recognize the need students have for trying to understand how to confront a moral quandary when they have one. This presupposes, however, that in terms of human development, students understand the goods that are (or ought to be) at stake. Invariably students are primarily concerned about relationships, and loyalty and fidelity are important values for those relationships. Ought those values be contested or confronted when one's circle of friends intends to endanger another? Though students might study in their ethics classes methods of moral reasoning or case studies regarding the world of ethical choices in a variety of professions, rarely do they engage directly the cases that affect them as university students, mostly because neither faculty nor administrators have university ethics on their radar.

Allan and Iverson found that hazing cases helped students to understand newer ethical issues because it "forces students to reexamine values and beliefs in the face of challenging moral situations." They report that students who became involved with antihazing efforts are precisely the students who "experience[d] dissonance as a result of a moral dilemma related to hazing—and this dissonance contributed to their motivation to take action." They learned their lessons not in the classroom but in the singularity of their own experience. Their crisis occurred as they recognized an "opportunity to speak out against hazing but also wanted to preserve their membership in the hazing organization." They truly faced "the moral dilemma when they realized that their silence was making them complicit with the problem of hazing and, in turn, contributing to an environment that placed others in danger."[58]

Students who spoke out of their experiences of having been hazed and having hazed, of going through the delusional and humiliating practices of hazing, only could do so by being transparent about their participation in them and by subsequently repudiating them. They in turn became, in a manner, role models for others who recognized the dilemma but did not know how to resolve it. The accompaniment that these role models provided in time prompted the development of a counter-culture, a group of rebels ala Horowitz, against the hazing college insider.

In "Hazing and Gender: Analyzing the Obvious," Allan looks first at sorority hazings but quickly turns to the objectification of women and the commodification of women's bodies to be the object of men's desires. Here she notes that women often collaborate or initiate the staging of hazing episodes (often enough connected to athletic teams or sororities) that humiliate women with men as witnesses, and there, she identifies the "paradox of sexism": "[W]omen themselves actively participate in sustaining the 'object' status of other women."[59]

Along with the objectification of women, she finds homophobia also embedded in the culture of hazing and therein attempts to identify the subject of manliness that presides over these cultural themes. Similarly, she sees much of the contours of hazing humiliations aiming for practices that objectify women and debase homosexuality. For this reason she turns to the question of what constitutes the underlying campus culture that promotes collective practices of humiliation and asks readers to recognize how "rigid and narrow versions of gender work in tandem with homophobia to create environments that are more likely to tolerate and perpetuate hazing practices." She concludes by inviting us to be committed to promoting common ethical stances and practices across university campuses that promote respect for all people, especially against the vicious prejudices that are based on race, gender, and social class.[60]

Clearly in the general ethical wasteland of college campuses where student life is not a concern of faculty and where college men and women collectively engage in increasingly disturbing practices of humiliation while outsiders take cover, Nuwer, Allan, and Iverson stand as models of intellectual engagement of the ethical challenges that face the American university. They also show us that faculty can in the classroom, on the Internet, on campus, or through publishing enter into university ethics with some effect. Yet the entire challenge of hazing cannot be met by only four faculty. They need others to stand with them and their students.

RACIALLY THEMED PARTIES

Lest we think that hazing practices are the only forms of humiliation that college collectives engage in, one of my undergraduate assistants in this project, Catherine Larrabee, introduced me to another fraternity infraction, themed parties. These racially and ethnically class-themed parties have kept blogs going for years. For instance, Jacob Hawley reports on "Frats in Trouble for Sexist, Racist Parties," in *Higher Ed Morning* that the University of Chicago's Delta Upsilon fraternity invited people to a party themed "Conquistadors and Aztec Hoes." Partiers were encouraged to bring "an unlimited need to conquer, spread disease and enslave natives."[61] Google the University of California–San

Diego "Compton Party" and you will find literally thousands of posts on one party, covered even by *The New York Times.* [62]

One report caught my eye: Katie Baker's "'Pedo Parties' and Racist Ragers: Why are Frat Bros Fixated on Fucked up Theme Parties." [63] Baker mentions a number of these parties and asks, "Why are privileged undergraduates at elite colleges unable to resist the lure of 'subversive' theme parties even though the potential repercussions could last a googled lifetime?"

Katie Baker, a writer for *Jezebel,* manages to provide perspectives that other journalists miss. As a good feminist, she knows about power and sex. Explaining the function of a frat party, she writes that "fraternity men need women to fuck . . . in order to fulfill the strict codes of masculinity which they reproduce." One junior added that alcohol is not all that you need for the environment: "Your party theme can't just be 'Powerful Men and Submissive Women,' . . . so other powerful-powerless relationships become necessary." [64]

Another student thought that undergraduates "are drawn to racist and sexist themed parties because the concept of breaking social rules intrigues kids who are book-smart but haven't experienced real struggles." "No matter where we come from, a Montessori school in Portland or small prep school in Virginia, we all have a background in the politically correct," she added. "Dressing up in a ludicrous summation of an entire people and culture just seems like another crazy risk, getting laughs from your peers for creativity or absurdity. It is laced with the subversive, your parents wouldn't approve, you wouldn't put it on your resume, but for awhile 'but it's college!' is enough of an excuse for a lot of questionable behavior."

Katie Baker keeps her *Jezebel* readers mindful of these parties. She notes those fraternity parties that target the poor or minorities living in their vicinity, for instance, the infamous "Compton Cookout" at the University of California–San Diego or the University of Texas chapter of the Alpha Tau Omega themed party that focused on immigrants crossing borders. [65] Later she published pictures of an Indiana University sorority party where the girls "smudged dirt on their faces and fake-begged for food, money and prayers during a *homeless*-themed party this week." The student who sent in the photos gave Baker some background: "Just so you know, Bloomington, IN (home of IU) has a disproportionately high homeless population. They're typically the target of a lot of shit from students. They get treated pretty badly. It's actually really sad—one of the places homeless people tend to hang out is right across from the most popular student bar in Bloomington, and on pretty much any given night, you can hear students loudly ridiculing the homeless population while they sip their drinks."[66] When they can attack not only their classmates but also their environs, these girls give new meaning to Horowitz's "college women."

Baker reports that one reader sent her a photo of a poverty party at a fraternity at Tufts, taken at the start of the Depression. Commenting on the photo, Baker notes, "Apparently, making fun of those less fortunate than you has long been a favored frat party theme."[67]

These parties have made the news for decades. Since 1989, the *Chronicle of Higher Education* has published articles and blogs on the parties. In 2007, for instance, in "Racial-Themed Parties Draw Fury on Campuses across the Country," the *Chronicle* reported that a party at Clemson University, where students wore blackface and padded their trousers to make their rumps appear larger, caused exceptional bitterness because it was held on Martin Luther King Day.[68] A year earlier, the *Chronicle* reported how a fraternity at Johns Hopkins held a "Halloween in the Hood" theme party "which featured a skeleton hanging, lynch-style, from a rope noose."[69]

While Dartmouth[70] and Duke[71] have been covered in the media for more than one of these parties, many universities do not have multiple offenses. Still, the sheer fact that annually these racist parties are held at many of our finest institutions, often deriding and demeaning the neighboring people who themselves do not have the income or the education that would admit them to these universities, is disturbing. Moreover, anyone following these parties notes that they are getting more provocative, more hateful, and more reckless. These are not toga parties. These have targets: freshmen, women, and neighbors. They are predatory.

Though coverage of these parties is fairly widespread, still I found only one article by academics addressing racially themed parties at American universities. Gina Garcia, Marc Johnston, and others report in "When Parties Become Racialized: Deconstructing Racially Themed Parties" that "racially-themed parties are all-too-common occurrences on college campuses."[72] They note that these are "not isolated incidents" and that they "have been disproportionately sponsored by mainstream Greek-letter organizations and directed toward Communities of Color."[73] They write, "Whatever the original intentions by party planners, these events can be characterized as campus hate or bias-motivated incidents due to their offensive nature." They also note the absence of proactive leadership from the university in dealing with race relations. They write: "Additionally, many institutions find themselves in a reactive (rather than proactive) position in addressing the conflict that can arise from racially motivated incidents."[74]

Through the lens of Critical Race Theory, they deconstruct the parties, raising matters of race and racism, and then turn to a discussion about "who ultimately decides whether or not the event was racist? The responses from both administrators and students send messages about whether those in power believe these incidents to be harmful." Here they turn to the "embedded nature of racism" and propose matters for research and practice.[75] They argue that "despite historical efforts to desegregate colleges and universities, racial hierarchies exist and prevent the true realization of equity in higher education."[76] They conclude, noting the potential significance of research by faculty on campus events and how that can have a transformational effect on our students: "Utilizing this understanding of our everyday interactions with students and furthering the discourse through research to promote transformational change in higher education may influence positive campus racial climates, improve institutional responses, and ultimately prevent future racially themed parties from occurring."[77]

These faculty working together and weighing in on these racially themed parties give us a way of appreciating the parties' significance and impact, and provide administrators and other faculty with resources to use in the classroom to address these issues not only when they happen but before they happen. This type of academic work is precisely what I think we need more of from faculties across the university. We need faculty to use their academic resources to discuss campus ethical challenges and to show, first, an awareness of these things happening; second, a reflective estimation of why they are problematic; and third, a strategy for the university community to address them effectively, responsibly, and transparently.

THE FRATERNITY AND THE UNIVERSITY

I will develop these racially themed issues further in Chapter 9, but now we return to the essay by Flanagan mindful that fraternities and sororities are clearly the cultural and institutional substantiation of Horowitz's "college men" and "college women." As if taking a page out of *Campus Life,* Flanagan writes:

> From the very beginning, fraternities were loathed by the grown-ups running colleges, who tried to banish them. But independence from overbearing faculties—existing on a plane beyond the reach of discipline—was, in large measure, the point of fraternity membership; far from fearing the opprobrium of their knock-kneed overlords, the young men relished and even courted it. When colleges tried to shut them down, fraternities asserted that any threat to men's membership in the clubs constituted an infringement of their right to freedom of association. It was, at best, a legally delicate argument, but it was a symbolically potent one, and it has withstood through the years.

Like Horowitz, Flanagan finds that fraternities root themselves in the original instincts of the founding of the American university, more so than the pious ministerial studies. In fact, since 1825 with the founding of the first fraternity, Kappa Alpha Society, at Union College when there were only 4,600 university students in the United States, fraternities have proven a more robust legacy within the academy than the ministerial trend itself has. Flanagan writes: "[F]raternities exist as deeply in the groundwater of American higher education as religious study—and have retained a far greater presence in the lives of modern students."

Flanagan likewise highlights the lack of an ethical backbone in the university, in the absence of a credible, articulated objective argument that addresses the grounds for the issues that the university believes are in jeopardy by the practices of their local fraternities. She writes:

> Fraternity tradition at its most essential is rooted in a set of old, deeply American, morally unassailable convictions, some of which— such as a young man's right to the freedom of association—emanate from the Constitution itself. In contrast, much of the policy governing college campuses today is rooted in the loose soil of a set of

political and social fashions that change with the season, and that
tend not to hold up to any kind of penetrating challenge. And this is
why—to answer the vexing question "why don't colleges just get rid
of their bad fraternities?"—the system, and its individual frats, have
only grown in power and influence. Indeed, in many substantive
ways, fraternities are now mightier than the colleges and universities
that host them.

The lack of a compelling argument to evaluate the practices of fraternities resonates with the claims of this book. From the start, we have
seen that ethics is simply not a default value for universities, whether in
censoring abusive faculty, validating high tuitions or even higher salaries, or negotiating contracts with adjuncts. Universities do not invoke
ethics or any language of moral accountability or responsibility that are
rooted in objective standards that transcend particular localities. Even
though university professors teach that other professions should follow
such objective standards in the development of those professions, university administrators rarely make that pitch about the academy and
faculty do not comment on the lack of an administrative summons to
professional ethical conduct.

If university administrators and faculty were to look at ethics, not
only as they engage local fraternities, but as a bedrock for the delibera-
tions of what is best for the university's mission to collectively educate
and form their students for the common good, then, I believe universities would be able to counter an array of ethically challenging realities
on their campuses.

Yet, as in the cheating scandals, individual university presidents insisted that cheating was not what people at their own university did.
You can hear them: "This is not how 'fill in the name of the university'
acts!" Besides wanting to respond, "Sorry, but they do," the more important issue is to acknowledge that cheating is wrong not because
Harvard or the University of Virginia opposes cheating but because by
objective ethical standards the human community has always and will
continue to reject cheating as a valid means for any form of accountability for human flourishment. Rather than invoking ethics, administrators
remain in their lone university mission statements with their private
language trying to address public actions. The university has to realize
that ethical norms transcend their campuses, but that may be a claim
they do not want their profession to recognize.

What would be an overall ethical concern about fraternities that a university might want to consider? Throughout this chapter we have seen the blinding effect that social pressure has and while we can recognize that a university does not need to have the Greek system in order to have offensive theme parties, fraternities and sororities are the most evident instantiation of the type of social pressure that comes especially from Horowitz's "college men" and "college women."

I found the description of that "social pressure" evident in a provocative essay from 1997 in the *New York Times*. In "Drinking to Fit In," Walter Kim shared his reflections on social pressures, drinking, and the fraternities, which were prompted by the death of 18-year-old Scott Krueger who "died after attending an M.I.T. fraternity party at which freshmen were supposedly required to collectively consume a certain amount of liquor. It has been reported that he didn't even like to drink."

Kim captures the delusion underlying the social pressure: "[T]he strange thing about drinking oneself into unconsciousness while fraternity buddies are standing by offering support and shot glasses is that most people are not drinking to get drunk. They think they are doing something more meaningful: vowing their loyalty to new friends, winning the respect of others, building a zany memory they'll later cherish."[78]

Reflecting on his own undergraduate time in Princeton, Kim argues that the social institutions of the fraternities are effectively predatory: he calls for the university "to do away with the selective campus fraternities and sororities that have bullied, insulted and hazed their students for generations. It's not the clubs' liquor licenses, but their status, their promise of social elevation, their ability to prey on the insecurities of young adults that need to be revoked, and then, if possible, filled by other, less destructive means."[79]

I think Kim names well "their ability to prey on the insecurities of young adults." Their extraordinary predatory capacities are evidently well protected. We could not imagine how, in any other setting, a national club that claims the lives of twenty-four freshmen remains active. Imagine if the initiation rites of the Boy Scouts or the Girl Scouts had such horrendous identifying statistics. Would they survive such reports? Imagine if an all-black club, Hispanic club, or Native American club had these statistics. They would never survive the sanctions or the animosity that would be unleashed on them. Only fraternities at American universities are protected in their luring students into life-threatening and death-causing practices that would give them the delusional self-understanding of having "made it."

Yet fraternities have been and remain birthing grounds for powerful sets of relationships operative today in the corporate world. Maria Konnikova reports in the *Atlantic Monthly*,

> Fraternity men make up 85 percent of U.S. Supreme Court justices since 1910, 63 percent of all U.S. presidential cabinet members since 1900, and, historically, 76 percent of U.S. Senators, 85 percent of Fortune 500 executives, and 71 percent of the men in "Who's Who in America." And that's not counting the 18 ex-frat U.S. presidents since 1877 (that's 69 percent) and the 120 Forbes 500 CEOs (24 percent) from the 2003 list, including 10—or one-third—of the top 30. In the 113th Congress alone, 38 of the hundred Senate members come from fraternity (and, now, sorority) backgrounds, as does a full quarter of the House.[80]

Fraternities also remain the social location for major university decision makers to behave badly, as a recent exposé illustrated of Kappa Beta Phi, "a secret fraternity, founded at the beginning of the Great Depression, that functioned as a sort of one-percenter's Friars Club."[81] The *Chronicle of Higher Education* researched the list of the 423 Kappa Beta Phi members and found that 1 in 5 "had served on college governing boards. . . . Forty-two of them are current trustees." In an essay on the evident differences between the cultures of the academy and Wall Street, the writers asked: "To the extent that the goings on of *Kappa Beta Phi* embody the ethos of Wall Street, concerns may be raised about the seriousness with which trustees from the finance sector would treat issues of diversity and discrimination."[82]

Fraternities' ability to remain standing despite the enormous settlements and their financial payouts is not simply due to their financial assets of three billion dollars nor to the insurance policies and indemnity trails that national fraternities have developed over recent years.[83] Before national fraternities made these moves, Flanagan notes, "Liability insurance became both ruinously expensive and increasingly difficult to obtain. The insurance industry ranked American fraternities as the sixth-worst insurance risk in the country—just ahead of toxic-waste-removal companies."[84]

In an essay titled, "Animal House on Steroids," David J. Leonard and Richard C. King, colleagues from Washington State University, ask two evidently emerging questions: "[D]on't these parties seem to be getting much worse and more harmful and how much do the universities really want to shut down fraternity culture?"[85]

They acknowledge that "collegiate partying is nothing new. It is the stuff of local legend and school tradition, woven into the mythos of American life." The partying was a complement to education that students pursued. Noting the reality at today's campuses, however, they argue "that balance has begun to break down, as universities have begun to actively contribute to a new formula that often embraces entitlement and indulgence over learning and hard work." Not only media like *I'm Shmacked* but universities themselves "promote an atmosphere that puts fun and experience ahead of academics and learning. In an era of increasing tuition and shrinking job prospects, universities can no longer promise a certain path to the American Dream."

Leonard and King turn to the works of other faculty to make their claim. First they invoke the work of two sociologists, Elizabeth A. Armstrong and Laura T. Hamilton in *Paying for the Party: How College Maintains Inequality*, to argue "that America's universities use the 'party pathway' to lure upper-middle-class students onto campus."[86] Armstrong and Hamilton write: "At the heart of the party pathway was a powerful Greek system, a residence-hall system that fed students into the party scene, and numerous 'easy' majors. As the most visible and well-resourced route through the institution, the party pathway was impossible to avoid—even by those who wished to."[87]

Then reflecting that the priorities of institutions are evident in their investments, they turn to the Ohio University economist Richard K. Vedder who commented on a recent report by the Delta Cost Project that showed that colleges spend a declining share of their budgets on academics. Vedder noted: "This is the country-clubization of the American university. A lot of it is for great athletic centers and spectacular student-union buildings. In the zeal to get students, they are going after them on the basis of recreational amenities."[88]

Leonard and King conclude, "Leisure, consumption, comfort, and pleasure have become the means to attract students, and the university has turned into a yearlong party. Attending sporting events and concerts, winterfests and spring flings, every undergraduate can go on to earn a postmodern Ph.D.—Party Hard Degree."

The absence of ethics on university campuses can be found not only in the actions of students and the silence of faculty but also in the decisions of university administrators.

DENOUEMENT: RAPE

This chapter is not only about partying; throughout it has also been about power: the power between faculty and students; the power of college men over outsiders, especially incoming women; the power of sophomores over freshmen; the power of fraternities over their pledges; the power of fraternity brothers over women at their themed parties; the power of gown over town; the power of privileged students over their neighbors.

It is also about administrators and faculty not responding well, competently, or at all, and as we have just seen, even profiting from the power inequities at work in the partying.

Everything about the use of power on campus changed on January 22, 2014, when the Associated Press reported from the White House Council on Women and Girls Report, *Rape and Sexual Assault: A Renewed Call to Action* that "No one is more at risk of being raped or sexually assaulted than women at our nation's colleges and universities."[89]

The Report is riveting. Special attention is dedicated to campus sexual assault that deserves to be cited in full:[90]

> Sexual assault is a particular problem on college campuses: 1 in 5 women has been sexually assaulted while in college.[91] The dynamics of college life appear to fuel the problem, as many survivors are victims of what's called "incapacitated assault": they are sexually abused while drunk, under the influence of drugs, passed out, or otherwise incapacitated.[92] Perpetrators often prey on incapacitated women, and sometimes surreptitiously provide their victims with drugs or alcohol.[93] Perpetrators who drink prior to an assault are more likely to believe that alcohol increases their sex drive—and are also more likely to think that a woman's drinking itself signals that she's interested in sex.[94]

Most college victims are assaulted by someone they know, especially in incapacitated assaults.[95] And parties are often the site of the crime: a 2007 study found that 58% of incapacitated rapes and 28% of forced rapes took place at a party.[96] Notably, campus perpetrators are often serial offenders. One study found that 7% of college men admitted to committing rape or attempted rape, and 63% of these men admitted to committing multiple offenses, averaging six rapes each.[97]

College survivors suffer high rates of posttraumatic stress disorder, depression, and drug or alcohol abuse, which can hamper their ability to succeed in school.[98] Depression and anxiety are linked to higher college dropout rates, as is substance abuse.[99]

Reporting rates for campus sexual assault are also very low: on average only 12% of student victims report the assault to law enforcement.[100]

This is a report that students, parents, and faculty need to read. As the report states:

> Change the Culture: Sexual assault is pervasive because our culture still allows it to persist. According to the experts, violence prevention can't just focus on the perpetrators and the survivors. It has to involve everyone. And in order to put an end to this violence, we as a nation must see it for what it is: a crime. Not a misunderstanding, not a private matter, not anyone's right or any woman's fault. And bystanders must be taught and emboldened to step in to stop it. We can only stem the tide of violence if we all do our part.[101]

The summons to all applies to all at the university, to look at its culture that has allowed this phenomenon to persist. This means not only the students, the administration, and those in student affairs, but also faculty stepping up as well, in their classrooms, in their lectures, in their panels, their research, and their publications.

However, the federal government is so concerned about universities on this matter that universities are no longer being allowed to monitor themselves. As the report notes:

> The Federal Government enforces laws that oblige universities to combat campus sexual assault. Title IX requires schools receiving federal funding to take necessary steps to prevent sexual assault on their campuses, and to respond quickly and effectively when an as-

sault occurs. The Clery Act promotes transparency and therefore requires colleges and universities that participate in federal financial aid programs to report annual statistics on crime on or near their campuses, to develop and disseminate prevention policies, and to ensure victims their basic rights. [102]

On May 1, 2014, so as to guarantee "that students are not denied the ability to participate fully in educational and other opportunities due to sex," the Department of Education's Office for Civil Rights posted fifty-five colleges and universities with open Title IX sexual violence investigations. The list is staggering: Harvard, Dartmouth, Princeton, University of Chicago, Catholic University of America, University of Virginia, Emory, and Southern Methodist University, among others. While the website informs us that "a college or university's appearance on this list and being the subject of a Title IX investigation in no way indicates at this stage that the college or university is violating or has violated the law," they explain, "We are making this list available in an effort to bring more transparency to our enforcement work and to foster better public awareness of civil rights. We hope this increased transparency will spur community dialogue about this important issue." [103] On July 2, the Office added another twelve institutions to their list of schools under investigation. [104]

Furthermore, the Office is also posting at *Notalone.gov* those court filings being arbitrated between universities and the government watchdog. [105] Finally, at the request of Chairman Claire McCaskill, the Senate Subcommittee on Financial and Contracting Oversight launched in April 2014 a national survey to assess how colleges and universities are currently handling sexual violence. The survey also assessed how institutions work with law enforcement to ensure that reports of rape and sexual assault are investigated and prosecuted. Among the findings:

More than 40 percent of schools in the national sample have not conducted a single investigation in the past five years.

More than 20 percent of the nation's largest private institutions conducted fewer investigations than the number of incidents they reported to the Department of Education, with some institutions reporting as many as seven times more incidents of sexual violence than they have investigated.

Experts agree that annual climate surveys—confidential student surveys regarding behaviors that constitute or are associated with sexual assault—are one of the best ways to get an accurate portrait of sexual assault issues on a campus. However, only 16 percent of the institutions in the Subcommittee's national sample conduct climate surveys.[106]

After years of doing things their different ways, the universities now have to follow the federal government's lead.[107] Clearly, this is an issue that women undergraduates, long dissatisfied with their universities,[108] have driven to the federal government.[109] Whether they find better responses from the federal government is not yet clear, but these women now understand that they have rights and that will change the discourse on campuses in the years to come.[110]

As we close this disheartening chapter, we might think on the following, words of Derek Bok that are an extension of the very insight with which we started:

> Universities should be among the first to reaffirm the importance of basic values, such as honesty, promise keeping, free expression, and nonviolence, for these are not only principles essential to civilized society, they are values on which all learning and discovery ultimately depend. There is nothing odd or inappropriate, therefore, for a university to make these values the foundation for a serious program to help students develop a strong set of moral standards. On the contrary, the failure to do so threatens to convey a message that neither these values nor the effort to live up to them are of much importance or much common concern. This message is not only unworthy of the academy, it is likely in the atmosphere of a university to leave students morally confused and unable to acquire ethical convictions of their own.[111]

8

GENDER

"People tend to think that the problem has gone away, but alas, it hasn't."
—Dr. Nancy Hopkins[1]

Women undergraduates are now able to get a hearing in Washington about sexual assault on campuses because they have become collectively aware about the ethical issues around sexual assault. They learned from hearsay, personal testimony, and actual experience that sexual assault was and is an issue on campus. They learned too about the ethical issues of consent, reporting, confidentiality, and their rights. They communicated with one another what the issues were, created networks of solidarity, and sustained a discourse appraising others about the matters of justice that were at stake in responding to a reported sexual assault.

Though the data shows that, for a variety of reasons, few students still report sexual assault (on average only 12 percent of student victims report the assault to law enforcement), many students recognize that the silence on campus regarding reporting is part of the problem. They also know the awful experiences of women who reported at universities that were not prepared or competent to arbitrate the claims in those reports, as the White House Report and the McCaskill report make clear, and as the *New York Times* conveys with great clarity in their account of one woman's attempt to report, "Reporting Rape, and Wishing She Hadn't: How One College Handled a Sexual Assault Complaint."[2]

Their collective awareness of this issue has progressively developed over the past decades. It has developed into a discourse that has broadened and deepened with a more and more diverse confluence of voices and insights. Many of those voices originally came from the "campus rebels," as Horowitz named them.

Horowitz's rebels have long been a campus phenomenon and indeed a group much more alert to gender issues than the "college men and women." In the 1970s some of these rebels became educators, while others became writers and activists. They brought the discourse about the wrongness of sexual violence along with the wrongness of misogyny to their colleagues and students on campus and to their public. They brought also the languages of rights, of ethics, and of law, and the skills of social media and community organizing.

One very concrete instantiation of this work of consciousness-raising comes from organizations like the Take Back the Night Foundation, an international organization with roots stretching back to the 1970s in the cause to create safe communities and respectful relationships through awareness events and initiatives. Their marches, rallies, education programs, vigils, concerts, imagery, and events unite those around the globe who seek to end sexual assault, domestic violence, dating violence, sexual abuse, and all other forms of sexual violence. On college campuses they provide fairly sophisticated and engaging programs to raise campus consciousness starting with freshmen about the reality of campus sexual violence.[3]

This collective consciousness-raising did not happen, therefore, overnight. For instance, a look at the board of directors of the Take Back the Night Foundation highlights the names of many who in the 1970s first worked to end sexual violence but now do so today by teaching or working precisely on university campuses to help end sexual violence. While others brought violence onto the campus, these faculty and administrators brought the ethical issue of sexual violence into campus discourse. Yes, the injustice of sexual violence is the subject of university teaching, lecturing, and publishing as the educators at Take Back the Night highlight.[4]

Women (and men) faculty were not only listening and participating in student consciousness-raising, they were also speaking, writing, and networking about ethical matters dealing with exclusion and at times even assault on campus.

As an ethicist, I find the general question of gender and the more specific topic of sexual harassment and assault to be *the* issue in university ethics where faculty, staff, and administrators, in particular women faculty, are already involved. If there is one topic that shows the richness and promise of faculty involvement in addressing the university about its own ethics of fairness, it is not cheating, adjunct faculty, students behaving badly, athletics, or even tuition; it is gender. The discourse about gender at university campuses is the entry point for further discourse on university ethics.

And yet what this chapter shows, I hope, is that for all the work, by concerned faculty, administrators, and students, as well as their allies, the university's profound disinterest in ethics continues to try to push even this issue to the sidelines.

FACULTY CONSCIOUSNESS RAISING TO THE ISSUE OF SEXUAL ASSAULT

In 1984, a professor of literature, Billie Wright Dzeich, and a university administrator, Linda Weiner, together penned *The Lecherous Professor: Sexual Harassment on Campus*.[5] The book is a comprehensive exposé of sexual assault as it is found on campuses across the country; it prompted considerable discussion and even some change. But both authors realized that the needed change will not come from women alone, but from the more senior, male faculty and male student body. Linda Weiner, reflecting in the second edition on the "success" of the book, writes: "Sexual harassment takes what has long been within the range of normal male behavior—if not practiced by a man himself, then tolerated in others—and makes it illegal. For many, that puts the personal and the professional in disturbing conflict. Institutional change always comes slowly; in the case of sexual harassment, resistance to change runs particularly deep."[6]

For someone like Dzeich, these matters of change are a no-brainer. For instance, when she was interviewed by the *Chronicle of Higher Education* and asked for her position on faculty dating students, she simply responded: "Wal-Mart says managers may not date cashiers. That's it, end of discussion. I don't understand what makes educators think they are an exception to that rule."[7] Nonetheless, even though

professors in business, legal, and medical ethics teach that power diffe-
rentials and evident boundary violations must be routinely regarded in
the workplace, they do not by extension apply it to their own workplace
or their colleagues' conduct. While university faculty teach that dating
is inappropriate in other professions, they are reluctant to teach it about
their own profession.

Before *The Lecherous Professor,* other women had already written
on sexual harassment in the workplace.[8] Dzeich and Weiner took the
work of previous academics who saw harassment as pervasive in society
and applied it to the university. This, in my eyes, is one of the first
instances of bringing ethics into university life. Later, Michele Paludi
witnesses to how many faculty entered into the question of campus
sexual harassment with her edited collection, *Ivory Power: Sexual Harassment on Campus.* Published in 1990, only six years after *The Lecherous Professor,* Paludi's volume has twenty-seven contributors and refers to extensive writings elsewhere on sexual harassment on campus.
Then, in 1996, she expanded the collection and titled it *Sexual Harassment on College Campuses: Abusing the Ivory Power.*[9]

Several other academics authored other related works on campus
sexual assaults shortly after Paludi.[10] In 1997, for instance, two crimi-
nologists co-authored an important work explaining and proving the
pivotal role that male peer support on campus has in legitimizing their
sexual assault of women.[11]

In 2000, Leslie Pickering Francis wrote *Sexual Harassment as an
Ethical Issue in Academic Life* that appeared in Steven Cahn's book
series *Issues in Academic Ethics.*[12] Francis's book studies potential ethical issues about reporting policies especially as they relate to consensual
relationships as well as to concerns about academic values like academic
freedom. As a law professor, she tries to wake up universities to their
ethical and legal responsibilities regarding campus sexual assault despite arguments to the contrary. In Judith Glazer Raymo's review of the
book, she wrote, "The extent of institutional responsibility for the actions of its faculty, staff, and students should make Chapter 3 ("Sexual
Harassment in the Law") required reading for university administrators, including deans and department chairs."[13] Finally in 2010, three
other professors of criminal justice wrote *Unsafe in the Ivory Tower:
The Sexual Victimization of College Women.*[14] Their work refers to over
three hundred writings related to the topic.

Clearly we can see some degree of effectiveness of faculty entering into the research work regarding sexual assault on campus. As professors of criminology, counseling, ethics, women studies, sociology, philosophy, and psychology, these scholars brought their research to the fore legitimizing the move by earlier academics who argued that the assault of women on campus could no longer be tolerated. They in turn emboldened their students to see what their expectations ought to be from the university in the face of sexual harassment and assault. They seemed to have convinced some university administrators that they needed to make policy changes on their campuses in light of these proven ethical violations. Moreover, their work in ethics and law as it pertained especially to Title IX, gave the larger community firmer footing to express their expectations that universities must be responsive to matters of sexual assault on campus.

Still, as the White House Report shows, these works were not sufficient to make most universities realize that looking for the ethical solution is *the* way to find the solution.

Why did the universities not take the right road but rather let the federal government launch investigations of one university after another to compel them to protect their students?

One reason is that men, and in particular those on universities, are still not convinced of the seriousness of the issue. Linda Weiner wrote that men not only have to stop harassing and assaulting as well as stop permitting, promoting, and tolerating harassment, they also have to be part of the change itself. She writes:

> Dealing with sexual harassment means dealing with sexism. . . . Dealing with sexual harassment on campus means dealing with our institutions. It's rude to point, but men have the lion's share of power on most campuses. They are the chancellors, presidents and vice presidents. They are also the deans, the full professors, the grievance chair, not to mention the student affairs officer, student body president, and the important alumni. And there is both personal and institutional resistance to changing the distribution of power.[15]

As a case in point, witness the now infamous response to the White House initiative, by George Will on June 6: "Colleges Become the Victims of Progressivism." Though not a member of the academy, Will wrote: "Colleges and universities . . . are learning that when they say campus victimizations are ubiquitous ('micro-aggressions,' often not discernible to the untutored eye, are everywhere), and that when they make victimhood a coveted status that confers privileges, victims proliferate." Will also took issue with "the supposed campus epidemic of rape, a.k.a. 'sexual assault.'" He concluded: "Academia is learning that its attempts to create victim-free campuses—by making everyone hypersensitive, even delusional, about victimizations—brings increasing supervision by the regulatory state that progressivism celebrates."[16]

Will's essay caused a stir: some newspapers cancelled his column, the blogs tore into it, Senators wrote letters about it, and survivors tweeted about their "privilege."[17] But Will did what he wanted: He provided men, and in particular "college men," a text to respond to the White House. Here is the resistance.

The universities' inability to address the sexual assault issue without federal oversight is a combination of "old boy" resistance and the university's general disinterest in ethics that together leaves the university incompetent in adjudicating fairly the reports it receives. They could more fairly resolve these reports but, as the *New York Times* illustrated in its stunning article on reporting, universities are still leaving the woman victim out in the cold. Eventually, if the issues of ethics and sexism do not move the university to more just policies, the law will compel it into compliance.[18]

Still, many have worked to get the university to be ethically a better place. Rightly, Billie Dzeich gets the last word on this: "The only way in which people can rescue themselves from the confusion and controversy over sexual harassment is to stop attacking one another and start talking. If academicians really believe their own rhetoric about collegiality and rational discourse, the American campus should be the place where that dialogue begins."[19]

THE STATUE AT WELLESLEY

While working on this chapter, I became absorbed by a story about a statue called the "Sleepwalker" that was placed on the nearby Wellesley University campus. The work, by the Brooklyn artist Tony Matelli, was created for his solo exhibition, "New Gravity," at the Davis Museum at the college. The *New York Times* described the art work this way: "The sculpture, 'Sleepwalker,' is 5 feet 9 inches tall and made of epoxy, fiber-glass and paint. The figure, with a bit of a paunch, is clad only in tight white briefs. His arms are stretched out in front of him, his face red-dened and miserable."[20]

The "Sleepwalker" was not placed in the Davis Museum with the rest of the show, but rather on the campus greens. Actually, the pictures that I saw of it has him seemingly crossing a campus in nearly knee-deep snow, with flakes still on his head, shoulders, and extended arms.

The article went on to report that the women students at the univer-sity immediately started a petition to put the statue indoors in the Davis Museum where the rest of the show is appearing.[21]

I found the petition online; in it the students wrote:

> Within just a few hours of its outdoor installation, the highly lifelike sculpture by Tony Matelli, entitled "Sleepwalker," has become a source of apprehension, fear, and triggering thoughts regarding sexu-al assault for some members of our campus community.
>
> While the sculpture may not trigger, disturb, or bother everyone on campus, as a community it is our responsibility to pay attention to and attempt to answer the needs of all of our community members.[22]

While nearly one thousand students signed the petition, the university administration refused to cede to the students' demand.

I had a double reaction to the news and debate about the "Sleep-walker." First, I could imagine how incredibly startling it would be for anyone to suddenly see this lifelike statue, especially at night. In other words, their reaction was, in my mind, perfectly understandable. Sec-ond, I predicted the response: ridicule of the petition, by men and by women.

From the neighboring *Go Local Worcester,* Tom Finneran dared the reader "to take a look at the statue and ask yourself if this is a 'source of fear and apprehension.'" He suggested, "the guy could probably be their father, beleaguered, bedraggled, and wondering what he's spend-ing $50,000.00 a year for. The poor shnook. He has yet to realize that he must suffer yearly impoverishment so his daughter can learn to manu-facture outrage on demand."[23]

In "Fear and Loathing at Wellesley," Lenore Skenazy in the *Wall Street Journal,* while arguing that art is itself a trigger, belittled the women. "Behind the 'hide that thing!' demand lies the crippling new conviction that what doesn't kill you makes you weaker. . . . [T]here's a great irony in hearing that so many Wellesley students, espousing feminist rhetoric, want to be treated like Victorian maidens, too delicate to view a statue of a guy in his undies."[24]

Fortunately, Wellesley's president, H. Kim Bottomly, responded to Skenazy in the *Wall Street Journal* in an article in which she "calls attention to how the reactions of Skenazy and other critics reflect a history of silencing women." Elsewhere, Bottomly reported that she decided she could not move the statue because it would "destroy the artistic integrity" of the exhibition.[25]

Throughout the entire discussion, I thought it all metaphorically ironic. Here is a statue of a man in briefs sleepwalking across an all-women campus just as sexual assault *finally* is making headlines and *he* gets to stay where he is. The women who petition that the statue be incorporated into the show are rebuffed. Isn't this a metaphor for the state of the American university today during the entire sexual assault debate?

Those who put him there—Matelli, the artist and Lisa Fischman, the museum director—were surprised by the women's reception of the show. Matelli said, "What they see in the sculpture is not in the sculpture." Fischman said, "I was completely taken aback by this response."[26] In neither case did they think the women were seeing the statue rightly. Are they kidding us? Do they read the newspapers? Are they any different from Skenazy? Who has purchase on what viewers should and do see? Doesn't context have anything to do with art in the twenty-first century? In fact, did Matelli and Fischman understand the context in which they placed the statue? A statue of a man in briefs walking unimpeded across a woman's campus? What were *they* thinking?

The Wellesley women were quite articulate in what they encountered. Annie Wang, a senior, said, "I think art's intention is to confront, but not assault, and people can see this as assaulting. Wellesley is a place where we're supposed to feel safe. I think place and a context matters, and I don't think this is the place to put it."[27]

While I applaud the president's defense of the students against Skenazy, I did not see the university acknowledge that they made a mistake in putting the statue there in the first place. If the university were to assume professional ethics, then transparency and accountability would require them to apologize and to acknowledge they should have been more predictive of how the students might have acted to such a provocative installation.

OUTSIDERS IN A CHILLY CLIMATE

The statue in the snow takes me back to the "Chilly Climate" discussions that were first launched in the mid 1980s when Roberta Hall and Bernice Sandler wrote about the experience of women at American universities. In 1982 they first wrote for the Project on the Status and Education of Women of the Association of American Colleges, *The Campus Climate: A Chilly One for Women?* In 1984, they titled their next study *Out of the Classroom: A Chilly Campus Climate for Women?* Two years later, they revisited their project with less of a question: *The Campus Climate Revisited: Chilly for Women Faculty, Administrators, and Graduate Students.*[28]

The concept of *campus climate* allowed them to look not only in the classroom but also outside it, across the university. Their use of *campus climate* allows them to go beyond the academic context to the entire university community. They use the concept *chilly* simply to convey a constant experience of not being treated equally to men; it evokes images of no warm welcome or of being left out in the cold.

In their papers, Hall and Sandler look at a variety of practices on campus that create the chilly climate. Jennifer Freyd and J. Q. Johnson who later assembled "References on Chilly Climate for Women Faculty in Academe" explain the concept of chilly climate this way: "Gender bias and discrimination against women in academia take many forms, from overt sexual harassment to the much more ubiquitous and insidious problem of subtle and unconscious sexism impacting daily life, work distribution, student evaluations, and promotion and hiring decisions. This confluence of problems has been called the problem of the 'chilly climate.'"[29]

From the very beginning, Hall and Sandler helped educators recognize a variety of practices that put women at a disadvantage. Three of the common issues that were raised involve the questions of (1) representation on faculty, (2) curriculum, and (3) faculty–student interactions. They argued that in order to understand the chilly climate, we need to ask how well gender equity appears in university departments:

are as many women hired as are men? Is equity also evident regarding
tenure, promotions, and university appointments? Do departments that
hire fewer women have fewer women undergraduates and graduates as
well? Regarding curriculum, we have to ask whether the texts that the
students engage are at all inclined to a more inclusive agenda, that
recognizes the academic achievements and relevance of research by
both men and women. Finally, we need to ask whether there are gender
differences in the way faculty call on students, mentor students out of
class, invite students into existing projects, and so on.

Annemarie Vaccaro notes that much has changed since Hall and
Sandler published their original chilly climate series.[30] She notes for
instance that some women have heard the call to be rebels as a way of
moving from being outsiders by invoking the cry of social justice.[31] Yet
hostility, invisibility, and the feeling of being an outsider are still realities for many other undergraduate and graduate women. Interested in
climate surveys that try to portray a growing tolerance and disposition
for gender and racial diversity on campuses, Vaccaro did a climate study
at one predominantly White university. She wanted to know "what lies
beneath" the surface of those claims to a growing appreciation of diversity. Her analysis "exists against a backdrop of official reports that described the climate as 'positive' and 'accepting.'"[32] Though previous
studies showed that women are more open to diversity than are men,[33]
she writes that:

> gender differences uncovered in this study went deeper than those
> described in the literature. In addition to women having more inter-
> group contacts and less negative stereotypes, female participants in
> this study desired deeper processes through which diversity was
> shared. Women longed for more in-depth diversity conversations,
> including discussions that moved beyond tolerance to acceptance
> and appreciation. From open-ended comments it was clear that
> many men (mostly White) considered the absence of dialogue and/or
> the lack of depth in diversity discussions as a positive aspect of the
> climate. Moreover, male respondents showed signs of symbolic ra-
> cism, hostility toward diversity efforts, and resentment toward the
> university's liberal bias.[34]

She concludes with a warning against thinking that biases against race,
class, or gender can be addressed separately or resolved singularly. "In

this study, men's symbolic racism, resentment of liberal bias, and resistance to diversity efforts emerged as strong themes alongside embedded issues of institutional sexism and an unwelcoming climate. To address any one topic without the others is myopic and will likely result in continued oppression, not just of women, but of other marginalized groups on campus."[35]

Vaccaro's study is stunning. Against the claim that things are getting better she finds that the college man is very much in the background, making sure that whatever developments in tolerance occur on a campus remain shallow and without any deep traction. The intransigence of some men with power on universities remains a continuous obstacle toward forging greater consensus for the key ethical insight of equity at the university. Moreover her warning against seeing the issues of race and class as distinct from gender is also terribly important, because, we will see that, though women made gender a university ethics issue, they are certainly not giving race and class the attention these issues deserve. In fact, we saw plenty of evidence in the tenure and tenure-line disinterest in adjunct faculty situations to recognize that many women faculty, like their male counterparts, do not recognize class as a university ethics issue.

Throughout her essays, Vaccaro also acknowledges that narratives of exclusion are very much found among women students and faculty of color. In *Standing on the Outside Looking In,* Mary Howard-Hamilton and four other colleagues edit a collection of essays that describe the many ways women of color experience the climate as unwelcoming.[36] Oiyan Poon and Shirley Hune recount how Asian women on campus are treated as perpetual foreigners and members of a "model minority."[37] Latinas find the rich forms of cultural and social capital they possess devalued in the academy.[38] Venice Sulé, who titled her dissertation "Black Female Faculty and Professional Socialization,"[39] writes now about how black women may feel compelled to rely on oppositional stances to succeed in hostile climates.[40]

Diane Dean, Susan Bracken, and Jeanie Allen show real hope for the future in their collection titled *Women in Academic Leadership: Professional Strategies and Personal Choices.*[41] In her foreword to the book, Claire Van Ummersen notes that several authors "highlight the barriers women face in institutions with rules created by and for the comfort of men. Academic careers are structured around an outdated assumption that academics are either single or have at-home partners. It is critical for all to understand that society has changed. No longer are stay-at-home wives the norm."[42] She adds: "The challenge of navigating the male norms that define the academy can be daunting."[43]

What is so salutary about this collection, however, is its inclusive attention to women of color. Van Ummersen writes:

> the lack of women of color in the professional faculty ranks choke the pipeline, leading few to advance to academic leadership positions. In chief academic officer roles, for example, women of color remain anomalies. Most women who rise to this critical position and the formal leadership positions below it are the first within their institutions to hold that role. For women of color, barriers to these roles and the pressures within them are more intense as they face the overwhelming responsibility of breaking gender and color barriers.[44]

The first of two essays addressing women of color concerns preparing them for leadership and the authors found three salient features: the importance of effective mentorship, the lack of emphasis on color throughout leadership programs, and negative ramifications with regard to outspokenness on racial and ethnic issues.[45] The other essay is a powerful advisory one from Yolanda Moses based on her twenty-five years in academic leadership. In almost any review of the book, her essay is singled out for its challenges to find the right starting place, to determine one's long-range goals, to seek out the right mentors, and to develop the right networks.[46]

Finally Vaccaro also comments that the "climate for lesbian, bisexual, and transgender students can be hostile, unwelcoming, and downright dangerous."[47] She adds that "lesbian and bisexual women must contend with both sexist and heterosexist language. They also face a multitude of stereotypes, including assumptions that lesbians are hypersexual, sexually confused, sexually deviant, and angry."[48]

Finally few studies focus specifically on college women with disabilities. In their review of the literature, Nichols and Quaye describe how institutional, physical, and attitudinal barriers that originate with peers and faculty keep students with disabilities from fully engaging on campus.[49] More specifically, Vaccaro writes that "feminist disability literature shows how women with disabilities experience unique forms of objectification, such as stereotypes that they are unattractive, dependent, or asexual."[50]

STUDIES AND REPORTS OF GENDER INEQUITY

In the fall of 2010, the latest year for figures available from the Department of Education, there were 21.6 million undergraduate and graduate students at the 1,505 colleges and universities in the United States. Of those students, 57.2 percent were female and 42.8 percent were male.[51] Women also earned 60 percent of all master's and 52 percent of all doctoral degrees, including doctorates in professional fields like medicine and dentistry.[52] With majorities like that, one would think that women could influence such schools, but as a matter of fact, they still do not.

I find that the "chilly climate" captures well a variety of practices at play that inhibit and compromise the feasibility of gender equality at the university. In order to make this point, we now review a variety of reports that highlight interpersonal, social, and structural factors that contribute to the chilly climate.

A variety of studies appear in 2012's *Gender Issue* of the *Chronicle of Higher Education*. Their titles tell the story of their own studies and they convey that the *Gender Issue* is dedicated not to the victories, but to the struggles.[53] In "Despite Efforts to Close Gender Gaps, Some Disciplines Remain Lopsided," Katherine Mangan gives us a general idea of the gaps by comparing the 2010 Education Department reports that women received 80 percent of the undergraduate degrees in education, 77 percent of the master's degrees, and 67 percent of the doctoral degrees, but in engineering, they earned 18 percent of undergraduate, 22 percent of master's, and 23 percent of doctoral degrees.[54] In the article "In the Humanities, Men Dominate the Fields of Philosophy and History," we see that just 29 percent of the bachelor's degrees in philosophy and 41 percent of those in history go to women. Women make up 21 percent of the philosophy faculty.[55]

In "Is Biology Just Another Pink-Collar Profession?" Marlene Zuk and Sheila O'Rourke note that in 2009 women received a majority of the degrees awarded in biological and biomedical sciences, from associate to Ph.D. degrees, and earned 53 percent of the doctorates; in health professions and related clinical sciences, 59 percent went to women. While "the number of women in undergraduate and graduate programs in the life sciences has been increasing for the past several decades," the rise of women in the fields of science "has not translated into proportionately more women in post-doctoral or faculty positions."[56]

Marc Bousquet provides an essay on business schools not unlike the others. In "Lady Academe and Labor-Market Segmentation: The Narrative of Women's Success via Higher Education Rests on a House of Cards," he argues simply: "Women still have to get a lot of education to outearn men who don't." It is a story we see time and again. He adds:

> Sure, there are more women in business administration, but they are far more common in the dead-end administrative and supervisory ranks of lower management. At graduation, women with new business B.A.'s earned $15,000 less than men with the same degree. Only a third of M.B.A.'s are awarded to women, and a longitudinal study of University of Chicago M.B.A. holders found that men with the degree earned 40 percent more than women 10 years later.[57]

But Bousquet, who wrote *How the University Works: Higher Education and the Low Wage Nation,*[58] sees that tenured women faculty are far more interested in themselves than in women colleagues in adjunct or staff positions. "At nearly every college I've ever visited, the women's faculty group was a more comfortable home for faculty administrators than for female faculty serving contingently." After referring to the experiences of women in contingent roles, he simply states that "women in academic leadership positions have on balance done little for women in super-exploited segments of academic labor." He concludes: "I believe in academic feminism. I think it will have more impact on campus when it does more to articulate and remedy the relationship between the most and least privileged women in its own steadily more feminized workplace."[59]

In all the essays on gender in the university, the themes are the same: Whether women are undergraduates, graduate students, postdocs, or junior faculty, they will receive less recognition or pay for their work than male counterparts. Consider the only article ever to appear in *Nature* on gender inequity, "Data Show Extent of Sexism in Physics."[60] There we learn that the study of Fermilab suggests "that female postdocs had to be three times as productive as male postdocs in order to be granted the opportunity to present work at academic conferences."[61]

While there are certainly, as in Bousquet's study on schools of business, significant growth in entry level areas, the developments to incorporate more women plateau too early. Thus in another issue of the *Chronicle of Higher Education* we find another essay echoing the same reality: "Women and Minorities Lag in Appointments to Top Fund-Raising Jobs."[62] Sustained struggles peak before they should.

Hopefully matters about the lack of fairness and equity are clearly evident to us, and this could mean that the university has a profound ethical liability when it comes to gender equity, particularly when 57 percent of its student body are women. But is this lack of fairness something that the university causes? Is the university itself at fault, or is this just the way things are meant to be? Does gender just break down "naturally" this way at universities? Or is the inability to attain equity actually due to the agents of the university? Is Vaccaro's study at one university, for instance, a key to what happens at other universities? Are university communities themselves responsible for the gender inequity?

If the universities are at fault, then the perpetuation of these chilling practices is as unethical as the inequity itself.

There is much evidence that gender inequity at the university is primarily due to bias and discrimination. In fact the studies on gender at the university are so eye-opening, one wonders why we have not yet seen a real ethical conversion at our universities.

Dan Berrett tells, for instance, the interesting story about Ben Barres. A scientist listening to Barres's talk at MIT commented that Ben's work was much better than his sister's.[63] The scientist did not realize that Ben Barres himself had had a sex-change operation and he was in fact the woman to whom the scientist was referring. Berrett writes:

> Though Barres's gender has changed, he says that the quality of his work certainly has not. But the underlying assumption . . . that women have less innate intellectual prowess or ability to conduct scholarship, both in science and in academe more broadly—is alive and well even as women are gaining a stronger foothold in academe, accord-

ing to a recent MIT report on the status of women in science and engineering.[64]

That report, *A Report on the Status of Women Faculty in the Schools of Science and Engineering at MIT, 2011,*[65] noted the great gains for women in science and engineering over the past twelve years, but also an "unwanted consequence: the perception that hiring and promotion standards are more relaxed for women than they are for men." That is, the study found that these scientists and engineers, who make it harder for women to get the recognition that men get, believe that the standards against women are not hard enough.

The 2011 report from MIT is followed by the 2012 study by Yale researchers. In many ways it reflects and validates the experience of Ben Barres. Wanting to avoid questions of preferential treatment or of "innate differences" between genders, the Yale researchers sought to design the simplest study possible. Kenneth Chang of the *New York Times* reports:

> They contacted professors in the biology, chemistry and physics departments at six major research universities—three private and three public, unnamed in the study—and asked them to evaluate, as part of a study, an application from a recent graduate seeking a position as a laboratory manager.
>
> All of the professors received the same one-page summary, which portrayed the applicant as promising but not stellar. But in half of the descriptions, the mythical applicant was named John and in half the applicant was named Jennifer.
>
> About 30 percent of the professors, 127 in all, responded. . . . On a scale of 1 to 7, with 7 being highest, professors gave John an average score of 4 for competence and Jennifer 3.3. . . . The average starting salary offered to Jennifer was \$26,508. To John it was \$30,328.[66]

The authors of the study "Science Faculty's Subtle Gender Biases Favor Male Students," acknowledge at the outset their basic finding: "Despite efforts to recruit and retain more women, a stark gender disparity persists within academic science." They then highlight how this study differs from previous ones: "Abundant research has demonstrated gender bias in many demographic groups, *but has yet to experimentally investigate whether science faculty exhibit a bias against female stu-*

dents that could contribute to the gender disparity in academic science."[67]

In their study they found that the "gender of the faculty participants did not affect responses, such that female and male faculty were equally likely to exhibit bias against the female student."[68] In his interview with Corinne Moss-Racusin, the lead author of the paper, Chang notes that the "bias had no relation to the professors' age, sex, teaching field or tenure status" and then quotes Moss-Racusin: "There's not even a hint of a difference there."[69]

Thus they were left with nothing to conclude but that "Mediation analyses indicated that the female student was less likely to be hired because she was viewed as less competent."[70]

The researchers added: "We also assessed faculty participants' preexisting subtle bias against women using a standard instrument and found that preexisting subtle bias against women played a moderating role, such that subtle bias against women was associated with less support for the female student, but was unrelated to reactions to the male student."[71]

Chang interviewed another researcher, Dr. Handelsman, who stated that:

> previous studies had shown similar subconscious bias in other occupations. But when she discussed the concerns with other scientists, many responded that scientists would rise above it because they were trained to analyze objective data rationally.
>
> "I began to, on the one hand, wonder, 'Well, perhaps that's true: maybe people who are trained to be objective have some way of ferreting these out," she said. "But on the other hand, if scientists were no different from all the other groups that have been studied, that's something that we should know.'"[72]

The study generated and supported other research findings.[73] For instance, in "How Stereotypes Impair Women's Careers in Science," the researchers "designed an experiment to isolate discrimination's potential effect. Without provision of information about candidates other than their appearance, men are twice more likely to be hired for a mathematical task than women."[74]

The editor of the *Journal of General Physiology*, Sharona E. Gordon, published an editorial, "Getting Nowhere Fast: The Lack of Gender

Equity in the Physiology Community." After lamenting the findings of Moss-Racusin and other researchers, she insists that by the time women are done with graduate studies, they begin to opt out of teaching position applications. "Interventions to achieve gender parity in academia must therefore start no later than graduate school and should continue at least through women's decision to apply for faculty positions."[75]

She then expresses poignantly her own experience:

> As a scientist who is a woman, I believe that my every professional step is affected by my gender. No matter where I am or what I do, my perception is that I am seen as a woman scientist rather than as a scientist. When I face rejection, I wonder whether gender bias played a role. When I succeed, I ask myself whether I have received favored treatment as a minority. In a conference room full of male speakers, I feel that I don't belong. Yet I find it unbearable to be the token woman.

She concludes noting, "When I earned my PhD in 1993, I was not aware that I would be a pioneer."[76]

She offers the ethical hard work of facing and overcoming culturally rooted bias and discrimination as the only legitimate course of action. "Achieving gender equity will require a cultural change in the academic workplace. The first goal is for both men and women to recognize implicit and explicit bias in their actions. I believe this will require vigilance and many uncomfortable conversations."[77]

THE PIPELINE

No matter the field, no matter the professional school, across the university we find gender inequity and discrimination in faculty appointments and advancements. Take engineering. Commenting on the study, "Professional Role Confidence and Gendered Persistence in Engineering,"[78] Erica Perez writes "It's pretty well documented that women are less likely than men to pursue engineering as a career, more likely to leave the engineering major once they enter it and less likely to go into the field after graduation."[79]

Schools realize that they need to address these issues. Perez notes, for instance, how the University of California (UC)–Berkeley College of

Engineering has realized a need to study sexism in practice in their school of engineering.[80]

Any department, professional school, or university, when it addresses sexism inevitably begins to ask itself questions about the pipeline. As Kristen Renwick Monroe and William Chiu explain it, "The image of a pipeline is a commonly advanced explanation for discrimination that suggests that gender inequality will decline once there are sufficient numbers of qualified women in the hiring pool."[81] These authors argue that we have to ask whether the pipeline is functioning, because if it is just a matter of time before numbers of women undergraduates will get through the pipeline to doctorates and subsequent appointment in universities, then time and not policy will correct the situation.

As we have seen in this chapter, however, the numbers of women interested in the academy and in teaching positions is extremely high. Available candidates are routinely and nearly universally discriminated against.

Monroe and Chiu report in their study: "Our analysis uses aggregate data collected by the [American Association of University Professors] on the status of women in higher education in the United States over roughly the last 30 years—years that saw increased efforts to expand the pool of women entering the academic market." Using this data, they found "that the percentage of women in the academy remains disproportionately low, and that those women who do succeed in finding an academic job still earn less for the same job than their male counterparts."[82]

This use of aggregate data allows us to get a view of the big picture of the context in which faculty operate. What does the big picture tell us?

> National statistics clearly show that fewer women work in the academia than would be expected, given the relatively comparable numbers of male and female graduate students currently entering the market. Overall women are employed at lower status institutions. Women are ranked at lower grades, and they earn less at each grade than their male counterparts.[83]

They add that things get worse as one rises in university hierarchy. "As women move from lower to higher ranking institutions, pay inequalities increase. A 3% average gap at the community college level becomes an 8% gap at research I institution level."[84]

The fact that things get tighter as one ascends suggests another finding: the glass ceiling "that manifests itself as a filter at the highest rank and levels of prestige." The authors expand on this point: "Women participate at deteriorating levels as ranks rise at colleges, universities, and research institutions. At the highest level—the research I institution—women constitute 10.9% of assistant professors but only 7.2% of full professors."[85] They conclude that universities need to more actively address the disparities of gender inequity.[86]

Monroe and Chiu's study raises questions about salaries, hiring, promotions, and appointments that, we have seen, are prompted by gender bias. But other scholars have looked at the pipeline to ask whether there are other factors that prompt unfavorable results. One set of researchers from UC–Berkeley, Mary Ann Mason and Marc Goulden, have posed the question, "Do Babies Matter?" In 2002, they published their first read of the research of the Survey of Doctorate Recipients biennial weighted, longitudinal study, which follows more than 160,000 PhD recipients across all disciplines until they reach age seventy-six.[87] In their first study they reported:

> that babies do matter for men and women PhDs working in academia. They matter a great deal, especially their timing. We found that men with "early" babies—those with a child entering their household within five years of their receiving the PhD—are 38 percent more likely than their women counterparts to achieve tenure. Moreover, the pattern of tenure achievement for women and men stayed almost identical in the humanities, social sciences, and hard sciences. It also held true across four-year institutions, from large research universities to small liberal arts colleges.[88]

In 2004 they asked a second question: "[W]hat happens to the men and women who secure that first assistant professor job before becoming parents?" They found, "Only one in three women who takes a fast-track university job before having a child ever becomes a mother. Women who achieve tenure are more than twice as likely as their male counterparts to be single twelve years after earning the PhD. And, women who are married when they begin their faculty careers are much more likely than men in the same position to divorce or separate from their spouses." They add, "Women, it seems, cannot have it all—tenure and a family—while men can."[89]

Mason and Goulden noted an exception: "On the other hand, the 'second tier' of women PhDs—those who are not working or who are adjunct, part-time, or 'gypsy' scholars and teachers—looks very different. Second-tier women have children and experience marital stability much like men who became professors."[90]

Mason and Goulden acknowledge that a gender equity that only looks at careers without looking at family expectations misses true gender equity. They therefore propose, "A true measure of gender equity in the academy would look at both career and family." They add, "We call this two-pronged measure the 'baby gap test,' because it takes into account both the gap in professional outcomes for women with children compared with men and the gap in family formation for academically successful women. We need to ask not only how many women are professors and deans relative to their male counterparts; we also need to ask how many women with children are in high places compared with men with children."[91] They conclude: "Achieving gender equity in terms of careers and families in the academy requires a restructuring of the workplace."[92]

In 2013, Mason and Goulden with Nicholas Wolfinger brought together their entire research on the *Do Babies Matter? Project* and have published their *Do Babies Matter? Gender and Family in the Ivory Tower.*[93] Among their findings were that 44 percent of female tenured faculty were married with children versus 70 percent of male tenured faculty.

On the occasion of its publication, Colleen Flaherty at *Inside Higher Ed,* interviewed the authors. Goulden stated, "Certainly our most important finding has been that family negatively affects women's, but not men's, early academic careers. Furthermore, academic women who advance through the faculty ranks have historically paid a considerable price for doing so, in the form of much lower rates of family formation, fertility, and higher rates of family dissolution."

Commenting on women in the academy, Mason said, "At every stage, there's a 'baby penalty.' In the earlier stages, graduate students have children and drop out or grad students get turned away from the academic profession, in terms of the [lack of family-friendliness] they see around them." She adds, "Concerns about time demands in relation to caretaking, and worries that advisers, future employers, and peers would take their work less seriously were all reasons female Ph.D. students, more than male, cited for not having a child or being uncertain about having a child."[94]

All three referred to recent projects by universities that were becoming more family-friendly of its faculty, including providing paid maternity leaves and other options for women faculty.

Finally, how do all these statistics compare to other professionals? In 2008, the three academics reported in a paper, "Alone in the Ivory Tower: How Birth Events Vary Among Fast-Track Professionals,"[95] that male and female faculty members are less likely than their counterparts in the fields of medicine and law to have children.

Both *Inside Higher Ed* and the *Chronicle of Higher Education* reported on the paper. From the *Chronicle,* Robin Wilson wrote this brief summary of the striking report:

> The paper says that male faculty members are 21 percent less likely than male physicians and 12 percent less likely than male lawyers to have children. The paper attributes the difference in part to doctors' and lawyers' higher incomes, which give them more money for day care.
>
> In addition, the paper says, male doctors are more likely to have children because they are also twice as likely as male professors to be married to wives who do not have jobs. Male professors, by contrast, are more likely than male doctors or lawyers to be married to female professors, who are the least likely of women in the three professions to have babies.
>
> In fact, the study found that female professors are 41 percent less likely than female doctors and 24 percent less likely than female lawyers to have children. Female faculty members, says the paper, are also more likely than their female counterparts in medicine and law to be divorced or separated.[96]

CONCLUSION

Unlike the other chapters in this book, the reports, studies, and arguments of this chapter on gender do not come from journalists who recognize how ethically scandalous some of the activities of universities are. This chapter is basically the research and arguments of mostly women faculty fighting for equity within their own ranks.

Here we can see the significance of faculty using their own research, teaching, and mentoring skills to better their own situation, especially in the light of the ethical issues of gender bias and discrimination. We can also see that their long-standing fight for fair treatment has not been easily won and that in fact the struggle highlights, I think, the lack of familiarity that the university has with issues of justice in the first place.

Still, it cannot be ignored that the voices of those women have changed to some extent the overall lay of the land for faculty, at least highlighting that the land is not only for men. Moreover, these women have brought their research into the classroom and into public places on the university, especially in the fight for undergraduates to protect themselves and others from sexual assault. Here we see the true beginning of ethics when faculty women (and men) work for the just treatment of not only themselves, but of others.

Nonetheless, other than working for students to be free from sexual assault, there are other instances where women faculty and administrators are conscious of other challenges that women students might have at a university where sexual assault is more common on their campus than in most neighborhoods in America. In particular, faculty and administrators at Princeton University, following the lead of President Shirley M. Tilghman, developed the *Report of the Steering Committee on Undergraduate Women's Leadership* (March 2011).[97] Effectively, this is one of the first reports to look at women undergraduates as their own cohort, no longer *like* college men, no longer finding their place as outsiders or as rebels. For the first time, women leaders at a university are carving out a specific place and role for women students. No longer do women students, even though they are the majority, need to look at the university as basically for men. The Princeton project is an instance of what Aristotle promoted in his *Nicomachean Ethics* in advancing that a community working for ethics works effectively for its own flourishment (though for Aristotle, they were mostly college men).

These women faculty and administrators moved outside their own offices and even their own classrooms. Though they have taken to the campus on matters of sexual assault and the well being of their students, they, like their male counterparts, are pretty absent, as we saw earlier, from the struggles of men and even more so of women who are staff and contingent faculty. I do not think they are necessarily callous, though the staff and contingent faculty might think that. Rather the university geography keeps us in our fiefdoms, which are convenient for many, including the faculty who should, I think, ask more questions about ethics on campus.

   If they did, the university would be a better place.

9

DIVERSITY AND RACE

"As undergraduates progress in higher education, they become less interested, on average, in promoting racial understanding."
—Scott Jaschik[1]

In 2012, the *Chronicle of Higher Education* published the news that "Women Are Still Underrepresented as Medical-School Deans, Study Finds." The article was brief. "Despite the increased participation of women in academic medicine, they remain significantly underrepresented among the deans of medical schools and take longer to advance through their ranks than their male counterparts."[2] It referred to the study, "The Impact of Cross-Cultural Interactions on Medical Students' Preparedness to Care for Diverse Patients," which appeared in *Academic Medicine* and found that just 7 percent of medical school deans were women from 1980 through 2006. On average, they only lasted for a three-year tenure, while their male counterparts lasted just over five years.[3]

That study was part of *Academic Medicine*'s entire issue dedicated to diversity and inclusion in medical schools. Among the articles was a commentary about diversity and inclusion by Marc Nivet, the chief diversity officer for the Association of American Medical Colleges, who immediately noted the ethical mandate to attend to diversity and inclusion: "Fairness will always be a fundamental argument at the heart of diversity work. This moral imperative has been well articulated in the academic medicine literature, framing diversity in health care as a means to increase access to care for underserved populations, reduce health disparities, shape a more inclusive biomedical research agenda, and enhance the cultural competence of providers."[4]

Many of the goods that diversity brings to health care parallel those related to higher education. That is, the compelling interests that health care and education have in serving and bettering the common good prompts both institutions to realize that a commitment to the future of diversity is a commitment to the future of the common good.

Nivet asks us to see, however, that underlying our concern for diversity is a recognition that in the United States, often enough, attention to diversity is mandated by a recognition about fundamental inequities:

> At the root of this social justice rationale are two important social realities: gender, racial and ethnic inequities persist as demographics continue to shift. Facing these realities are two important societal realities: our collective history of inequities on the basis of gender, race, and ethnicity, and the rapid demographic changes taking place nationally. The moral imperative recognizes that unequal educational opportunities and other forms of exclusion and discrimination persist and must be addressed.[5]

Nivet argues rightly that unequal educational opportunities must be corrected. We need to bear in mind that the issue of American inequity is not singular or occasional, but rather systemic. What we need to erase are the differences that are long embedded in the social fabric of our nation. These differences in gender and in race run across the campus, whether in the arts, sciences, or professional schools. Even more important than these broad instances of discrimination across the American university spectrum is the impact that these inequities have on the common good.

Still, in responding to social inequities, the expectations of the universities ought to be high. If women do not find equity in the institutions that teach, promote values, and set standards, where will they find equity? If African Americans do not find equity in the institutions that teach, promote values, and set standards, where will they find equity? But in fact, they do not find it in American universities.

In *Diversity's Promise for Higher Education: Making it Work*, Daryl G. Smith argues: "Diversity represents one of the most dramatic societal changes in the twenty-first century, with significant implications for

American higher education. It is not only shaping higher education but higher education's role in society."[6]

Smith's interest in diversity first arises from the interest of diversity in the student population, recognizing that diversity is the future of the American university. He immediately recognizes the mutually dependent relationship that diversity among students needs to be reflected also among university hires. Recalling Vaccaro and others, we cannot treat the matter of gender inequity without recognizing its intrinsic dependency on other matters of diversity and inequity. Whether talking about gender, race, class, or sexual orientation, the practices of discrimination are fundamentally similar, as Smith notes: "The hiring and retention literature stresses the barriers to hiring, including the myths given for limited hiring, the passive nature of searches, biases in how excellence is defined and sought, and embedded cultures that privilege existing norms over change."[7]

There need to be signs of equity not only in hiring and retention, but also in leadership. In a section titled "Developing Human Capacity: The Rationale for Leadership Diversity," Smith writes, "The important role of leadership in building capacity for diversity is discussed in virtually all of the research and field work in higher education."[8]

Certainly, when we turn to leadership diversity, we think of a variety of women who rose to the presidencies of American universities. In 2001, the *New York Times* noted that when Princeton president Shirley Tilghman appointed Amy Guttman as provost, it became the first research university to have its two top positions held by women. At the same time, with University of Pennsylvania's Judith Rodin and Brown's Ruth J. Simmons, there were three Ivies with women presidents. Additionally, noting that 19 percent of American college presidents were women (up from 9.5 percent in 1986), the *Times* added with high expectations: "With the number of women presidents, faculty and doctoral students all on the rise, the academic world seems to be dismantling what was once seen as a veritable old-boy network."[9]

In 2012 the news was less optimistic. First, in the fall of 2011, Ruth J. Simmons, the first black president of an Ivy League institution, announced she would step down as president in June 2012 after eleven years at Brown and six earlier years as president at Smith. When she announced she was stepping down, she remarked, "When I went to my

first Ivy League presidents' meeting, I didn't feel particularly welcomed."[10]

Then there was the announcement of Massachusetts Institute of
Technology (MIT) president Susan Hockfield's intention to step down
in June 2012 after eight years as president.[11] On September 11, 2012,
Shirley M. Tilghman announced she would step down as Princeton's
president in the following June.[12]

Around the same time, The American Council on Education re-
leased a report on American university presidencies: "[T]he typical
American college or university president is a married white male who is
61 years old, holds a doctorate in education, and has served in his
current position for seven years—a profile that has not varied greatly
over the previous 25 years." The report was sobering: "While women
have increased their representation (26 percent in 2011, up from 23
percent in 2006), the proportion of presidents who are racial or ethnic
minorities declined slightly from 14 percent in 2006 to 13 percent in
2001."[13] The expectations of 2001 were not really met by 2012.

HOW SUCCESSFUL ARE UNIVERSITIES ON
MATTERS OF DIVERSITY?

Vaccaro's study of "What Lies Beneath" turns out to be more accurate
than many would believe. Many outside the university think that diversity is well received at the university, but her study, like the reports on
theme parties, ought to dispel such beliefs. Worse, more recent studies
confirm that undergraduates are less interested in diversity than many
would think. In fact, the longer they are in college, the less interested
they become.

Scott Jaschik with *Inside Higher Ed* reflects on a recent study[14] that
reports "as undergraduates progress in higher education, they become
less interested, on average, in promoting racial understanding."[15]

In the study, students were asked, "How important to you personally
is helping to promote racial understanding?" They were asked the question upon arriving at college, at the end of their freshman year, and at
the end of their senior year.

Jaschik reports, "Ranking the importance of promoting racial understanding on a four-point scale, African American students started off

with the highest score (above 3.2), followed by Hispanics (just below 3.2), Asians (around 2.9) and whites (just under 2.5). All four groups were lower at the end of their freshman year, and lower as well by their senior year."[16] In other words, the longer they were in college, the less interested they became in racial understanding.

Jaschik quotes the researchers Jesse Rude, Gregory C. Wolniak, and Ernest T. Pascarella: "Contrary to our expectations, the average change in racial attitudes during the first year and over the entire four-year period is in a negative direction." Jaschik reports, "In between the start and end of freshman year, 30.5 percent said that promoting racial understanding was less important at the end, while only 17.3 percent thought it was more important. (The rest didn't change.) Between the start and end of college, more students 'trend negative' (33.8 percent) than positive (21.4 percent), the study finds."

The typical assumption that mixing students together would prompt an appreciation for racial diversity is incredibly presumptuous. It effectively left students less inclined toward racial diversity than when they arrived. The researchers write: "These findings cast doubt on research and conventional wisdom that argues for the liberalizing effects of higher education on racial attitudes. Instead, it suggests that, for some students, negative experiences with diversity may dampen the relatively progressive racial views they hold when entering college."

Mandating more culturally diverse classes is not the answer. Rather, the university needs to commit itself to promoting racial understanding as a good and to ensuring that good is visible across the campus in a variety of ways. As we saw in Chapter 6, "Cheating," the university needs to invest itself in developing witness to the value of racial understanding across the university. Rude, Wolniak, and Pascarella write: "An implication of these findings for postsecondary institutions with racially diverse campuses is that efforts to broaden students' racial views should extend beyond multicultural course requirements. Colleges that can take steps that promote environments conducive for cross-race friendship and other forms of positive interaction may have an even greater impact on students' racial attitudes."[17]

The findings of these researchers should have been expected because American universities were warned ten years earlier about the need to anticipate the challenges that would arise from increasing campus diversity. In 1996, Ernest T. Pascarella, one of the researchers of the 2012 study, led a study titled, "Influences on Students' Openness to Diversity and Challenge in the First Year of College."[18] They found what we are constantly finding: "[W]omen had higher levels of openness to diversity/challenges than men, and nonwhite students had somewhat higher levels than their white counterparts."[19] The white college male is less interested in diversity and racial understanding than universities will admit. Their study of roughly four thousand students at eighteen institutions over the course of four years led Pascarella to make a variety of fundamental assertions about what a university needed to do to become a place that promotes racial understanding.

For instance, Pascarella's group wrote that "joining a fraternity or a sorority had a modest but significantly negative effect on openness to diversity/challenge." In particular "for white students the influence was strongly negative."[20] While acknowledging that their data was not explicit on the causes, they conjectured, "[O]ne possible explanation is that they provide essentially homogenous and insulating environments that minimize the opportunities that white students have to interact with people of diverse backgrounds and philosophies." But then they added, "Irrespective of the cause, the findings on membership in fraternities and sororities suggest the potential need for programmatic interventions or policies that might counteract the negative influence of these organizations." They then recommended racial or cultural awareness workshops that in their study had a positive effect that "was particularly strong for white (versus nonwhite) students." Similarly, they mentioned occasional conversations among students of diverse backgrounds on value-laden or controversial issues also had a strong effect on white students.[21] That is, they found that putting racially and ethnically mixed students together to face a controversial issue actually had a positive impact on the participants. Leaving them alone, however, only increased the negative stances from disinterest to suspicions and intolerance.

What I found most interesting, however, were Pascarella's group's concerns about the institutional policies. They believed that their study called for "more broad-based policies aimed at influencing the overall institutional environment." They found that "the extent to which an institution's environment was perceived as racially non-discriminatory positively influenced students' openness to diversity/challenge." They recommended "purposeful policies and programs that both sensitize faculty, administrators and students to what constitutes racial discrimination and demonstrate unequivocally that such behavior is anathema to the institutional ethos." In a clear nod to ethical foundations for these endeavors, they write that "institutions should develop policies and programs aimed at creating a nondiscriminatory racial environment primarily because it is the right thing to do, not simply because it enhances the student development." Their research shows that the isolating feudal structures of the university campus do not promote anything but isolation. If the university wants a nondiscriminatory racial environment, it will not happen on its own; the administration will have to create it.

Pascarella and his colleagues are not at all naïve about the scale of their cross-campus recommendations: "Alterations in an institutional environment, however, will require substantial collaboration among a number of campus divisions and units." Taking aim at the inhibiting departmental structures of the university, they add, "Academic and administrative units that now think of themselves as separate will have to learn to plan and work together. Programmatic and policy interventions that are mutually supportive and reinforcing across organizational units will have to be developed."[22]

The study in 1996 by Pascarella and colleagues is similar to another in 1999. Sylvia Hurtado, Jeffrey Milem, Alma Clayton-Pedersen, and Walter Allen published their study, "Enacting Diverse Learning Environments: Improving the Climate for Racial/Ethnic Diversity in Higher Education."[23] Their overall finding was that issues of racial diversity are interconnected across the entire campus. "Campuses can no longer speak about changes in the number of diverse students without recognizing how this change affects the psychological climate or opportunities for interaction across different groups on campus—and ultimately changes in educational outcomes for students."

They found that different racial and ethnic groups view the campus differently and they predicted in 1999 what we now know to be the experience on campuses today: "[T]hat increasing the racial/ethnic diversity on a campus while neglecting to attend to the racial climate can result in difficulties for students of color as well as for white students."

Moreover, Hurtado and colleagues found that where diversity functioned well—that is, when students have diverse peers in the learning environment—"students' ability to engage in more complex thinking about problems and to consider multiple perspectives" evidently improves. They concluded that "providing opportunities for quality interaction and an overall climate of support results not only in a better racial climate but also in important learning outcomes for students." In a word, diversity could actually be good news for educational goals.

Hurtado and colleagues have a bottom line: The most basic fundamental change that we need to see in colleges and universities is "a conceptual shift in thinking about how diversity is central to the institution's overall priorities for teaching and learning which also requires a change in how students are regarded or valued."[24]

Both studies warned us that if we increased racial diversity without attending to the overall campus climate we would create a more negative atmosphere at the university. That there are theme parties, diminishing interests in racial understanding, and overt signs of intolerance of racial diversity highlights how their recommendations went unheeded and that, in fact, the climate is worsening.

DIVERSITY: THE FUTURE FACE OF THE AMERICAN UNIVERSITY

Diversity is not going away. In fact it is increasing as a reality in two very significant ways: First, the domestic population of the United States is becoming increasingly diversified. Here is the news in a nutshell from a 2012 report by the U.S. Census Bureau.

> The non-Hispanic white population is projected to peak in 2024, at 199.6 million, up from 197.8 million in 2012. Unlike other race or ethnic groups, however, its population is projected to slowly decrease, falling by nearly 20.6 million from 2024 to 2060.
>
> Meanwhile, the Hispanic population would more than double, from 53.3 million in 2012 to 128.8 million in 2060. Consequently, by the end of the period, nearly one in three U.S. residents would be Hispanic, up from about one in six today.
>
> The black population is expected to increase from 41.2 million to 61.8 million over the same period. Its share of the total population would rise slightly, from 13.1 percent in 2012 to 14.7 percent in 2060.

The Asian population is projected to more than double, from 15.9 million in 2012 to 34.4 million in 2060, with its share of the nation's total population climbing from 5.1 percent to 8.2 percent in the same period.

Among the remaining race groups, American Indians and Alaska Natives would increase by more than half from now to 2060, from 3.9 million to 6.3 million, with their share of the total population edging up from 1.2 percent to 1.5 percent. The Native Hawaiian and Other Pacific Islander population is expected to nearly double, from 706,000 to 1.4 million. The number of people who identify themselves as being of two or more races is projected to more than triple, from 7.5 million to 26.7 million over the same period.

The U.S. is projected to become a majority-minority nation for the first time in 2043. While the non-Hispanic white population will remain the largest single group, no group will make up a majority.

All in all, minorities, now 37 percent of the U.S. population, are projected to comprise 57 percent of the population in 2060. (Minorities consist of all but the single-race, non-Hispanic white population.) The total minority population would more than double, from 116.2 million to 241.3 million over the period.

Projections show the older population would continue to be predominately non-Hispanic white, while younger ages are increasingly minority.[25]

The statistics are astonishing.

Yet we see in our own data that facing diversity, universities apparently thought that they did not need to do anything at the university but recruit a more diversified student body and occasionally require a multicultural course. It is as if the administrators were thinking that if at day care centers 4-year-olds get along with one another regardless of diversity, what's the difference in bringing in diverse 18- to 20-year-olds. The only problem is, for better or worse, American young adults come to college having been socialized by the biased perspectives of their own demographics. Unlike a 4-year-old who doesn't see color, these young people do.

Moreover, the last sentence of the Census Bureau report is telling. Inasmuch as diversity grows the younger the population is, the challenges of diversity will hit educational structures before they hit business, health, and other sectors.

The American university is facing diversity on a second front: the call of globalization. More and more students around the world want to attend American universities and more American universities want to recruit these international students who often pay full fare. The same naïve and irresponsible assumptions that we saw with universities admitting more and more racially diverse students without the needed cultural climate change within the university are at play with the recruitment of international students, yielding similar repercussions. The university recruits students from around the world but the support they provide for these students and the way they prepare the university's campus climate are still problematic.

We cannot underestimate how the recruitment of international students is affecting the contemporary American university. In 2011, the Institute of International Education reported robust numbers of international successful student recruitment. "The number of international students at colleges and universities in the United States increased by five percent to 723,277 during the 2010/11 academic year. . . . This represents a record high number of international students in the United States. This is the fifth consecutive year that figures show growth in the total number of international students, and there are now 32 percent more international students studying at U.S. colleges and universities than there were a decade ago."

The Institute particularly noted that the "increased numbers of students from China, particularly at the undergraduate level, largely accounts for the growth this past year. Chinese students increased by 23 percent in total and by 43 percent at the undergraduate level. . . . Chinese student enrollment in the United States rose to a total of nearly 158,000 students, or nearly 22 percent of the total international student population, making China the leading sending country for the second year in a row." Nearly half of all international students in the United States come from China, India, or South Korea.

The Institute explains the enormous economic impact that these international students make, usually paying full tuition. "International students contribute more than $21 billion to the U.S. economy, through their expenditures on tuition and living expenses." They add, "Higher education is among the United States' top service sector exports, as international students provide significant revenue not just to the host campuses but also to local economies of the host states for living expenses, including room and board, books and supplies, transportation, health insurance, and support for accompanying family members."[26]

Here we can wonder: What does ethics expect of us when our country together with our universities recruits over seven hundred thousand 18- to 21-year-olds from foreign cultures to pay roughly $60,000 a year for an American education when we also believe that they lack the maturity to drink a beer? Maybe even more to the point, do we believe we have any specific ethical responsibilities regarding their welfare at the university?

A number of studies suggest that their travels here are not without incident. In "Welcome to America? International Student Perceptions of Discrimination," Jenny Lee and Charles Rice consider a range of difficulties international students encounter "from perceptions of unfairness and inhospitality to cultural intolerance and confrontation." They "find that not all of the issues international students face can be problematized as matters of adjustment, as much research does, but that some of the more serious challenges are due to inadequacies within the host society."[27]

Later they write:

> Our study reveals some of the worst hardships in negotiating university life as due to the foreign national status of some of our international guests. As we have discussed, these difficulties run from students being ignored to verbal insults and confrontation. This research also shows how this occurs in a range of contexts, both in and outside the classroom, by peers, faculty, and members of the local community.[28]

They conclude: "The most obvious first step is for institutions to become more aware that discrimination based on nation of origin exists in many forms."[29]

More recently, Elizabeth Redden wrote "I'm not Racist, but." The title is taken from a tweet by a student at the University of Nebraska at Lincoln, "I'm not racist, but one thing I did not miss was all the Asians." Redden recounts a variety of episodes at college campuses that show little hospitality and a fair amount of aggression toward new Chinese, Indian, or South Korean students.

Moreover she also reports, dishearteningly, that a recent study "found that nearly 40 percent of international students reported having no close American friends."

Though she reports some colleges and universities trying to help students, faculty, and administrators better welcome and support these growing populations, she warns that "experts suggest that as international students become more numerous and visible on North American campuses, there will be an increase in nasty culture clashes."[30]

Elisabeth Gareis's study found that nearly 40 percent of international students had no American friend. She also noted, "Participants from English-speaking countries were most likely to report having three or more close American friends, whereas students from East Asia often had no close American friends." Clearly, if the overall average was 40 percent, then the Asian students had even less of a chance of friendship with an American. Gareis also reported:

> Friendship numbers and satisfaction levels were highest in the South, with the nonmetropolitan Northeast ranking second, and the New York City metropolitan area ranking lowest.
>
> Among all races and ethnicities, 46 percent thought that the reason for their friendship problems was an internal factor, such as low language proficiency or shyness. However, among East Asian students, that percentage was much higher, at 78 percent.
>
> The most common reasons why students attributed their friendship difficulties to Americans or to U.S. culture were superficiality (32 percent) and not being open-minded or interested in other cultures (25 percent).[31]

In an essay based on that study, Gareis concluded "Considering that East Asians are the largest contingent of international students in the United States and the least satisfied, special attention should be paid to furthering their integration."[32]

This recruitment of international students bears further reflection. While appreciating the evident way that universities have made international students as much a commodity as the degree the universities proffer them, Philip Altbach warns that international student populations are more volatile than other populations and that their growth rates will eventually ebb. Underlying all this are Altbach's concerns about the humanity and very human needs of these international students. He writes, "Many assume that expansion will continue indefinite-ly—and indeed that has been the trend in the era of massification of enrollments and globalization. Yet, international student flows can be quite volatile. The more countries and institutions think of international students as commodities to be traded, the more this volatility may have consequences for budgets and academic programs." Altbach refers, for instance, to the United Kingdom whose international student enroll-ments fell during 2013.[33]

Altbach highlights what so many others on campus do not really appreciate. It was not a simple move recruiting these students to American universities. Young people overseas did not wake up one morning with a sudden desire for Boston or Chicago. It took more than a village to recruit them; it took an industry:

> An entire industry has been built around international students. Eng-lish language programs, some offered by universities and many spon-sored by private companies, are a significant part of the mobility nexus. Agents and recruiters, some of them with questionable ethical standards, increasingly funnel students to universities abroad. Transi-tion programs that prepare undergraduate students for overseas study have sprung up in many countries. All of these providers de-pend on a growing flow of internationally mobile students.

Altbach concludes with a warning about the difficulties that arise when the reductive work of commodification inhibits us from seeing what may have been the promises recruiters made or what may have been the challenges in language acquisition that were not anticipated. These are young people, not objects to be traded. These are students we want to teach, not entities coughing up $65,000 a year. "We have seen the emergence of a wide range of ancillary services—many of them driven more by commercial opportunities than educational goals. And we have seen international students, to some extent, become another commod-ity to be traded on global markets with the aim of earning a profit."

Certainly we do not want to be naïve about the financial ramifica-tions of such recruits, but as Altbach warns and as our data shows, young people, particularly Asians, are having a harder time at our uni-versities than we are acknowledging and inasmuch as we are mission-driven and not for-profit institutions, their educational needs and gen-eral well being, and not their role as a resource, ought to be our first consideration. They ought not be simply a set of numbers in the growing commodification of the American university system.

Zach Ritter offers us a view from another perspective; he has published an essay on his findings of how some international students view American diversity. He argues that racial misunderstandings happen in many situations and that universities must be attentive to the racial understandings of incoming international students.

For his dissertation at the University of California–Los Angeles (UCLA), Ritter studied forty-four Chinese, Japanese, and Korean international students' experiences with cross-racial and ethnic interaction at UCLA. He found the following:

> More than half of students interviewed in my dissertation study held negative stereotypes of African-American and Latino people. This stemmed from little to no interaction with individuals of a different racial/ethnic background, combined with media images of African-American and Latino people as poverty-stricken or criminals—images found both in Asian and American media. A racial hierarchy emerged as students explained that white people were on the top of this status pyramid because of the perceived wealth, beauty, and education portrayed in American and Asian film and television. East Asians and Asian Americans came second, Latinos third, and African Americans as well as Southeast Asians were lowest on this hierarchy. Southeast Asians were placed at a low level due to the developing economic conditions of many Southeast Asian nations as well as an Asian racial hierarchy based on phenotype, with darker skin being less desirable.

He acknowledges a rising awareness of these challenges of racial misunderstandings that have been accompanied by some interesting programming, but writes, "[T]here must be a culture of sensitivity and cultural awareness on the part of professors, students affairs officers, and students to make international students feel welcome. Building a culture of tolerance takes time, but as the number of international students grows, colleges and universities will have to adapt quickly to serve the needs of these students or else face a decline in revenue from this unique population."[34]

While student affairs personnel are rather informed about these significant shifts in the US American university population and while they have studied and prepared worthy responses to assist and welcome the more diversified student populations at American universities, the rest of the university population—administration, faculty, trustees, and staff—have really no institutionally guided appreciation of the challenges that American and international students of color experience. White students have some experience, usually in the form of mandated multicultural courses that often many students of color are not required to attend. In other words, even the students are not institutionally guided to any encounter with their fellow students, with white American students left talking among themselves about the multicultural students not in their courses.

What about the faculty and administration? At American universities, as I'm sure we would find at other universities around the world, there is a presupposition of intellectual competency, which says, though the students might need some multicultural diversity, faculty and administrators are so smart that they do not need an orientation to the newer types of students they are meeting. This is the same presupposition that faculty and administration don't need any training in professional ethics, because, well, they are smart enough to learn that on their own. But are they? Do they?

Just as few faculty and administrators are trained in professional ethics, neither are they trained to learn the challenges in and expectations of learning that students of color have. But why should this surprise us? Faculty are in the dark about what their students get from their classes. Derek Bok offers great insight when he claims that faculty have never really appreciated the challenges of any students when it comes to their learning processes: "The most common method instructors use in conducting their classes is the lecture, a method repeatedly shown to be one of the least effective means of developing higher-level thinking skills or helping students to achieve a deep comprehension of challenging subject matter." He adds, "Lecturing appeals to instructors because it is the most efficient way to cover a lot of material. The catch is that students retain very little of what they hear."[35]

RACE AT THE AMERICAN UNIVERSITY AS INEVITABLY CONNECTED TO US HISTORY

We cannot talk about race on campus adequately until we address the often wildly overlooked fact of America's history of slavery. Underlying most of the phenomena that we have seen previously is the fact that the long-standing exclusion of African Americans from American campuses has had enduring and broad-ranging effects on the profoundly unethical cultures found in American universities.

In the history of the United States, no group of people has been more continually unwelcomed at the American university than African Americans. African Americans during slavery and later with the thirteenth amendment understood that education was deeply connected to their freedom and their flourishment. History documents well the odds that African Americans fought and fight against today for education in this country.[36] But often enough, even the philanthropist who appears as benevolently appreciative of the African American struggle managed to enhance the white supremacist structure that steered African Americans away from the road to true equity in educational access in the United States.[37]

With rare exceptions, African Americans were not accepted on American campuses. Two exceptions come to mind: Oberlin College and Berea College. Oberlin College was founded as co-educational in 1833. Two years later, the trustees voted to admit African Americans. In time, Oberlin became a stop on the Underground Railroad.[38] Before the Civil War, Oberlin had enrolled more African American students than any American university and by 1900, as Oberlin's Alumni Association of African Ancestry reports, Oberlin had graduated one-third of all African American undergraduates.[39]

From its one-room school house in 1855 to its original articles of incorporation in 1859 to its opening a few years later, Berea College, named after the town where Paul and Silas went and found a people who "received the word with all willingness and examined the scriptures daily to determine whether these things were so" (Acts 17:11), was from its inception a school for white and black students. In its 1866–1867 catalogue, it listed ninety-six black students and ninety-one white students in its enrollment. Berea took many of its faculty from Oberlin.

Elsewhere, African Americans attended historically Black colleges and universities founded across the United States. Three colleges were established before 1862. Cheyney University of Pennsylvania was established in the 1830s. Lincoln University in Pennsylvania and Wilberforce College in Ohio were established in the 1850s.

Before the Civil War, few African Americans were at any other northern institutions, while in the south, African Americans were forbidden even to read. Black leaders along with the American Missionary Association and the Freedmen's Bureau fought to establish schools and between 1861 and 1870 seven Black colleges and thirteen teaching colleges were started. Though the Morrill Land-Grant Act of 1862 became the foundation for the development of American university life by training Americans in the applied sciences, agriculture, and engineering, in the segregated South, African Americans were unable to benefit from it. Later, the passage of the second Morrill Land-Grant Act in 1890, which specified that states using federal land-grant funds must either make their schools open to both blacks and whites or allocate money for segregated Black colleges to serve as an alternative to white schools, gave to sixteen exclusively Black colleges the opportunity to survive.[40]

These historically Black colleges and universities became the foundations for the higher education of African Americans. African American leaders like Frederick Douglass, Booker T. Washington, and W. E. B. Du Bois would be at the forefront of campaigning for education though even among them there would be debate over how to access education in white America.[41]

There are today a variety of studies about the success of African American graduates from historically Black colleges and institutions versus predominantly white institutions of higher education.[42] We have much to learn from them, but here in this book on university ethics we must look at the predominantly white institutions that are continuing to recruit African American students and that certainly had a less receptive stance toward them than their counterparts.

Before going to recent reports on race at predominantly white institutions in the United States, I want to posit that, unlike gender or other American racial biases in America, the history of white supremacy over the African American is a history that is still not accountable or recognized. Of course, so much of the bad behavior and harm done by "the college male" at the university has not been accountable or recognized, in part because, as we saw in the last chapter, they have a considerable legacy of control at the university to this day.[43]

White supremacy is much different. It did not begin in the university, though the university has practiced it from the first day it used slaves, made money in slave trading, and excluded African Americans from their campuses. David Gillborn of the University of London writes that, according to Critical Race Theory (CRT), "white supremacy is conceived as a comprehensive condition whereby the interests and perceptions of white subjects are continually placed centre stage and assumed as 'normal'." As such, I think many can view white supremacy throughout America and across our campuses.[44]

I find the term *white supremacy* helpful to get whites to think more concretely about how race plays out across the country. Many writers have commented on how preferable *white supremacy* is to *white privilege,* but I want to signal two faculty members who have helped me to appreciate the lack of attention by the US polity to our white history of enslaving black people. M. Shawn Copeland, who first opened my eyes to university ethics, gives us *Enfleshing Freedom: Body, Race and Being* in which she reflects on embodiment and race to consider the truly awful stories of black women in the time of slavery and its enduring aftermath.

In their bodies, black women were treated as objects of property, production, reproduction, and sexual violence. By turning to the lives of the long dead in a meditation that could accompany, as she suggests, Toni Morrison's Pulitzer Prize winning novel, *Beloved,* Copeland seeks to liberate us from a house, the United States, "haunted by the ghosts of slavery." Knowing that the "political memory of the nation suppresses our deep entanglement in slavery," and that the attempt to totally erase any reminder of slavery is doomed to failure, she raises "the aching memory of slavery" and "interrogates memory and history for the sake of freedom." In the midst of stories of torture, sexual assault, and lynching, Copeland notes that therein, "black women began the healing of their flesh and their subjectivity in the *there and then*, in the midst of enslavement."[45]

Copeland, like many others, believes that our nation suffers from all that we did during slavery and the deep, on-going effects of that history. Trying to forget that history only makes the effective history of slavery deeper and stronger; only by facing it do we encounter the possibility of healing, reconciliation, and freedom. Facing the white supremacy in our country both historically and contemporarily, we, whether white or black, Latino or Asian, can change the course of history only if we first acknowledge it.

Like Copeland, Bryan Massingale offers a manifesto for recognizing the historical effectiveness of racism, while proposing significant strategies for racial solidarity.[46] Together they help us to see the deep and abiding ghosts of slavery that haunt our country, including our campuses.

One of the great ethical problems on our campuses, the indwelling of racism, will never be overcome until there is a recognition of our racist history. There are high stakes here because the American university is precisely the place in America that could provide hope to subdue the ghosts of racism and encounter solidarity with a reconciling spirit of accountability and forgiveness.

For instance, the report from the Brown University Steering Committee on Slavery and Justice serves as an instructive lesson on what a university could do to awaken its own identification with racism in a positive, constructive, truthful, and reconciling way. The committee documents its charge in their report, "Slavery and Justice: A Report of the Brown University Steering Committee on Slavery and Justice":

> Our primary task was to examine the University's historical entanglement with slavery and the slave trade and to report our findings openly and truthfully. But we were also asked to reflect on the meaning of this history in the present, on the complex historical, political, legal, and moral questions posed by any present day confrontation with past injustice. In particular, the president (Ruth J. Simmons) asked the committee "to organize academic events and activities that might help the nation and the Brown community think deeply, seriously, and rigorously about the questions raised" by the national debate over reparations for slavery.[47]

The Committee concluded that its task was "to provide factual information and critical perspectives to deepen understanding and enrich debate on an issue that had aroused great public passion but little constructive public dialogue." Through President Ruth J. Simmons's charge, Brown University provided a model an American university could look to as it examines its own history of racism through the lens of slavery.[48]

Brown University is hardly the only university with a deep historical link to slavery. In a National Public Radio interview with Craig Steven Wilder over his recent book *Ebony & Ivy: Race, Slavery, and the Troubled History of America's Universities*,[49] Wilder introduced readers and listeners to how closely other universities like Harvard, Princeton, Columbia, Yale, Dartmouth, Pennsylvania, and William and Mary were connected to slavery.

Wilder, who chairs the history department at MIT, writes: "The academy never stood apart from American slavery. In fact, it stood beside church and state as the third pillar of a civilization built on bondage."[50]

Not only did these universities receive financial support from slaveholders and traders as they recruited and educated their sons, but Wilder argues that the academy was largely responsible for substantiating the credibility of racial supremacy or the natural inferiority of certain racial groups. These arguments furthered the ethical legitimacy of slave holding and trading. Though there were those on campus arguing against slavery, they were undermined by those other professors.

"There were real struggles about this," Wilder said in his interview. "There were lots of people on campus who argued vehemently against the expansion of the slave trade and the expansion of slavery." But they lost that battle in part because of those faculty developing "the emerging intellectual defense of slavery that was rooted in racial science." Wilder adds, "The perverse irony of that is that they're defeated by a body of ideas that are emerging on campus itself."

Wilder reminds us that, were American universities more vigorous in addressing their own unethical entanglements with slavery, racism, and white supremacy, they could help respond to the unaddressed but constant US racist ethos that inhibits much of the possibility of true diversity in the United States.[51] Because the universities do not, they become victims of themselves and to the ongoing historical effects of America's deep relationship with slavery and racism.

RACISM AT THE UNIVERSITY TODAY

In 2008, Gloria Gadsen wrote "A Minority Report" for the *Chronicle*. In it she argued that a diversity among students requires a diversity among faculty, and she added that administrators who hired minority faculty had to realize ways of retaining them, especially when the new faculty encounter antagonism from students. She writes:

> I have experienced another common problem: antagonism from white students who feel threatened by professors from minority groups. Some students—both in groups and individually—have confronted me in class, typically with a great deal of hostility and a complete lack of respect. Others have gone to department chairs with a barrage of complaints in an attempt to undermine my authority and credibility in the classroom, saying that I am biased or racist, that I am intimidating, and that I cannot teach. Those complaints have consistently been made part of my annual evaluations.
>
> In addition, I have been verbally assaulted and threatened outside the classroom by white students, most of them male. One student called me the N-word while passing me in the hall. Another threw something at me as I was walking to my car. And a third told me that his father knew the college's president, and that I would certainly lose my job if I didn't change the student's grade. Those are only a few examples out of many.[52]

Gadsen's experiences help us to hear what is often not easily transparent or reported. More recently a group of minority faculty have shared their experiences on campus and called their collection, *Presumed Incompetent: The Intersections for Race and Class for Women in Academia*. The book is divided into seven parts. The first, "The General Campus Climate," has seven essays on topics from "White Face Multiculturalism" to "The Racial and Gender Politics of Elusive Belonging." "Faculty–Student Relationships" has another seven essays and ranges from "The Silence of the Lambs" to "The Student Teaching Evaluations" and "The Perils of 'Doing' Gender and Race in Classroom." The third, "Networks of Allies," has five essays, which include, "Working across Racial Lines in a Not-So-Post-Racial World." The fourth is briefly on "Social Class in the Academy," and the final section has eight essays on "Tenure and Promotion" that leads with "The Making of a Token." The essays show the often unnoticed struggles of women of color working at American universities; the only real success stories here are the women's.[53]

The on-going effects of America's racism remain apparent at our universities, not simply as evidenced by racist actions like theme parties or the growing disdain for diversity at universities, or the diminishing interest in racial understanding, but also in the experiences, progressively being acknowledged by university faculty and administrators.

The basic question about whether predominantly white institutions have any interest in diversity in their administrations received a blistering report from the *Chronicle of Higher Education* on diversity's ceiling at today's Ivies.[54] This report was accompanied by an essay, "At the Ivies, It's Still White at the Top," which Stacey Patton authored. Patton refers to a "diversity" dinner party held a year earlier by University of Pennsylvania President Amy Guttmann. Patton writes:

> The president said that she would love to see a person of color in that dean position, and that she was committed to diversity, "but she would not just bring in someone who is not qualified," recalls Camille Z. Charles, a professor of sociology and director of Penn's Center for Africana Studies. Ms. Charles says she asked herself at the time: "Did I really just hear that?" She adds, "Why would there even be the need to talk about qualified? We don't say we need qualified applicants to recruit white males. It's assumed."[55]

The scene basically captures an ineptitude in the academy that one finds in the awkward relationships that the faculty have with others not like them. It gives us an idea again of what we saw earlier as the nature of faculty work: highly individualistic and fundamentally noncollaborative. Faculty do not understand much outside the silos in which they remain and when they are invited out of them, they are pretty awkward. The more that faculty are invited into collaborative work such as interdisciplinary teaching or university committees, the healthier they become. But they do not go easily.

Things do not change easily at a university because the faculty have already set up structures and machinery by which they don't hire women, don't hire faculty of color, and don't collaborate or socialize with adjuncts. Faculty select again and again their own. They belong to an identified group. The group defines them.

When white women or men and women of color do get hired or do move up through levels of authority, they are not that free to be themselves. The pressures to accommodate to the style of being faculty and to doing things the way they are done, are part of the faculty ethos on campuses. Where there's little diversity, the diverse have little freedom. Yet some have succeeded.[56] One can only imagine, however, the times that they have been given advice to not rock the boat, to not change anything, to go slower. In short we can imagine any number of faculty being guided to going nowhere. One can only imagine the number of times that Ruth J. Simmons or Shirley Tilghman had to remind those who insisted on offering them unsolicited advice that they were capable of running their universities.

It's not simply racism or indifferentism, it is also the nature of the profession, which has not had sufficient critique about itself. And this is hard because long ago the faculty decided not to have any horizontal accountability after tenure. So there is little to incentivize people to renew or to invent. There is then something fundamentally conservative about faculty. We associate old boy networks with big business, but they are ripe at the university and they are not accustomed to change.

The old-boy networks among our faculty are but more civilized expressions of the fraternities that reside on our campuses. They are exclusive, with long traditions, not subject to anything other than their own legacies. They look for sameness, are uncomfortable with women as equals, and dismiss diversity. They are, in short, a boys club. Is it at all surprising, then, that fraternities are at universities? They are, after all, copycats of university old-boy networks. They are not found in other professions, not in medicine or law or journalism or nursing. They are found where they are bred, universities.

We can see, then, the need to create a culture of ethics on our college campuses. Our campuses are often considered insulated bubbles. Similarly, students refer to graduation as the time when they "go out into the real world." The world of the college campus is indeed somewhat unreal, isolated from the give and take of the world of commerce. That world of commerce learned over the years that it needed to construct cultures of ethics in each of its enterprises and to monitor the practices to effectively sustain these cultures.

Universities need to realize that the insularity of the campus mirrors the insularity of their faculty and administrators. As we saw in the fifth chapter, the feudal terrain of the university and the radically individual-ized work of the faculty are obstacles to building communities on our campuses. Getting faculty out of their individual offices and into inter-disciplinarity is a good first step in breaking the protective, isolating, and stifling environment of the university. If we were to have more collaborative opportunities, we might realize the true value of commu-nity and the virtue of hospitality, a practice that has not been well extended to women, students of color, international students, and other newcomers.

Certainly the predominantly white men who lead our faculties and our universities have to recognize women as equals and racial and eth-nic diversity as a good. They cannot do it with simple practices but rather they must promote a supportive climate that is engaging and welcoming, and they must believe that that climate or culture is neces-sary for the university of the twenty-first century.

Today white male faculty and administrators need to shoulder the responsibility that until now has been borne predominantly by women and people of color at our universities. The latter have worked toward a greater inclusivity and parity for all. They have worked to model a respect for what one brings to a campus rather than for whether one belongs to the club. Until white men at our universities actively work to secure gender and racial equity, their unspoken biases are recognized and validated by their white male students.

Similarly, we know from the studies that we have seen in these last two chapters that setting up encounters that promote bridge-building in universities among students of diverse backgrounds would alleviate the often unspoken and equally unaddressed tensions that our campuses experience. Trying to move our students and their faculties and admin-istrators to greater partnership and community are first steps toward developing a culture of ethics. And as we take these steps, we might see the truth of Wayne Meeks's insight that making morals means making community.

10

COMMODIFICATION

Have we arrived at a point in higher education where we will see increasing divergence between degrees meant for the masses and those for the elites? How will a Wal-Mart-type degree ("Always low prices") differ from high-end products with status value à la Lord & Taylor ("The Signature of American Style") and those targeted, Macy's-like, to folks in the middle ("Way to Shop!")?
—Mary Cayton[1]

Commodification has been in the background of many issues in this volume. The recruitment of international students, for instance, is in part due to a marketing suggestion to bring fresh cash from new consumers into the university. They are lured into a new market. They get commodified to the extent they become simply objects that keep the university afloat with cash.

The turn to more and more adjunct faculty to replace tenured faculty allows administrators a way of reducing expenses for faculty who now receive compensation solely for the specific courses they teach. No health care benefits, no phones, no offices, an easy commodity. Disposable too, with piece work contracts.

Administrators provide more and more of the university's budget for student services and student recruitment than for student teaching, further alienating the faculty but further empowering the student as a consumer with purchasing power. In turn the administrators hire more and more managers for student affairs and for admissions and these managers hire their staffs and launch their mini-fiefdoms. More managers, more business-like, more commodification.

The university aims not at its mission, that is, the education of its citizenry so as to promote the common good, but at its own financial survival. Subsequently the geography of the campus shifts, with more staff and more managers providing students a wider array of services, from health care, extracurricular activities, police safety, varied dining service, sports facilities, housing opportunities, career and personal counseling, and technological support, among other services. It takes a village to entertain a university student today.

The students as customers come more to see how they will pass their four years there. The end point is still getting the degree, but the experience of learning is mixed considerably with the other goods used for recruiting the customers. No wonder fraternities cannot be suppressed; they remain bait for financially worried institutions wanting to ensure successful enrollments.

Commodification is a mindset, a critical one, which looks at the university in the twenty-first century and contends that for its survival higher education has become simply a commodity and its goods from the degree to education itself gets commodified. Commodification is basically a way of philosophically reflecting on the growing emergence of the administration of the university as a corporate business.

To appreciate how wide the net of this critique goes, I offer three rather interesting reflections on commodification, one from a historian, another from a scientist, and the third from a blogger on matters of higher education. They give us, I think, a way of seeing developments at the university as related to one another inasmuch as they tend toward greater business efficiency in a consumer-oriented society.

One final prefatory remark is in order. We saw earlier how many think of the history of American higher education as basically being about recruiting young men to do serious ministerial studies. Though there is some truth in believing those were our beginnings, soon after the American Revolution a new type of student, the college man, arrived. The sons of businessmen were sent to university not to become ministers but because their fathers saw education as a purchasable commodity that would enhance not primarily the common good but rather the opportunities their sons would have in advancing the family's prospects. Of course, the ends of the family fortunes and the flourishment of the common good were not inimical, but there was a hierarchy of ends there then as there is today.

Some of the writers on this topic seem to suggest that this commodification of higher education is new, that interests in education before were never tainted with money issues. Therein we should recognize a somewhat naïve presupposition that university education until recently was about sitting in one's dorm room, studying 24-7, and sharing with one's classmates the wisdom uttered by Socrates, Plato, and Aristotle so that we could all build a new Athens. Pining for the elysian fields of the university campus, some of the critics sound like guardians at the campus gate, thinking that they have kept the industrial revolution forever at bay.

While there have always been serious, studious undergraduates wanting to make the world a better place, and among them some who were hoping for business success, there were also those who saw the pursuit of a degree as no more than a launching ground for business and marriage.

The real issue of commodification today is not that university education comes down to getting (as opposed to earning) a degree (many have thought that for decades), but rather how pervasive and reductive the mindset of students and administrators, staff and trustees, and faculty are when they consider the goods of education as marketable commodities. It's as simple as that, the new, all-inclusive bottom line.

THREE INTRODUCTIONS TO COMMODIFICATION

In a reflective essay, "The Commodification of Wisdom," Mary Kupiec Cayton writes about the unfortunate reality of trying to restore confidence in higher education by standardization. She writes:

> When higher education was thought to be mainly about educating citizens, standardization wasn't much of a concern, either. The professoriate, trained to pursue and disseminate knowledge, enjoyed enormous latitude. The curriculum provided structure, but that structure was flexible. Although a class in biology or theater might deliver two or four hours' worth of credit, courses were not seen as interchangeable units for delivering a certain amount of content in a certain way. The credentials of the institution and the instructor's

membership in a professional guild underwrote the value of the instruction. Standardization wasn't an issue.[2]

Cayton sees that the credibility issue now has shifted. No longer is the university and the professor that which attracts potential students; now it is *US News and World Report Rankings* that tell us a whole set of factoids about enrollment, satisfaction, retention, and job placements. As she writes, "Standardization has come later to higher education than to other commodities markets, but it has arrived. As with other commodities, unit cost matters, as do how 'goods' are produced, measured, and sold."

She sees a relatively significant shift here. First she sees how universities on their own initiative are moving in this direction in terms of faculty staffing: "For example, many for-profit universities are driving down the cost of instruction by outsourcing it to part-time workers, often with lesser qualifications than those of faculty members at more traditional four-year degree-granting institutions. In so doing, those universities are forcing a reconsideration everywhere of how to cut labor costs in order to compete."

Then she turns to the matter of government interventions and cites her own state of Ohio, which, she writes:

> has developed an articulation-and-transfer policy for postsecondary institutions that guarantees the ability of credits for certain courses—for instance, U.S. history surveys—to transfer between institutions and apply directly to the major at any public postsecondary institution in the state. Professor Smith's lecture on Jamestown and Professor Jones's module on the Industrial Revolution, no matter where in the state they are taught, may now be considered educationally equivalent within a standardized delivery system meant to ensure that consumers receive common value for their tuition dollar. Your course is now educational legal tender, whether you take it at a selective university or at a community college.

Cayton's concern is not simply with the reductive capacity of standardization, that is, that two very different courses can be reduced to the same transferrable three credits. Nor is her concern with the wistful summons of the past. She is more concerned with the future, that is, that education will be used to further the inequality gap that so dominates American culture. In her 2007 essay, she predicts well the effectiveness of standardization in being marketed *not* to make everything fair, but to make everything saleable. She asks:

> Have we arrived at a point in higher education where we will see increasing divergence between degrees meant for the masses and those for the elites? How will a Wal-Mart-type degree ("Always low prices") differ from high-end products with status value à la Lord & Taylor ("The Signature of American Style") and those targeted, Macy's-like, to folks in the middle ("Way to Shop!")?
>
> Past patterns of consumption suggest that as education becomes increasingly commodified, the gap will widen between most public institutions on the one hand and elite colleges subsidized by high tuition, big endowments, or both on the other. The former will offer bare-bones, interchangeable, standardized packages of credit hours that are supposed to be roughly comparable to one another; the latter, special programs in Namibia and value-added paid internships for those who can already afford them. The degrees will be called the same thing, but the quality of "higher education," the experience, will differ significantly.

While she is sympathetic to the fact that parents especially who spend great amounts of money for their children's education would like some guarantees that they received an "itemizable" education, she believes that the end will not be fairness or accountability but rather the runaway marketing of education for the haves and a radical diminishment of education for the have-nots.

In *The Commodification of Academic Research: Science and the Modern University,* Amsterdam's Hans Radder edits a collection of thirteen essays by philosophers, sociologists, scientists, and ethicists wrestling with the corruptive influence of commodification on universities. Overall, he brings his panoply of scholars into one conversation to examine effectively under the aegis of the philosophy of science whether commodification is good for science. He furthermore charges the contributors that if they determine it is not good for their particular field of study, they must name its more corruptive practices and suggest alternatives as mainstays in the defense of higher education.[3]

In an interview with Scott Jaschik of *Inside Higher Education,* Radder elaborated more specifically on his concerns:

Commodification means that all kinds of activities and their results are predominantly interpreted and assessed on the basis of economic criteria. In this sense, recent academic research is far more commodified than it was in the past. In general terms, one can say that the relation between "money" and *specific* academic activity has become much more *direct*.[4]

Then he demonstrates how commodification functions in a science department.

Consider the following examples: first, the amount of external funding acquired is often used as a measure of individual academic quality; second, specific assessments by individual scientists have a direct impact on departmental budgets; for instance, if I now pass this doctoral dissertation, my department receives a substantial sum of money; if not, it ends up with a budget deficit; third, the growing practice of patenting the results of academic research is explicitly aimed at acquiring commercial monopolies.

Finally, he applies the term to the overall function of the university:

Related to these financial issues are important and substantial changes of academic culture. Universities are increasingly being run as big corporations. They have a top-down command structure and an academic culture in which individual university scientists are forced to behave like mini-capitalists in order to survive, guided by an entrepreneurial ethos aimed at maximizing the capitalization of their knowledge.

Radder then enters into the question of utility and how utility so often has a limited appreciation of research and that if something is not deemed immediately useful, it is not at all considered a merit-worthy proposal. This enormously foreshortens the function of research at a university, because often enough it is not until the end of our investigations that we fully appreciate the applicability of our findings. Thus he comments that this preempting of research does not "just apply to the study of ancient languages but also to research into the social (rather than the physical) causes of illness."

Radder believes that the world of academic research "needs to re-uphold the values and basic standards of good research rather than just economic goals."

Radder concludes his interview arguing that the challenge of com-modification calls us to return to ethical standards. "A big step in the right direction could be made if universities would consistently adhere to the ethical codes of good scientific conduct they have developed over the years, not merely in assessing the behavior of individual scientists but also, or even primarily, in the structural measures and policies taken by academic institutions and governmental bodies."

Radder helps us to look not back to the romantic, idyllic (read: nonsensical) times when simply the reputation of a university and its faculty provided the standards of credibility. Radder believes that the university must return to the ethical standards that governed research so that we will not do a wholesale abandonment of the grounds for academic research.

While Cayton sees the challenge as one between the traditions of higher education on the one hand and accountability to the consumer on the other, she also fears that the present course will further alienate those who can barely afford higher education. Radder suggests that the conflict is the abandonment of ethical standards so as to do an end-run for needed university income versus the need for those standards to protect the quality of research. Both agree, however, that the present focus on making education more and more a commodity will actually do more harm to the already endangered good.

At the Brainstorm blog, one writer sees the commodification issue as fundamentally a debate between those who yearn for a world that never was and those who want efficiency and transparency.

The blogger, known as bzemsky bzemsky, claims "Most don't like markets, arguing that much that is wrong with higher education starts and ends with the commercialism and unbridled pursuit of economic advantage that have accompanied the academy's embrace of competi-tive markets. The most outraged even have a word for what has trans-pired: commodification."[5]

With irony he writes,

[C]ommodification is the sure sign that the nation's colleges and universities have gone astray. Money matters too much—values hardly at all. Students have been transformed into customers. Faculty have been told to become entrepreneurs, which is just a step above being money-grubbing ambulance chasers. The academy, which was once venerated as a scholarly community, is now little more than a business constantly worried about its bottom line.

On the other hand, bzemsky bzemsky cites "the efficiency pundits" like Richard Vedder, author of *Going Broke by Degree: Why College Costs Too Much,*[6] who argues:

> higher education is not really subject to market forces. A host of third-party payers—principally the states, the federal government, and subsidized loan programs—have largely allowed colleges and universities to raise prices at will. Thus shielded from the rigors of a truly competitive market in which productivity and efficiency convey substantial advantage, colleges and universities have grown slothful. Productivity is down, economic discipline is negligible, and far from favoring the entrepreneurial and efficient, universities use their near market monopoly to protect the outdated and outmoded.[7]

Here we see another side of the commodification discussion. Vedder and the blogger clearly believe that there has not been an economic accountability (feasibility? sustainability?) strategy incorporated into the entire structure of the contemporary university. Certainly any observer would grant some of their critique and many would like to see greater accountability and efficiency at the university. The issue, however, is whether making most of the educational goods at the university into commodities is the right solution to the financial challenges at the university.

THE DEBATE OVER COMMODIFICATION AND ACCOUNTABILITY

As one who is arguing that we need an ethics for the entire university, I find the commodification discussion very important, precisely because it gives faculty a leverage, a perspective, and a conceptual framework at least to discuss across the university the nature and the integrity of the university. In a way, it brings us full circle by allowing us to look again at the university's culture. Is the underlying culture of the university being compromised by commodification?

Essentially faculty writers and other commentators on the university recognize that there are and should be limits to commodification. In doing this they can do one of two things. First, they can simply reject commodification as an intrusion into the good of education. These rejections look a bit like the rants that we saw earlier in this book where writers tell us how bad higher education is today, how expensive it is, and so on. These are fairly emotive works that say things like "commodification is bad!" These are those texts to which bzemsky bzemsky ironically was referring. A good example of this is Carlos Alonso's critique, in which unfortunately he equates commodification with a culture of accountability. He writes:

> What is the place of graduate studies in higher education's current culture of accountability? At some level, at least, the question itself is moot, since there is no argumentative ground from which we could claim that anything is outside our current "culture of accountability." Culture, education, and the university have become commodities and purveyors of commodities; they must answer to the logic of accountability—and there is no space outside that logic.[8]

For Alonso this culture of accountability leads inevitably to commodification: "[I]ts underlying assumptions make the project of accountability a questionable strategy for the specific crisis of social legitimation with which the university is contending." Alonso explains what he means by a culture of accountability:

> In other words, the crisis of legitimation we are confronting today is related more to the product that we are selling than to our inability to make that product worth buying. Accountability presumes that if we are able to show the effective transmission of knowledge and skills to our students, we will satisfy the market's requirement for verifiable results. But what if the market has already devalued from the start the knowledge on which the entire operation of outcomes and accountability is based, as well as the institution where it is produced?[9]

My problem with his claims is with a presumption in the sentence "Accountability presumes that if we are able to show the effective transmission of knowledge and skills to our students, we will satisfy the market's requirement for verifiable results." He has identified accountability with outcomes assessment, an attempt to measure the product of teaching and learning. Clearly the accountability he has in mind is a reductionist market accountability. Unfortunately, in identifying accountability with this form of accountability he has reduced accountability itself; in short, for him, we need to stay away from accountability and commodification.

I think this is an especially problematic identification, because those like Cahn who were trailblazers in the field of academic ethics were precisely raising accountability as an issue in keeping office hours, in writing letters of recommendation, in terms of integrity of research, in relations with students, and so on. Accountability is at the heart of professional ethics. Therefore, when academics using ethics critique commodification, they cannot deny the rightful expectation of accountability. They may, of course, take aim at particular forms of accountability like outcomes assessment as unworthy categories of accountability for a university.

Cayton and Radder are clearly different from Alonso. Cayton believes that parents have a right to ask why tuition is so high or whether their child will get a good education; but she is concerned that commodification is not the singular answer for the needed forms of accountability. In fact, her rejection of the commodification trend is precisely on ethical grounds: Commodification will only promote the marketing of inequities in education. Radder, too, sees that market efficiency is sometimes a real good for the university but other times, as it tries to be financially accountable, academics may actually overstep the ethical standards of research to which they also ought to be accountable. The issue is, then, in searching for different forms of accountability, are there not limits to the present rush toward commodification?

ETHICS AND COMMODIFICATION

As we consider the clash of expectations, goods, and forms of accountability and how they ought to be played out university-wide, we enter the realm of ethics. Ethics, with its principles of fairness and responsibility, and its virtues of justice, honesty, respect, and fidelity, helps us to negotiate the conflicting claims. This has been in fact the case in discussions of commodification that have developed elsewhere.

The discussion on the limits of commodification did not start with the matter of higher education. People in the fields of medical and legal ethics first saw the problem of treating some goods as matters of exchange. They started with questions about commodifying our bodies, our body parts, our sexuality, and our reproductive capacities, to say nothing of our children and our very selves.

Stanford's Margaret Radin, in her landmark work *Contested Commodities: The Trouble with Trade in Sex, Children, Body Parts, and Other Things,* raises the fact that marketing goods that are closely connected to our personhood compromises our pursuit of human flourishment. She argues that such marketing ought to be prohibited or, at best, strongly regulated. [10]

More recently, with Madhavi Sunder, Radin co-authored a paper on "The Subject and Object of Commodification." [11] There she explained that in her book, she "worried about the effects of commodification—or the denial thereof—on the poor, but also the effects of commodification on everyone, through the shifting understanding of human relationships it entailed." [12]

In the article, however, Radin and Sunder explained how the issue of commodification first prompted scholars to ask questions about whether matters not simply about education but our humanity were at stake:

> In the latter part of the 20th century, academic attention to commodification grew in response to increasing calls to turn over more and more of human life to the invisible hand of the market. Where some saw freedom in markets, others sensed despairing capitulation or inexorable dehumanization. Contrary to the liberatory economic rhetoric, the ability to sell anything and everything might—commodification theorists argued—prove ultimately disempowering. When this discourse entered the legal arena, the question was to what extent legal limits on commodification should exist. Commodification scholars focused our attention on the choices made, and consequences felt, of reducing aspects of our lives to market exchange. [13]

More than anything, the bottom-line concern was whether there were some ways that through commodification, the market was able to reduce our own humanity to a thing.

Viewed this way, the topic of commodification is reduction of the person (subject) to a thing (object). Viewed in terms of society as a whole, the inquiry is who would be the subjects of commodification—controlling the terms of the sale—and who would be its objects—turned into mere commodities in a global trade? The answers to these crucial questions determine the distribution of wealth in society, and indeed throughout the world. They also determine how we conceive of ourselves (and others) as persons, and therefore bear deeply on the meaning of human life itself.

In particular, the real ethical matter is that the subject whose humanity has been reduced by the market is a person who is already marginalized or alienated from the common good and then commodifies the self further as when he or she sells a kidney, child, or self into slavery. Radin and Sunder write: "Often, those whom commodification objectifies become entrenched as society's subordinated class. Conversely, those who control the terms of commodification secure their position as society's ruling class. Market relations reflect, create, and reinforce social relations."[14]

These ethical issues then help us substantiate where and when lines ought to be drawn and where some human interactions ought to be prohibited or regulated as market exchanges. Outside of the market, then, we find a context to arbitrate matters that try unsuccessfully to be measured solely in terms of market efficiency. Ethics helps us to make these decisions.

Others have entered the discussion, specifically invoking ethics to limit the claims or options of commodification. Harvard's Michael Sandel in *What Money Can't Buy: The Moral Limits of Markets* raised provocatively a number of issues that money can but should not buy.[15] Even more comprehensively, Stanford University's Debra Satz writes *Why Some Things Should Not Be for Sale: The Moral Limits of the Market*. There she dedicates a chapter to each of the following topics: women's reproductive labor, women's sexual labor, child labor, voluntary slavery, and human kidneys.[16]

She begins her work praising markets: "Markets are important forms of social and economic organization. They allow vast numbers of people who are otherwise completely unknown to one another to cooperate with one another in a system of voluntary exchange."[17]

Then Satz introduces the idea that markets not only make possible efficient strategies of exchange, but they also shape our communities, cultures, and identities. She writes:

> Markets not only allocate resources among different uses and distribute income among different people but particular markets also shape our politics and our cultures, and even our identities. Some markets thwart desirable human capacities; some shape our preferences in problematic ways; and some support objectionably hierarchical relationships between people.[18]

This leads Satz to argue that efficiency is not the only measure of the markets: "[W]e have to think about the effects of markets on social justice, and on who we are, how we relate to each other, and what kind of society we can have."[19]

Satz continues, "In this book I challenge the one-dimensional view of markets found in many economic textbooks and seek to address markets as institutions that raise political and moral questions as much as economic ones."[20]

These writers make even more clear the claims and concerns that Cayton and Radder raised, that is, that inevitably our concerns about commodification are related to other claims about the political community and how it needs to ethically aim for an inclusive agenda of human flourishment. Thus as we turn now to precise issues related to commodification and the university, it will be ethical concerns that prompt us to ask the question: But is this growing marketability on the campus always a good?

We need to note, however, that the faculty's concerns on commodification are generally more based on their own experience, as we will see, whether it be with students' attitudes or administrative expectations, as well as with concerns about intellectual property and the pursuit of grants. Though journalists and other public intellectuals raise concerns about commodification elsewhere on the campus, faculty generally do not address other matters like the international student body, the fragile inequity that adjuncts encounter, or the experiences of other universities whether public or private, that suffer in a more and more economically competitive environment. To these array of issues we now attend.

COMMODIFICATION AND THE MISSION OF HIGHER EDUCATION

Here I want us to consider several different issues related to commodification and the mission of higher education. None of these issues can be resolved here, and not even an entire book on this issue can be adequate. In fact, the best we can do is appreciate that these are among the key issues that we need to address when looking at this topic. First, we need to look at an economically sustainable university that does not compromise its mission. Second, we need to examine briefly questions that arise regarding for-profit attempts in higher education. Finally, we have to view higher education itself not primarily as a private purchasable commodity but as an accessible good deeply related to the common good and therefore carrying rights and responsibilities for those who engage it. Here, we need to ask questions about hiring priorities in education, particularly the expansionism of the administration and the diminishment of faculty both by posting fewer tenure track lines and by recruiting adjunct faculty for piece labor. We close with a few examples concerning research goods that must be protected.

Clearly rising tuition and rising competition for a university education lead to urgent questions about sustainable futures. In light of attempts to make educational institutions more financially and ethically accountable, strategic plans are being articulated that aim to convey the university not as a business but as an organization.

A key innovator here was George Keller, author of *Academic Strategy: The Management Revolution in American Higher Education,* who began that book with the words, "A spectre is haunting higher education, the spectre of decline and bankruptcy."[21]

In a tribute to his legacy, Wilfred McClay reminds us what the early 1980s in education were like: "After years of rampaging growth, colleges were gripped by declining enrollments, increased competition, inflating costs, diminishing government support, and shifting priorities among those increasingly regarded as higher education's 'consumers.' The future of many traditional institutions—especially the venerable but chronically underendowed liberal-arts colleges—was in jeopardy."[22]

According to McClay, Keller warned that universities and colleges needed "to identify their particular areas of comparative advantage" and then "to recast their institutional life to emphasize those strengths."

McClay added, "Such reorientation would inevitably mean making an institution more responsive to the marketplace."

For Keller, the concepts of comparative advantage and strategic planning were "a middle ground between the idea of the university as a timeless repository, grandly indifferent to everything but its own internal imperatives, and the idea of it as a crass commercial operator, seeking above all else to increase its market share." American higher education needed to be "a complex mixture of the ideal and the practical."

Keller did not think that strategic planning made the university a business but rather recognized it as an organization. He saw the university needed to be an organic unity "animated by a sense of common purpose—one that is qualitatively different from the aggregate ambitions of individuals and the imperatives of their disciplines." This unified identity is captured, I think, by the sense of the common culture of a place.

McClay notes, however, despite *Academic Strategy*'s popularity, the lessons taught there were not well learned. "Many institutions survived the structural challenges of the 80s not by strategic concentration but by indiscriminate diversification—finding new constituencies of nontraditional students and inventing programs to attract them, thereby keeping enrollments up. They also began to rely more heavily on less-expensive adjunct faculty members to carry the teaching load."

McClay laments then that by not following the strategies that Keller suggested, the schools made a double error: they contradicted market decisions and they ethically compromised their own mission. "Such adaptations exacted a price by eroding institutions' sense of their core mission and making them more bottom-line oriented, more like diversified corporations of any other kind."

For Keller, management skills and tools were to be incorporated into the strategic plan based on developing one's comparative advantage as expressive of the school's mission. The goals of efficiency and mission were integral, not competitive and certainly not contradictory. Perhaps returning to this "organizational model" might be a worthy initiative.

Keller's last work was the study of a school that did follow his plan, Elon University in North Carolina. Published originally in 2004, a second edition was just published celebrating the school's 125th anniversary with a foreword and afterword by Elon University president, Leo

Lambert.[23] In a subsequent tribute to Keller, the president of Florida's Lynn University, Kevin Ross, wrote to the *Chronicle* how his university succeeded in identifying their comparative advantages to their strategic planning.[24] In 2008, James Doti, president of Chapman University, wrote in the *Chronicle* about his success in focusing on their "comparative advantage."[25]

These accounts help us to realize that university "commodification" is a critical concept for naming when a university's use of market strategies oversteps its own mission. The real problem is not using the market strategies; it is rather when mission is compromised by their use. But then, Keller would add, that's not good marketing sense!

Two striking instances of a marketing strategy that undoes mission come from university presidents who complain against Barack Obama's initiative to rank colleges "by several factors, including tuition, their percentage of lower-income students, affordability, graduation rates and earnings of graduates. Student aid will be tied to the rankings, which will be announced in 2015."[26]

Connecticut's Sacred Heart University president, John Petillo, tells the remarkable story of one of his graduates, a noted leader in social justice, who raises funds for children in countries without adequate educational systems. While remarking that it is hard to get rich while saving the world, he notes that this student's idealism puts at risk his university's future federal funding, "which is built on a formula that will reward schools whose graduates make the most money."

He concludes by writing, "The government's formula discounts the personal development of the individual and the need for social consciousness. . . . Equally frightening, some small independent colleges that produce teachers, clergy and social workers will face the prospect of having to close."[27]

Raynard Kington, president of Grinnell College, takes up nearly the same issue concerning the pay-for-performance model that the Obama initiative proposes, that is, that college rankings will depend on "completion rates, graduate earnings and advanced degrees of graduates." His concern revolves around rewarding those colleges whose students already have large reserves of social and financial capital that is used precisely to secure well-paying positions in the future.

He contrasts schools like that, which he refers to as "Silver Spoon College" to "Bootstrap College," which "provides opportunity to students with less social and financial capital—those needing an education to improve their economic condition," that is, those for whom federal funding could make education and social mobility possible. He suggests that some "well-tested, risk-adjusted college outcomes" ought to be applied, but notes that there are not yet any.[28]

In a very powerful essay, "Hard Times at Howard U," Charlayne Hunter-Gault writes about the challenges that Howard University faces.[29] In the light of our familiarity with the struggles of many universities, Hunter-Gault's study of Howard University, a veritable paradigm of the historically Black colleges and universities (HBCUs), helps us see the even more urgent challenges these schools have.

There is an irony in her essay. In 1961, Hunter-Gault was among those suing for entrance to the University of Georgia. For her, the university offered the only school of journalism in the South. Now, sixty-three years later, she writes, "The lawsuit made it possible for me and other students to pursue our dreams in places that had always been closed to African Americans. Little did any of us realize the price many black colleges would pay for equal opportunity."

Besides Howard University's own specific struggles, Hunter-Gault looks at many other challenges for the HBCUs. The first among many is enrollment: "Take Fisk University, a leading Black college in Nashville that graduated an army of freedom fighters who risked their lives to bring about equality and change in the South. . . . Enrollment reached a little over 1,500 in the '70s. Today, Fisk has 645 students. And like other HBCUs whose enrollments are 1,000 or less, the prognosis for survival is not good."

She then turns to financial issues: "The economic issues that bedevil higher education in general are even more disruptive in the HBCU community, in part because many of the students are first in their families to go to college. Forty-six percent of students at historically black colleges come from families with incomes lower than $34,000, and half qualify for federal low-income Pell grants, according to the United Negro College Fund, which finances scholarships for 37 private black colleges."

The instability of available funding exacerbates the situation. Hunter-Gault notes, for instance, that "many families have had to scurry for alternative financing, or had to leave their dreams behind altogether, after the Department of Education recently toughened eligibility criteria for Parent Plus loans." This change resulted in "some 17,000 fewer students attending black colleges, costing the institutions more than $150 million in revenue, according to the United Negro College Fund. Howard lost 585 students, though about half were readmitted thanks to an intense fund-raising campaign."

Asked whether Howard is right to remain dependent on federal support, Howard's interim president, Wayne A. J. Frederick, responded, "Students at HBCUs account for approximately 3 percent of all students enrolled at colleges and universities in the United States, but account for 18 to 20 percent of African-American college graduates. So they represent a very important pipeline. Also, a large number of PhDs in STEM are coming from HBCUs, of which Howard is the No. 1 producer. So it's definitely in the national interest. No doubt about that."

As these university presidents make clear, many of the colleges and universities that have worked to define the richness of the fabric of our population and its common good are precisely those that stand to lose as market strategies work themselves out in our broadening spectrum of inequity in the United States. And sometimes, as with new federal mandates, these strategies purport to be rescuing our educational institutions.

We see the profound awkwardness of our country's inability to find the appropriate standards to estimate how and why these schools and their students receive federal and state support. We see university presidents struggling to make sense of shifting enrollments and changing financial aid requirements. But it is remarkable how few faculty comment on these issues. Again, only journalists and a few administrators sound the cry that the very question of the integrity of the American higher education system is at stake in shaping our nation's future. Will the survival of our schools simply be decided through a market-driven, survival-of-the-fittest competition wherein those who win already are among the chosen?[30] In the quest for greater efficiency, Keller's vision of a strategy compatible with mission strikes me as the first ethical rule for navigating these decisions.

COMMODIFICATION AND FOR-PROFIT UNIVERSITIES

Commodification becomes incarnate in for-profit higher education. The latter's birth in the late 1990s is a strategy that purportedly embraced at once both the mission of higher education and the market itself. Its entry on the scene of higher education was significant.

A study published in 1999 tracking business schools from 1992 through 1997 showed a quick growth rate in for-profit's enrollment in business degree programs. One of their managers was quoted as saying, "Adult learners value convenience, access, and price value. For-profit schools have been more willing to meet potential students on those terms. They aren't as restricted by big investments in brick and mortar."[31]

Business schools became models for market wisdom in higher education. In 2008, for instance, Goldie Blumenstyk writes in the *Chronicle of Higher Education* about "Lessons from For-Profit Institutions about Cutting College Costs."[32] They are relevant and comprehensive:

Lesson 1: Create faculty pay plans that tie compensation to demand.
Lesson 2: Treat space as an asset with a measurable value.
Lesson 3: Use the college's buying power to get students' textbooks cheaper.

They are market insights at their best. But by 2008 there were signs of trouble. Early in 2005, Goldie Blumenstyk reported that some for-profit colleges were under scrutiny for their recruiting practices in California.[33] Later that year, Eric Wills reported in the *Chronicle of Higher Education* that the National Consumer Law Center had doubts about for-profits' job placement claims.[34] Then Wills reported that state agencies in New Jersey and Pennsylvania were "reviewing the recruiting or financial-aid practices of two colleges owned by the Career Education Corporation." Wills mentioned that these investigations came "a few weeks after a state consumer agency in California announced that it was restricting the license of another college owned by Career Education."[35]

In 2010, the Senate Health, Education, Labor and Pensions Committee, chaired by Tom Harkin, issued a report through the services of the Government Accounting Office (GAO), *Benefiting Whom? For-Profit Education Companies and the Growth of Military Education*

Benefits[36] "that portrayed the for-profit sector as ruthlessly exploiting federal programs intended to help veterans."[37]

That report, however, had its own errors and a coalition of the for-profit colleges sued the GAO for "professional malpractice."[38] On its own, the University of Phoenix fought back about other criticisms with a report from its Nexus research center. Blumenstyk writes that the report, "For-Profit Colleges and Universities: America's Least Costly and Most Efficient System of Higher Education," praises the University of Phoenix and other for-profit colleges, contends that concerns of their critics are not systemic and are reformable, and continues its assault on traditional schools of higher education as "studies in inefficiency."[39]

But in 2011, Kelly Field reported that the GAO had investigated some for-profit schools and found academic standards low. It found "widespread deception in recruiting by the colleges, with many employees providing students with false or misleading information about graduation rates, job prospects, or earning potential."[40]

In the same year, Frank Donoghue provided a profile of for-profit students that appeared when the Institute for Higher Education Policy issued a press release on June 14 bearing the headline "More Low-Income Students Begin at For-Profits." The key statistic that they relate: "low-income students—between the ages of 18 and 26 and whose total household income is near or below the poverty level—are more likely to be *overrepresented* at for-profit institutions and are *underrepresented* at public and private four-year institutions." Moreover, these representation ratios are part of a trend. From "2000 to 2008, the percentage of low-income students enrolling in for-profits increased from 13 percent to 19 percent, while the percentage enrolling in public four-year institutions declined from 20 percent to 15 percent." Were for-profits trying to lure students from community colleges to their own schools?[41]

The question is relatively important. In 2012, Dan Berrett reported, "Graduates of For-Profits Lag Behind Their Peers in Earnings and Employment,"[42] but then reported several months later that the two types of schools were faring about the same according to another study. Berrett pointed out that "in-state tuition and fees average $2,300 at community colleges, while costs at for-profits average $15,000."[43] When faring the same in job placement, it is hard to argue that paying quintuple the tuition makes sense.

Senator Tom Harkin and his Senate Committee appeared again. At the start of his essay, "Senate Report Paints a Damning Portrait of For-Profit Higher Education," Michael Stratford writes, "For-profit colleges can play an important role in educating nontraditional students, but the colleges often operate as aggressive recruiting machines focused on generating shareholder profits at the expense of a quality education for their students."[44]

In releasing the report, *For Profit Higher Education: The Failure to Safeguard the Federal Investment and Ensure Student Success,*[45] Harkin concluded "a two-year investigation into the operations of 30 for-profit higher-education companies from 2006 to 2010." At the conference, Harkin said "that federal student aid spent at for-profit colleges, which totaled $32-billion in 2009–10, had in many cases been 'squandered' by companies that failed to graduate a majority of their students and poorly prepared them for jobs. 'These practices are not the exception,' Mr. Harkin said. 'They are the norm.'" Harkin also criticized "the accrediting agencies that evaluate the colleges."[46]

Stratford writes: "The report says that more than half of the 1.1 million students who enrolled in the colleges under scrutiny in 2008–9 had withdrawn by mid-2010." He then quotes from the report: "While community colleges and two-year for-profit programs have similarly low retention rates, the cost of the for-profit programs makes those programs more risky for students and federal taxpayers." He adds: "Nearly all students attending a for-profit college take out loans to attend, the report says, compared with just 13 percent of community-college students."

Stratford reports:

> One of the most significant themes of the report is the role of marketing and recruiting at for-profit colleges. The investigation found that most for-profit companies devote more resources to attracting students than they do to instructing them. . . . In 2009 the education companies that the investigation studied spent $4.2-billion, or nearly 23 percent of their revenue, on "marketing, advertising, recruiting, and admissions staffing," compared with $3.2-billion, or more than 17 percent of revenue, on instruction.

The *Chronicle* cites a set of numbers from the report, including this related one: "In 2010 the for-profit colleges examined employed 35,202 recruiters, compared with 3,512 career-services staff and 12,452 support-services staff, which amounts to more than two recruiters for every student-service employee and 10 recruiters for every career-services staff member."

Finally, Stratford notes, "Senator Harkin singled out several institutions, including Strayer, Walden, National American University, and American Public University, as companies that are, in fact, doing a good job of educating students. He also cited Kaplan, DeVry, and the Apollo Group as companies that had 'very serious shortcomings in the past' but are making improvements."

Two years later, Harkin appears again, on August 5, 2014, on the heels of the financial collapse of Corinthian College. He writes to President Obama a letter lamenting the continuing lack of oversight of the for-profit colleges: "The recent announcement that Corinthian Colleges Inc. will largely cease operating while currently serving over 70,000 students has revealed a startling lack of liquidity and an unacceptable reliance on federal financial aid dollars for day-to-day operations." He immediately takes aim at the Department of Education: "It is also extremely troubling that recent press accounts revealed that the Department of Education did not have ample information, resources, or the expertise needed to properly assess Corinthian's dire fiscal condition. Though financial analysts were well aware of the precarious financial situation of Corinthian, the Department apparently was not. As one Department of Education official noted in a recent press article, the government's financial monitoring system 'didn't work in the case of Corinthian.'"[47]

Forecasting the closing of other for-profit colleges, particularly those publicly traded, he sounds a terrifying alarm for these lower-income students who have been recruited into a system in which frankly one can only wonder how well they will fare: "Corinthian Colleges Inc.'s failure raises serious questions about the financial integrity of other similarly situated, publicly traded, for-profit colleges. The Department's own records indicate that more than 23 additional companies that enroll 4,000 or more students currently have failing or close to failing financial integrity scores."

On this topic, Goldie Blumenstyk deserves the last word, in part, because she is so right: "For-profit colleges aren't going to disappear, not with a 13-percent share of all enrollments, and not while state support for public and nonprofit alternatives remains so anemic. Still, even more so than higher education as a whole, the colleges do have a credibility problem."[48] In addressing their credibility, Blumenstyk suggests they might be more interested in more truth and modesty in their expectations.

COMMODIFICATION AND HIGHER EDUCATION

The balance that Keller proposed and that McClay wishes schools sought remains elusive. Why? I think it follows the same fundamental claim that I have made throughout this book. The underlying cultures of our universities are not well defined and even were they defined, the fragmented nature of the university's geography inhibits the sharing of that culture across the campus. The cultures are not defined because they aren't present. Throughout, we have seen the profound reluctance of universities to see an ethical culture as constitutive of its fundamental identity. In the absence of a culture of integrity, cheating arises; in the absence of a nondiscriminatory appreciation of race, bigotry takes hold; in the absence of a culture of transparency and accountability, universities create a faculty of indentured servants and call them *adjunct.*

Of course there are signs of hope. Cultures of integrity are trying to be cultivated along with codes of honor at places that can afford to take cheating seriously. The federal government is forcing our universities to accountability regarding sexual violence, though only after the university was named the place in America where a young woman is most likely to be assaulted.

These are small gains and the absence of an identifiable ethical culture within a university is most patently seen by the creeping growth of commodification, which infects the entire undefended mission of the schools. Cheating, sexual assault, racism, and feudal structures have not threatened the university's integrity the way commodification has. Indeed, the unsustainable tuition that couples with diminishment of instruction along with the growth of adjuncts and the rise of much better paid managers in recruitment and in student services are all tangible effects of the growing commodification of the university. Unlike the academic strategies that incorporate market strategies so as to promote the universities' mission, commodification allows repeatedly a crude and naïve market strategy to override mission expectations. There is simply little to check commodification's growing claims.

Commodification plays out in the life of the university day by day. Rick Ayers, a professor in Teacher Education at the University of San Francisco, describes a more and more common experience in which a professor is asked by a student (or the parents), not "What did I learn?" but "Did I get what I paid for?"

Ayers' student wrote in his evaluation of the course, "I was looking back at my expenses this semester and I calculated that I pay $150 for each class session I have. Sometimes I wonder. . . . was it worth $150 for me to attend a movie (The Class) with you and chat about it afterwards? Did I get my $150 worth when we did that artifact share activity?"

Ayers mulls over the student's claim with the same financial logic. "I get paid approximately $200 for each class I conduct. . . . Hmm, let's see . . . with 20 students, I'm actually getting only $10 from each student for each class session I deliver. Ten stinking dollars! . . . But then I'm thinking: who got the other $140 that the student ponied up? The university, obviously. . . . But now I'm mad at the student. 'Hey, buddy,' I'm thinking, 'Don't lay that on me. Talk to your university. They're screwing us both over.'"

This leads him to think otherwise, about resisting the language of objectifying and commodifying education. He thinks of how the way we talk, as when we "deliver a lesson," suggests the transaction of some commodity and that maybe all education is nothing more than the transmission of an object. But then he writes, "But all the best educational experiences go outside this box, make something really happen, including deep, complex, and critical thinking, exploration, and reflection."

He sees that education cannot be simply reduced to a commodified good, because were it, then education becomes simply a transaction to be purchased individually, with no reference to anyone but the consumer. "Education is not seen as a public good—it is a private benefit that can be purchased in the marketplace. It's a system for handing down privileges to the next generation while masking as a meritocracy."[49]

Besides thinking of whether we are succumbing unnecessarily and wrongly to the language of commodification, the mission of the university strikes me as needing to ask questions about the hiring changes that we have seen across America, witnessing to a greater bureaucratization of the American university.

We can all admit that attracting a potential student to the university is an important priority, but as we saw previously, when the recruitment costs far outweigh the instructors' salaries we no longer have the mission of the university as our first priority. Rather than educating first, we are in the business of sales first. Moreover, while we can all admit that the student is not simply looking for an education but more broadly an "experience," still within that context, the lessons the students learn are, for the university, the student's most important experiences.[50] But what if recruitment costs and strategies are just so competitive?

In a blistering essay in the *New Republic*, William Deresiewicz, author of the new book *Excellent Sheep: The Miseducation of the American Elite and the Way to a Meaningful Life*,[51] argues that the recruitment processes of the top schools in the country are indicative of the type of education the students will have there. [52] He writes, "From learning to commodify your experiences for the application, the next step has been to seek out experiences in order to have them to commodify." The Ivy League schools, he believes, have so compromised themselves by commodification that they have only one aim: "The college admissions game is not primarily about the lower and middle classes seeking to rise, or even about the upper-middle class attempting to maintain its position. It is about determining the exact hierarchy of status within the upper-middle class itself."

He sees the university as effectively a race course, about winning a position ahead of most in the leading pack. He writes, "This system is exacerbating inequality, retarding social mobility, perpetuating privilege, and creating an elite that is isolated from the society that it's supposed to lead. The numbers are undeniable."

Then he provides those numbers:

> In 1985, 46 percent of incoming freshmen at the 250 most selective colleges came from the top quarter of the income distribution. By 2000, it was 55 percent. As of 2006, only about 15 percent of students at the most competitive schools came from the bottom half. The more prestigious the school, the more unequal its student body is apt to be. And public institutions are not much better than private ones. As of 2004, 40 percent of first-year students at the most selec-

tive state campuses came from families with incomes of more than
$100,000, up from 32 percent just five years earlier.

The numbers are clearly indicative of a greater and greater divide, as we
have seen throughout this book. We are here on the topic of commodification because it helps us to see whether the university stands to
promote the common good or to undo it. Deresiewicz writes, "The
major reason for the trend is clear. Not increasing tuition, though that is
a factor, but the ever-growing cost of manufacturing children who are
fit to compete in the college admissions game."

Deresiewicz sees that the sales pitch, from the admission's officer to
the president, is a sales pitch not about education, but about status,
because status and rank are what counts for these universities. Rather
than facing inequity, the Ivies are the promoters of the system of inequity in the United States: "And so it is hardly a coincidence that income
inequality is higher than it has been since before the Great Depression,
or that social mobility is lower in the United States than in almost every
other developed country. Elite colleges are not just powerless to reverse
the movement toward a more unequal society; their policies actively
promote it."

He concludes by urging today's students to think of second-tier, not
second-rate, schools that "have retained their allegiance to real educational values," schools that promote interest in serving the common
good, in providing actual service work, in learning core values. These
are the schools that today's students ought to attend. But he also calls
for the citizenry to recommit itself to public education.

We see all around indications that the sale of education as a commodity affects the hiring policies at our schools. Just as Deresiewicz
shows us that some universities promote the growing inequity of
Americans by the students they recruit, other universities are unable to
stay open unless they cut the cost of instruction, or so they believe. In
these schools, the justice issue that emerges from the narratives of
adjunct faculty is not only one that affects the faculty members themselves, but also the students pursuing an education at universities where
adjuncts are on the rise.[53] Cayton's fears about the growing commodification of our university leading to a further empowerment of the
wealthy and well-educated are already realized.

In an essay titled, "First Year Commodity: The Adjunct Professor Labor Crisis in Composition Departments," Josh Boldt, the Founder of the *Adjunct Project,* discussed earlier, sums up the way adjuncts develop from and depend on commodification and how the students at these schools suffer as well from the phenomenon:

> The new career track for university faculty is that of the Disposable Professor. As we rely more and more on adjunct professor labor, we slowly surrender our power on college campuses. Contingent faculty are, by definition, powerless. Completely replaceable. No tenure, no bargaining rights, no contract, no voice. First-year composition departments are all too familiar with this reality, as they are staffed predominantly by non-tenure track, contingent faculty. Adjuncts, and therefore the composition departments they staff, are powerless in the economic equation of the "corporatized" university.[54]

He gives us unsettling numbers of how elsewhere commodification affects our educational system. Reminding us that 70 percent of America's teaching faculty hold adjunct positions, he writes "This ratio has skyrocketed by 280 percent in the past 30 years. . . . And each year it's only getting worse. Non-tenure-track appointments have climbed 7.6 percent in the past three years alone. At this rate, it's only a matter of time before 'college professor' is no longer a viable profession."[55]

As the tenured faculty allow the commodification of the adjuncts, they cannot really think that their future is long lasting. In fact, the university's shift in hiring business managers over faculty continues unabated. In an essay in the *Chronicle,* Scott Carlson writes that "new administrative positions—particularly in student services—drove a 28-percent expansion of the higher-ed work force from 2000 to 2012."[56] The rest of his statistics show that "the number of full-time faculty and staff members per professional or managerial administrator has declined 40 percent, to around 2.5 to 1." He adds that faculty salaries were "essentially flat" from 2000 to 2012 and that "the rise in tuition was probably driven more by the cost of benefits, the addition of nonfaculty positions, and, of course, declines in state support."

There are positive signs of people, like Ayers, Clayton, Radder, and others fighting back. Duquesne's Jacob H. Rooksby blows the whistle at the universities' contemporary obsession of patenting their trademarks. As he writes, "Registrations and rights-claiming of this sort are unwarranted in higher education. Trademarks are meant to be vehicles for reducing consumer confusion, not rewards for brand-building." [57]

He highlights university pretensions as he offers examples of trademark registrations owned by colleges, which "include 'student life' (Washington University in St. Louis), 'students with diabetes' (University of South Florida), 'one course at a time' (Cornell College), 'touched by a nurse' (University of Colorado), 'we're conquering cancer' (University of Texas), 'working toward a world without cancer' (University of Kansas Hospital), and 'imagination beyond measure' (University of Virginia)."

Rooksby adds, "Little is to be gained from this growing commodification of language, despite the mostly vain hope that locking up terms that describe academic programs and research initiatives will lead to additional revenue. Most trademarks that go beyond the simple protection of institutional names, logos, and insignias present poor licensing opportunities, if any." It is not as if commodification is leading us to any good marketing sense.

Elsewhere the Modern Language Association (MLA) as well as the Association of American Universities worked to successfully stop the passage of the Research Works Act that would prevent "federal agencies from requiring researchers to make the published results of federally supported research available to the public without publishers' consent."[58] As MLA president Michael Bérubé stated, "Unnecessary limits on the free flow of ideas compromise a robust exchange of information and knowledge." In a similar way, the faculty at the University of California–Berkeley fought to preserve the university's libraries when faced with budget cuts, and won.[59]

These are all modest victories against the encroaching phenomenon of commodification, but to be sustained, universities and in particular their faculties need to enter into the fight to define the culture of the place where they are working. I suggest they find the grounds for that fight by looking at for what they want their university to stand.

11

A CONCLUSION: CLASS, ATHLETICS, AND OTHER UNIVERSITY MATTERS

"I have long wondered what the tipping point in intercollegiate athletics would be. Either it would move from the untethered pursuit of money and entertainment toward a model consistent with the soul of higher education, or it would separate from higher education and become professional. The time has arrived for us to move in one direction or the other."
—Nancy Hogshead-Makar[1]

When I began this project four years ago, I began with the argument of the first chapter: Regardless of the difficulties a university found itself in, it rarely referred to ethics to resolve the matter, even though the difficulties were about ethical matters. I also wanted to highlight the oddity of this lacuna, inasmuch as the university is where faculty teach and students learn ethics. The one place that those teaching ethics normally do not engage is precisely the place where they work.

This insight is riddled with ironies because we can hear professors in business, legal, social work, medical, and nursing ethics courses across American universities answering the questions of nervous students who ask, "But what if I face a situation at the place where I work as a professional and I realize that no one around me cares that the situation is unethical?" One wonders whether in answering that question responsibly those at universities teaching professional ethics ever have a reflective moment in which they ask themselves if they practice what they teach. Do they bother to assess the situations where they work as professionals to see whether those situations are ethical or not?

As we entered into the argument of this book, I tried to show first how ethics functions in other professional worlds like medicine and nursing to promote a culture of ethics and professionalism through structures like guilds and professional associations with practices and norms that guide professionals in their ethical conduct with their colleagues, clients, and institutions. I noted how that culture of ethics, along with its social structures, practices, and norms are absent from the university.

I then turned to the related literature on the university either by professors who write in the public forum their laments on contemporary education or by educators and sociologists who try to assess the state of contemporary higher education. I also noted that a few faculty entered into the topic of academic ethics and these were matters that basically aimed at the fiefdom of the professional faculty: their classrooms and offices where their work with students is assessed by critical ethics.

Wanting to open us up to university ethics, that is the whole campus and not just the professional faculty fiefdom, we considered the situation of adjunct faculty. I promoted that topic first because I wanted to show how little is really covered by academic ethics. Think of it, adjunct faculty are now the majority of faculty, but those writing in academic ethics about the ethics of faculty do not even mention them. Besides asking questions about the adjuncts' experiences of the university, where we see the first instances of the growing commodification of the university where adjuncts themselves are reduced to a commodity, we also asked questions about tenure-track faculty who show little interest in their colleagues' situation.

Their ability to ignore adjuncts has something to do with the phenomenology of the university campus. In considering the campus, I wanted us to get a sense of how ill-constructed the campus is for community building, transparency, and accountability. There is something about the very setting, the *sitz im leben* of university life, that allows people to work in their own fiefdom with their own caste owning up to their own bosses. For a place that houses wisdom, its terrain hardly speaks to the contemporary order, but rather reflects the medieval mentality that gave it birth. Somehow the university's tradition rather than its vision defined the communications world of the university's social structures.

We turned to the quintessential unethical vice of a university: cheating. I chose cheating so as to get to the relationship between ethical cultures and their practices. Not only do the university's inhibiting social structures that make transparency so difficult enable cheating, but the cultures that animate the university can promote cheating as well. On the one hand, peer pressure or a culture of cheating makes individual accountability harder to identify and easier to shrug off; on the other hand, a culture of integrity that engages with the practice of an honor code has proven successful. I wondered whether universities that had cheating scandals also lacked ethical cultures and practices. I was particularly interested in the claim that nature abhors a vacuum, and wondered whether I would find cheating where integrity and honor codes were not promoted. That appears to be the case.

I also thought that the American university's overall culture today is pretty shallow. One can feel the culture of the contemporary university: a decided air of privilege and self importance, but really little about how it serves the world or the common good. Without much of an ethical culture, other cultures creep in. Though a culture of integrity is an advance over a culture of cheating, still, integrity is fairly minimalist. Is integrity the best a university can give us?

As a faculty member, I know how little I know about my students' personal lives. I think most faculty members are at a loss about most of their students, but whatever the students do in their private lives is not apparent in the classroom. In this seventh chapter I try to cover a wide range of indicators that suggest a decline in the ethical conduct of university students, something that students know, but few others do. In very few instances could I find any faculty involved in ethical reflection on their students' lives, but those who did write on racist-themed parties, fraternities, or hazing, for instance, made significant contributions. Hopefully, any reader could see both how much faculty could do to promote the well being of their students were they to bring the students' out-of-class experiences into the classroom. Moreover, any reader of Julie Reuben realizes that inevitably faculty have to somehow, with the administration and with student affairs, face the question of the moral formation of the university's undergraduate population.

Where faculty are involved ethically is on the topic of women in the university. Whether we are talking about sexual assault or the promotion of women to tenure, women faculty are writing, speaking, teaching, and researching about women at the university. Ethical issues from the rights of victims of sexual assault to topics about the lack of equity in the academy's departments are well framed, discussed, and promoted by women faculty and their friends. If the role of faculty in contributing to the ethical life of the university has had any experienced traction, it has been overall on the topic of gender. Here we see—where faculty, students and administrators enter into discussion about the ethical and unethical issues related to gender—the gateway to university ethics.

Still, we are only at the gates. Speakers and writers on the topic of gender, ethics, and the university rarely if ever engage the plight of women as adjunct faculty, underpaid staff, or international students. The topics of gender at the university are, for the most part, still only about the white women in tenure tracks and their students. There are exceptions, but exceptions is what they are.

When we turn to race we find the startling, newly reported finding that students are less interested in race the longer they stay at a contemporary American university. But universities have ignored race for, well, centuries; why shouldn't their students do the same? That universities did not admit African Americans to their student body until rather recently is part of the often unacknowledged history of the American academy, but now through the work of administrators working with historians, we are learning how well major American universities profited by the slave trade. The American university houses the ghosts of slavery.

The growing instances of racism on campus again arise from the lack of an ethical culture, in this case one that actively promotes racial non-discrimination. In the absence of such a culture, white, Hispanic, and African American students frequently self-select and settle into greater segregated units. Despite warnings by researchers that adding racial diversity without addressing the cultural climate would lead to real clashes, universities again remained silent on ethical issues and let matters worsen.

As we have been seeing throughout this book, practices without cultures or cultures without practices are not sustainable. An active ethical culture, like academic integrity, has to have practices like an honor code and review boards. Neither cultures nor practices are in evidence on US campuses for promoting racial understanding.

Moreover, over the past ten years most universities have recruited actively international students predominantly because, again in a substantive nod to commodification, these are students paying full fare. But these students, especially from China, India, and Korea, enter into a world that's hardly hospitable as so much reporting records. Besides the ethical matters of race and diversity, one has to ask whether recruitment activities are honest and transparent about the challenges that these students have. That a recent report shows more than 40 percent of these students without an American friend highlights again that the culture of the university might have a sense of its own self-importance that it can attract so many students, but it hardly shows an ethics of hospitality or of care.

We conclude realizing that the lack of any defining culture at a university allows the creeping culture of commodification to reduce anything at the university to a commodity: from classes to adjunct faculty; from international students to the diploma itself.

While clearly acknowledging the need for greater financial efficiency and transparency at the university while facing universities' unsustainable trajectories of escalating tuition rates and cost-cutting of instruction, we also encounter resistance to strategies that are neither good for mission or for finance. Here the critique of commodification enters, which I find interesting inasmuch as it lets us see that a vicious culture like commodification is so pervasive. It's the untended crabgrass of the university campus.

Nonetheless, commodification is also targetable and most of the critique by interested parties at universities aims at the resulting inequities that commodification creates, above all the greater categories of class that our universities are jumping into. Of all the data we saw in the chapter on commodification, I found the following statistics the most disturbing: In 1985, 46 percent of incoming freshmen at the 250 most selective colleges came from the top quarter of the income distribution. By 2000, it was 55 percent. As of 2006, only about 15 percent of students at the most competitive schools came from the bottom half. The more prestigious the school, the more unequal its student body is apt to be. And public institutions are not much better than private ones. As of 2004, 40 percent of first-year students at the most selective state campuses came from families with incomes of more than $100,000, up from 32 percent just five years earlier.

College is more and more inaccessible to the working class and the ladder of social mobility is hardly advertised by the American university. I want to turn to this topic of class as well as athletics and competition in a moment, but as I conclude my summation of the investigation of this book, I want to suggest other topics than these that I did not examine.

OTHER TOPICS

I remember when I first discovered the Rowman and Littlefield book series that Steve Cahn edited, *Issues in Academic Ethics*. The series ran from 1994 to 2006, with fifteen contributions ranging from tenure, free speech, and sexual harassment to questions about sports, development, unions, and college presidencies. As series editor, Cahn easily defined the field of academic ethics.

There and then, I realized from Cahn not that I had so little material, but that I had so much to consider. As I expanded from academic ethics to university ethics, I raised ethical questions about adjunct faculty, commodification, racism, diversity, international students, and staff that are not found under the rubric of academic ethics. But the more I investigated, the more I found. I have spent the past four years combing the media and the library stacks and sending my students out as well to research daily the spectrum of university ethics. I would like to share what I found and what I still want to understand about university ethics.

I was at first interested in development and at the start I thought that I would find quite a number of scandals. For the most part, I found instances where donors made false assumptions about the influence they had on a campus because of a gift given.[2] Aside from these issues, I also found a few instances where a faculty publicly questioned a gift because of the donor's own character or because a university failed to spend endowment funds properly.[3] Finally, questions arose from time to time about conflict of interest with trustees' firms being contracted by the universities they serve.[4]

Despite these issues, I began to see that unlike other university departments, development has quite a system of professional ethics already operative, in part due to the fact that many personnel in development are educated in business schools where they learn, among other things, about the necessity of professional ethics. Though there are evident lapses of judgment and downright false reporting, for the most part, development personnel understand and appreciate matters like transparency, accountability, reporting, confidentiality, and fiduciary responsibilities. For instance, the *Council for the Advancement and Support of Education* posts on their website extensive guidelines, cases, norms, and related materials under the heading "Perspectives on Ethical Decision-Making in Fundraising."[5] If women championing the rights of women is the closest gateway we find to university ethics, I would suggest that development and advancement is a second gateway. It might be worth our while to consider some of the more problematic cases that development faces like donors who think their gifts give them more access to controlling the programs that their gifts benefit. Men and women working for gender equity and those active in university advancement seem to be those best versed on their respective sectors of university ethics.

At the start, I also became interested in dormitories. Throughout this book, the reader can see that I am interested in the university's social structures and geography. Nothing occupies the campus like its dormitories. Every faculty and administrative orientation ought to require a visit to one, preferably at the end of the day or better yet at the start of the weekend. These dormitories have their own cultures that student affairs, health facilities, and police officers know, but most faculty, staff, and administrators do not. We need to somehow understand better the specific cultures of our own university dormitories. They are very different from one another. Students know that; others in the university should know as well.

While talking about the way students live, we might ask how they drink. We live in a country that knows that young people drink, but insists that they do it clandestinely. Wouldn't it be remarkable if faculty knew, researched, and reflected with students and administrators about the university's drinking sanctions and asked whether they are ethical, realistic, and equitable?

I also wanted to work on tenure. But the debates for and against tenure have been covered time and again and it is not clear to me whether this is a debate about the ethics of tenure or its utility. I think the real ethical issue around tenure is how to hold tenured faculty to post-tenure accountability. I think that there are strong ethical grounds for instantiating the expectations that the university has of tenured faculty, and as we develop more and more university ethics I imagine some models will be articulated. In a similar way, questions of accountability for endowed chairs are also needed.

We could go into other topics like university investments; how ecologically sustainable and responsible the university is; what towns owe to universities and what universities owe to towns; the sustainability of tuition rates; whether states and counties have responsibility for funding community colleges; whether a college degree is an American right, option, or privilege; presidential salaries; and what we do with the student debt crisis; among many other issues. In other words, with this book I hope we now can appreciate how extensive are the ethical issues related to a university.

CLASS AND ATHLETICS

If there was one topic to which I would want to dedicate an entire book, it would be class, the most overlooked topic in university ethics, though it rides steadily beneath the surface of concerns in commodification. As the writers cited in Chapter 10 made clear, access to a major university diminishes year by year for lower-income and working-class people.

For this reason, President Obama in January 2014 pushed for reforms to help make higher education more affordable for lower-income people. As he said, "More than ever, a college degree is the surest path to a stable, middle-class life."[6]

The White House has a number of objectives to make college education more affordable for the working and middle classes. He wants to double investments in Pell grants, keep student loan rates low and help students manage their debt, and expand education tax credits. He wants to strengthen community colleges by promoting industry partnerships to foster career readiness.[7]

Incentives by the federal government as well as commitments by some colleges and universities are trying to turn things around. For instance, the *Chronicle of Higher Education* reports on federal initiatives to reduce the student loan debt: "The federal government now has three income-based student-loan-repayment programs. The most generous, known as Pay as You Earn, caps borrowers' monthly payments at 10 percent of their income and provides loan forgiveness after 20 years."[8]

And the President is not alone in his interest in college education. A new poll shows that 70 percent of the population believes that a college degree is a value for one's future, a huge difference from 1978 when 36 percent held the same belief. As one pundit said, "a college degree is now a part of the American dream."[9]

Still, these promising items stand in contrast to the actual data we have. In a recent article in the *New York Times,* Richard Pérez-Peña reports that "the nation's elite campuses . . . remain bastions of privilege." He writes, "Despite promises to admit more poor students, top colleges educate roughly the same percentage of them as they did a generation ago. Yet the percentage of high-performing, low-income students in the general population is twice that at prestigious campuses."[10]

His article is prompted by a series of federal surveys of selective colleges that "found virtually no change from the 1990s to 2012 in enrollment of students who are less well off despite a huge increase over that time in the number of such students going to college. Similar studies looking at a narrower range of top wealthy universities back those findings." Pérez-Peña explains that the interest in economic diversity and elite colleges exists "because students are more likely to graduate and become leaders in their fields if they attend competitive colleges. Getting low-income students onto elite campuses is seen as a vital engine of social mobility."

A host of experts agree with what we saw in Chapter 10: Elite universities are much more interested in the well heeled and the well educated. In fact, because of our elite universities, education and income are mutually defining. Thus Anthony P. Carnevale, director of Georgetown University's Center on Education and the Workforce, states, "Higher education has become a powerful force for reinforcing advantage and passing it on through generations."[11]

Similarly, Pérez-Peña quotes Michael N. Bastedo, director of the Center for the Study of Higher and Postsecondary Education at the University of Michigan: "A lot of it is just about money, because each additional low-income student you enroll costs you a lot in financial aid. No one is going to talk openly and say, 'Oh, we're not making low-

income students a priority.' But enrollment management is so sophisticated that they know pretty clearly how much each student would cost."

Moreover, rankings of American universities like those from *U.S.
News and World Report* are influential and result in competition. Pérez-Peña notes, "The rankings reward spending on facilities and faculty,
but most pay little or no attention to financial aid and diversity."

"College presidents are under constant pressure to meet budgets,
improve graduation rates and move up in the rankings," Dr. Carnevale
said. "The easiest way to do it is to climb upstream economically—get
students whose parents can pay more."[12]

As the divide in class continues, so does the racial divide. Georgetown University's Public Policy Center makes this clear in a paper by
Carnevale and Jeff Strohl titled "Separate and Unequal: How Higher
Education Reinforces the Intergenerational Reproduction of White Racial Privilege."[13]

The mission of the elite colleges and universities is now becoming
effectively different from those other universities and colleges where
young people of all backgrounds are attending. When pretense is
dropped, the success of one's own elite school is clearly its bare primary
goal and contributing to the common good is a consequential, but dis-
tant, second.

While studies help us understand where students from lower income
families fare at prestigious universities, we need to know more about
the impact of publicly funded schools. We can get some idea from what
we saw about the attraction of for-profit education. If students at community colleges are willing to pay for tuition at a for-profit institution
that costs roughly five times what community colleges cost *and* while
job placements for graduates from either institution are at parity, clearly they are looking for something better than the publicly funded community college.

Finally, I think we need to ask questions about who our elite schools
are leaving behind and why. And, as we ask it, we need the faculties,
administrators, and trustees of these schools to see that this is probably
their most urgent ethical question.

If class and race define categories of people alienated from our top
schools, then student athletes are the third group of persons often alienated from the university. And while I am interested in writing a book on
class and university ethics, I could never attempt one on college sports

and university ethics. The topic is so sprawling and constantly worsening that I have no idea of where to get traction on it.

As I was thinking of a chapter on sports, I thought of the entire Penn State affair. But then there was the mayhem over the University of North Carolina (UNC) scandal regarding alleged academic fraud that has gone on and on, saying worse things about the National Collegiate Athletic Association than about UNC.[14] As if to highlight my claim that things in athletics at universities continue to unravel, another university scandal about academic fraud just erupted, this time at another outstanding school, Notre Dame, where four football players were being kept out of practice because of "suspected academic dishonesty." Their case is under investigation.[15]

Then I saw that Taylor Branch in "The Shame of College Sports" prompted a firestorm when he claimed that "College athletes are not slaves. . . . Yet to survey the scene—corporations and universities enriching themselves on the backs of uncompensated young men, whose status as 'student-athletes' deprives them of the right to due process guaranteed by the Constitution—is to catch the unmistakable whiff of the plantation."[16]

While mindful of Branch's description of "the parasitic structure of college sports" and the attendant claims to just compensation, I think there are a host of other issues we need to ask about the education of a student athlete. So I considered a chapter that focuses on college athletes' graduation rates.

Or what about the health of athletes? Who goes to college and leaves with concussions? Athletes. But then I thought maybe I could couple their health with athletes behaving badly, for example, Duke's lacrosse team or Boston University's hockey team.

Perhaps I could do something positive on sports: Title IX. Brad Wolverton wrote an important essay about women's participation in college sports reaching an all-time high.[17] The essay was based on the longitudinal national study, "Women in Intercollegiate Sport."[18]

Or maybe I could take a shot at reforms of college sports, but then where to start? Brad Wolverton proposes in "A Student Centered NCAA" a return to values in which the athlete's education is brought into the equation, but this depends in large measure on the universities interested in doing this.[19] More recently he published a comprehensive essay titled, "How Should Big-Time College Sports Change," in which he called for strengthening enforcement, cleaning up academics, getting serious about players' rights, and improving safety protocols, among reforms.[20]

Earlier, in December 2011, the *Chronicle of Higher Education* hosted a forum titled, "What the Hell Has Happened to College Sports and What Should We Do about It?" asking a group of innovative thinkers to weigh in on an enterprise that makes over $10.6 billion annually.[21]

One of the contributors, Nancy Hogshead-Makar, in "Tie Money to Values," sees college sports now at a crossroads: either collegiate sports has to go off on its own or it must reenter the university's overall mission and value system:

> I have long wondered what the tipping point in intercollegiate athletics would be. Either it would move from the untethered pursuit of money and entertainment toward a model consistent with the soul of higher education, or it would separate from higher education and become professional. The time has arrived for us to move in one direction or the other.[22]

Another contributor, Frank Deford, offers his opening words in his essay, "Bust the Amateur Myth": "The situation in big-time college sports in the United States—essentially football and men's basketball—is not just scandalous. It is immoral." [23]

And then there was the O'Bannon ruling, which opened up the entire issue of whether this was commercial or collegiate sports when it determined that college athletes upon graduating should be compensated if the NCAA uses images of them for commercial purposes.

So I just could not cover athletics in one chapter, but lest anyone think that as university ethics develops its own field of inquiry, it will not have significant material from college sports, let me leave you with the recent *New York Times* story on 14-year-old Haley Berg who was recruited by a dozen college coaches of women's soccer before she started ninth grade. This story shows that college sports might itself make university ethics an industry.[24] Nathaniel Popper explains:

> The NCAA rules designed to prevent all of this indicate that coaches cannot call players until July after their junior year of high school.

Players are not supposed to commit to a college until signing a letter of intent in the spring of their senior year.

But these rules have enormous and widely understood loopholes. The easiest way for coaches to circumvent the rules is by contacting the students through their high school or club coaches. Once the students are alerted, they can reach out to the college coaches themselves with few limits on what they can talk about or how often they can call.

Haley said she was having phone conversations with college coaches nearly every night during the eighth grade.

Fraternities may be predatory, as one writer suggested earlier, but this story, together with Taylor Branch's, suggests the same about college sports.

IF I WERE A UNIVERSITY PRESIDENT

Some universities today are articulating university "codes of ethics," but as we already saw, codes are meaningless without a culture of ethics and its ethical practices. If universities wanted to start thinking through what a robust understanding of ethics looks like, they could start with the most hopeful sign on the campus, those working for the fair treatment of women.

If I had the authority of being a university president, I would form a University Ethics Committee to explore ways of making university ethics alive on a campus, and I would announce its formation at the university convocation. I would appoint someone who led the cause for equity for women on the committee and two ethics professors: one who taught ethics in the school of arts and sciences and another who taught professional ethics at either the law school or the school of business. I would choose two leaders each from among the tenured faculty, the adjunct faculty, and the staff. I would also appoint the vice president for student affairs, an athletic coach, and a respected university athlete. If there was any campus ministry office on campus, I would appoint its director to the committee. Besides a student leader from the student council, I would invite an international student and two other US students, different in color, one an undergraduate, the other from graduate studies. In all these appointments I would look to gender equity and diversity.

Finally I would invite two persons from the administrations of neighboring universities as well. I would appoint the committee for a two-year tenure.

For the first year, I would have the committee read reports like the White House Council on Women and Girls Report, *Rape and Sexual Assault: A Renewed Call to Action*, the report from the "Brown University Steering Committee on Slavery and Justice," and something from the Delphi Project or the New Faculty Majority. In other words, I would want them to look immediately beyond their own feudal camp to see how other institutions have expressed concerns about the nature of the university.

I would then invite them to look across the campus to consider the climate of the culture: Is it chilly, racist, homophobic, inhospitable, or predatory? Wherever they found a distinctively negative climate, I would ask them to name it, identify it, and then examine it to see if it is connected to any other source of harmful cultures or practices. I would ask them to categorize the practices that harm the flourishment of the university. I would not be looking at this stage for any personnel identification; I would rather identify locations where the ethical climate is unstable.

I would be especially interested in flagrant ethical violations. I would want to know whether the staff and adjunct faculty are paid living wages, whether student athletes are assured the resources to graduate from their degree programs, whether women are safe on campus and treated as equals, and whether students of color and international students have access to the same services that white students have.

I would ask the committee to consider identifiable social and structural issues like accountability, diversity, transparency, and equity. I would ask them whether the university was too hierarchical, insufficiently horizontally accountable, or simply too opaque. I would invite them to use the hermeneutics of suspicion that would lead them to look at what is below the surface of the geography of the university. I would ask them to consider whether the structure of our lines of accountability promotes mature responsibility or puerile fear.

I would also ask them to find out where there is a sense of ethical flourishment occurring on the campus. I would invite them to use the hermeneutics of generosity to name faculty, staff, administrators, and students who individually or collectively promote the ethical develop-

ment of the university. I would promote the leadership that they identified. I would harvest the university's ethical success stories and publish them.

I would ask them also to identify best practices of ethics, where
hospitality, transparency, and accountability were routinely present and
where the respect of persons was most in evidence.

Once they became informed of their initial studies, located sources
of hope and concern across the university, and collectively saw themselves as the "University Ethics Committee," I would invite them to
conduct a poll of everyone at the university from students and staff to
senior administrators and trustees. I would ask them to construct a poll
that asked each constituent what his or her hopes for the committee
were and what his or her concerns about ethics across the university
were. I would eventually ask the committee whether their poll reflected
well on the committee's own initial reading of the university.

I would ask them for quarterly reports and I would try to disseminate as much of each report as was prudentially possible so as to promote their work and engender discussion across the university. I would
try to make clear that creating a culture of ethics was for our good.

Throughout, I would promote academic freedom on the entire project. I would especially prompt staff and students to enter forums where
they could share with their colleagues their hopes and concerns for the
committee. I would not rule out any discussion, though there would be
no room for any character attacks or assassination.

I would hope to have these assessments by the end of their first year.
I would mark the reception of these assessments with the solemnity that
they deserve. I would especially seek to remedy as quickly as possible
those areas where flagrant violations were in evidence.

In light of these findings, I would ask the committee to spend its
second year promoting structures to support a culture of ethics. I would
first ascertain that there was a bidirectional, vertical accountability, that
is, I would make sure that any reports from below were answered by
accountable reports from above. I would try to solicit from the committee the practices that promoted fairness, accountability, and transparency. These would be the three overall values that would most guide my
own reception of their findings.

I would also ask the committee to name and promote those practices
that would promote horizontal accountability among faculty, staff, ad-

ministrators, and students. I would seek to develop bonds of collegiality among tenured and nontenured full-time and part-time faculty. In short, I would ask the committee to suggest ways that the university could fortify itself as a community.

I would be especially interested in developing how faculty and student affairs could become more knowledgeable of one another. I would be interested in making sure that faculty became more aware of the moral formation of their students not only through the programs of student affairs but also in their classrooms. Conversely, I would want to bridge student affairs with the academic formation of their students. I would certainly respect the distinctive competency of each but I would be less interested in isolating student formation from the academic experience of the classroom.

I would ask the committee to provide programs and practices that made sure that our students of color had access to all university services, that student athletes graduated from their degree programs, and that international students were welcomed.

I would ask them to suggest ways of rewarding leadership, moral courage, partnering in teaching, and human generosity, and I would ask them to suggest ways of reporting ethical infractions.

In short, I would make sure, as Ruth Simmons did with her steering committee at Brown University, that this committee was setting a charter for the university. And I would encourage everyone who belonged to the university to understand that the question, "But is it ethical?" was a question we should always ask when appointing new norms or practices for the life of the university.

And during this time, I would try to learn if any other neighboring campus was working to create a culture of ethics so as to ensure a place for university ethics.

But I am not a president. I am one of my university's hundreds of professors. While I hope that some university presidents will read this book, and maybe appoint committees like the one I suggest, I am just as interested in getting fellow faculty around the country who enjoy the right to exercise critical reflection on account of academic freedom to take a look at the community in which they work. I ask them to take a look at how athletes, women, people of color, adjunct faculty, international students, and others are treated on their campuses. I ask them to be less quiet about sexual violence and alcoholism; about sexism, racism, classism, and homophobia; and about the lack of transparency and accountability on our campuses. We see a good deal, but comment little. We can comment in our classes and offices, at department meetings and faculty forums, in our lecturing and in our writing. More than any other employee on our campuses, we enjoy the expressed right to comment. We have plenty of opportunities to raise the right questions at the right time. And in light of the stories we have read here *and* know of on our campuses today, that right time is now.

As we reflect that the time is now to raise the right questions about ethics and the university, we must remember that making ethics means making community and that the first step toward developing university ethics on our own campuses will be to appreciate that the university is more than its president and the faculty.

If we remember that it is only in systems with hierarchies that people insist on looking to the top for leadership, we can begin to look for university leaders among the real community builders on our campuses. We can find them among the people working for gender equity, the adjunct faculty connecting with others, the staffers welcoming newcomers, the student service personnel reaching beyond student affairs, the students working for social justice both off and on the campus, the athletes looking beyond the athletic fields to the campus asking what they can do, and the parents asking the right questions from their first visit to now.

Let the university community builders find in this book and our argument the support that they have been looking for. May they also find herein an invitation to go beyond their own context, to transcend the feudal landscape that so isolates and individuates us, and to get connected so as to push for a university ethics that makes us a true university system for the twenty-first century.

NOTES

1. THE ABSENCE OF ETHICS
AT AMERICAN UNIVERSITIES

1. Stephen Heyneman, "The Corruption of Ethics in Higher Education," *International Higher Education* 62, no. 4 (2011): 8.

2. I prefer throughout to use the word *ethics* so as to emphasize professional ethics. In speaking about university culture, I use *ethics* as well, though others use *morals,* as in "a culture of morals." I do not think there is much of a difference between the two phrases. At the end of the day, I use *ethics* in a rather broad, inclusive sense. If the word *morals* does occur, it is usually in the context of a passage or phrase that I quote.

3. Mary Carmichael, "Pushed Out of Harvard, Professor Returns Fire: Dismissal Stirs Debate over Free Speech," *Boston Globe,* January 2, 2012, 1, 8.

4. James Gentry and Raquel Meyer Alexander, "From the Sideline to the Bottom Line," *New York Times,* December 31, 2011; James Gentry, "In Coaching Contracts, Deals Within the Deal," *New York Times,* December 31, 2011.

5. Donald McNeil and Denise Grady, "How Hard Would It Be for Avian Flu to Spread?" *The New York Times,* C1, January 3, 2012.

6. Heyneman, "The Corruption of Ethics," 8.

7. Shailaja Neelakantan, "In India, Caste Discrimination Still Plagues University Campuses," *Chronicle of Higher Education,* December 11, 2011, http://chronicle.com/article/In-India-Caste-Discrimination/130061/.

8. Sebnem Burnaz, M. G. Serap Atakan, and Y. Ilker Topcu, "Have Ethical Perceptions Changed? A Comparative Study on the Ethical Perceptions of Turkish Faculty Members," 8, no. 2 (2010): 137–151.

9. Jeffrey R. Young, "Accrediting Agency Raises Questions About Chapel Hill's Compliance," *Chronicle of Higher Education,* November 22, 2014, http://chronicle.com/blogs/ticker/accrediting-agency-raises-questions-about-chapel-hills-compliance/90109.

10. Jack Stripling, "Widespread Nature of Chapel Hill's Academic Fraud Is Laid Bare," *Chronicle of Higher Education,* October 23, 2014, http://chronicle.com/article/Widespread-Nature-of-Chapel/149603/.

11. Jeffrey R. Young, "UVA Temporarily Suspends Fraternities in Response to Rape Allegations," *Chronicle of Higher Education,* November 22, 2014, http://chronicle.com/blogs/ticker/uva-temporarily-suspends-fraternities-in-response-to-rape-allegations/90097.

12. Sabrina Rubin Erdely, "A Rape on Campus: A Brutal Assault and Struggle for Justice at UVA," *Rolling Stone,* October 24, 2014, http://www.rollingstone.com/culture/features/a-rape-on-campus-20141119?page=4

13. Andy Thomason, "U. of Colorado Will Pay Philosophy Professor $185,000 to Resign," *Chronicle of Higher Education,* November 21, 2014, http://chronicle.com/blogs/ticker/u-of-colorado-will-pay-philosophy-professor-185000-to-resign/90081.

14. Dan Berrett, "Colleges' Prestige Doesn't Guarantee a Top Flight Learning Experience," *Chronicle of Higher Education,* November 20, 2014, http://chronicle.com/article/Colleges-Prestige-Doesn-t/150155/.

15. Rachel Louise Ensign, "2 Ivy League Drives Shame Seniors Who Don't Give," *Chronicle of Higher Education,* October 24, 2010, http://chronicle.com/article/Students-at-2-Ivy-League/125056/.

16. Brad Wolverton, "Faculty Reps Botch Sports-Oversight Role," *Chronicle of Higher Education,* October 31, 2010, http://chronicle.com/article/Some-Faculty-Athletics-Reps/125184/. That same issue of the *Chronicle* reported a very moving account of a faculty representative who sought grade changes from other faculty at the behest of coaches. It conveyed the ambiguity that faculty face at the academy when saddled with a new position for which they receive no ethical or professional training; see Libby Sander, "Complaints and Compromises Lead to an Abrupt Departure," *Chronicle of Higher Education,* October 31, 2010, http://chronicle.com/article/ComplaintsCompromises/125185/.

17. Paul Basken, "NSF Defers to Universities on Ethical Standards," *Chronicle of Higher Education,* August 20, 2009, http://chronicle.com/article/NSF-Defers-to-Universities-on/48095/.

2. ETHICS

1. Wayne Meeks, *The Origins of Christian Morality: The First Two Centuries* (New Haven: Yale University Press, 1993), 5.

2. James F. Keenan and Joseph J. Kotva, Jr., eds., *Practice What You Preach: Virtues, Ethics and Power in the Lives of Pastoral Ministers and Their Congregations* (Franklin, WI: Sheed and Ward, 1999).

3. For a look at confidences across the professions, see my "Confidentiality, Disclosure, and Fiduciary Responsibility in the Professions," *Theological Studies* 54 (1993) 142-159.

4. Michael Yeo and Anne Moorhouse, *Concepts and Cases in Nursing Ethics*, 2nd ed. (New York: Broadview Press, 1996).

5. Gerald R. Winslow, "From Loyalty to Advocacy: A New Metaphor for Nursing," *Hastings Center Report* 14, no. 3 (1984): 32–40. See also Jane Brody, "Virtue Ethics, Caring, and Nursing," *Scholarly Inquiry for Nursing Practice* 2, no. 2 (1988): 87–101.

6. See for instance Eileen Morrison, *Ethics in Health Administration: A Practical Approach for Decision Makers* (Burlington, MA: Jones & Bartlett Publishers, 2005); The American Association of Healthcare Administrators, "Code of Ethics," http://www.achca.org/content/pdf/Code of Ethics_non-member_Redesign Draft_100721%5B1%5D.pdf.

7. So much history could be offered here, but medical ethicist Albert R. Jonsen provides us much of the background for the evolution of contemporary bioethics: Albert R. Jonsen, *The Birth of Bioethics* (New York: Oxford University Press, 1998); *A Short History of Medical Ethics* (New York: Oxford University Press, 2000); *Bioethics Beyond the Headlines: Who Lives? Who Dies? Who Decides?* (Lanham, MD: Rowman & Littlefield, 2005); with Mark Siegler and William J. Winslade, *Clinical Ethics: A Practical Approach to Ethical Decisions in Clinical Medicine,* 6th ed. (New York: McGraw-Hill, 2006).

8. James Keenan, "Practice What You Preach: The Need For Ethics in Church Leadership," *Annual Jesuit Lecture in Human Values* (Milwaukee: Center for Ethics Studies, Marquette University, 2000); "Toward an Ecclesial Professional Ethics," ed. Jean Bartunek, Mary Ann Hinsdale, and James Keenan, *Church Ethics and Its Organizational Context: Learning from the Sex Abuse Scandal in the Catholic Church* (Lanham, MD: Sheed and Ward, 2005): 83–96; "Church Leadership, Ethics, and the Moral Rights of Priests," ed. Bernard Hoose, Julie Clague, and Gerard Mannion, *Moral Theology for the Twenty-First Century: Essays in Honor of Kevin Kelly* (London: T and T Clark, 2008): 204–219.

9. Meeks, *The Origins of Christian Morality,* 5.

10. Michael Papesh, *Clerical Culture: Contradiction and Transformation* (Collegeville, MN: Liturgical, 2004); David Gibson, "Clericalism: The Original Sin," *The Coming Catholic Church: How the Faithful Are Shaping a New American Catholicism* (San Francisco: Harper, 2003): 197–219.

11. William D'Antonio and Anthony Pogorelc, ed., *Voices of the Faithful: Loyal Catholics Striving for Change* (New York: Herder and Herder, 2007).

12. For narratives about the search for truth and faith during the crisis see Gibson, *The Coming Catholic Church* and Peter Steinfels, *A People Adrift: The Crisis of the Roman Catholic Church in America* (New York: Simon and Schuster, 2004). For a bibliographical review of the literature, see James Keenan, "Ethics and the Crisis in the Church," *Theological Studies* 66 (2005): 117–136.

13. Colleen M. Griffith, ed., *Prophetic Witness: Catholic Women's Strategies for Reform* (New York: Herder and Herder, 2009).

14. Donald B. Cozzens, *The Changing Face of Priesthood: A Reflection on the Priest's Crisis of Soul* (Collegeville: Liturgical, 2000); Cozzens, *Sacred Silence: Denial and the Crisis in the Church* (Collegeville, MN: Liturgical, 2002). See also Papesh, *Clerical Culture,* and Donald Dietrich, ed., *Priests for the 21st Century* (New York: Herder and Herder, 2006).

15. See Keenan, "Church Leadership," 77–90.

3. HOW THE LITERATURE ON THE UNIVERSITY IS MOVING SLOWLY BUT SURELY TOWARD UNIVERSITY ETHICS

1. Philip G. Altbach, "Harsh Realities: The Professoriate in the Twenty-First Century," ed. Philip G. Altbach, Patricia J. Gumport, and Robert O. Berdahl, *American Higher Education in the Twenty-First Century: Social, Political and Economic Challenges* (Baltimore: Johns Hopkins University Press, 2011), 243.

2. John Henry Newman, *The Idea of a University,* ed. Martin Svaglic (Notre Dame: University of Notre Dame, 1960), xxxvii.

3. Derek Bok, *Beyond the Ivory Tower: Social Responsibilities of the Modern University* (Cambridge: Harvard University Press, 1984); *Universities in the Marketplace: The Commercialization of Higher Education* (Princeton: Princeton University Press, 2004); *Our Underachieving Colleges: A Candid Look at How Much Students Learn and Why They Should Be Learning More* (Princeton: Princeton University Press, 2007); *Higher Education in America* (Princeton: Princeton University Press, 2013).

4. Theodore M. Hesburgh, ed., *The Challenge and Promise of a Catholic University* (Notre Dame: University of Notre Dame Press, 1994). See also

Cyril Orji, *The Catholic University and the Search for Truth* (Winona, MN: Anselm Academic Press, 2013).

5. Laurence R. Veysey, *The Emergence of the American University* (Chicago: University of Chicago Press, 1963), 338.

6. William James, "The Ph.D. Octopus," originally appeared in *The Harvard Monthly,* March 1903, http://grammar.about.com/od/classicessays/a/The-Ph-D-Octopus-By-William-James-Classic-Essays.htm.

7. Frederick Rudolph, *The American College and University: A History* (Athens: The University of Georgia Press, 1962), xxvi.

8. John Thelin, *A History of American Higher Education* (Baltimore: The Johns Hopkins University Press, 2011).

9. Helen Lefkowitz Horowitz, *Campus Life: Undergraduate Cultures from the End of the Eighteenth Century to the Present* (Chicago: University of Chicago, Press, 1987), 42.

10. Veysey, *The Emergence of the American University.*

11. Julie Reuben, *The Making of the Modern University: Intellectual Transformation and the Marginalization of Morality* (Chicago: University of Chicago Press, 1996).

12. Ibid., 13.

13. Ibid., 269.

14. Gina Kolata, "A Murder Suspect's Worth to Science," *New York Times,* February 22, 2010, http://www.nytimes.com/2010/02/23/science/23bish.html.

15. Andrew Hacker and Claudia Dreifus, *Higher Education? How Colleges Are Wasting Our Money and Failing Our Kids: What We Can Do about It* (New York: Henry Holt and Company, 2010). Earlier works in this genre include Allan Bloom, *The Closing of the American Mind: How Higher Education Has Failed Democracy and Impoverished the Souls of Today's Students* (New York: Simon and Schuster, 1987); Charles J. Sykes, *Profscam: Professors and the Demise of Higher Education* (Washington, DC: Regnery Gateway, 1988); Martin Anderson, *Imposters in the Temple* (New York: Simon and Schuster, 1992).

16. Mark C. Taylor, *Crisis on Campus: A Bold Plan for Reforming Our Colleges and Universities* (New York: Alfred A Knopf, 2010).

17. Andrew Delbanco, *College: What It Was, Is and Should Be* (Princeton: Princeton University Press, 2012).

18. Anthony Grafton, "Can the Colleges Be Saved?" *New York Review of Books,* May 24, 2012, http://www.nybooks.com/articles/archives/2012/may/24/can-colleges-be-saved/; see also Richard Wolin, "Democracy and Education: On Andrew Delbanco," *The Nation,* May 21, 2012, http://www.thenation.com/article/167679/democracy-and-education-andrew-delbanco.

19. Elaine E. Englehardt, Michael S. Pritchard, Kerry D. Romesburg, and Brian E. Schrag, ed., *The Ethical Challenges of Academic Administration* (New York: Springer, 2010), xiii. They refer to two earlier works, Rudolph Weingartner's *Moral Dimensions of the Academic Administration* (Lanham, MD: Rowman & Littlefield, 1999) and Paul Olscamp, *Moral Leadership and the Presidency* (Lanham, MD: Rowman & Littlefield, 2003). One text exists for all school administrators, Kenneth A. Strike, Emil J. Haller, and Jonas F. Soltis, *The Ethics of School Administration* (New York: Teachers College Press, 2005).

20. Englehardt, et al., *The Ethical Challenges,* 15. For a similar work designed for administrators of secondary schools, Kenneth A. Strike, *Ethical Leadership in Schools: Creating Community in an Environment of Accountability* (Thousand Oaks, CA: Corwin Press, 2007).

21. Donna Werner, "On The Dark Side: Lessons learned from an Interim Dean," in *The Ethical Challenges of Academic Administration,* ed. Elaine E. Englehardt, Michael S. Pritchard, Kerry D. Romesburg, and Brian E. Schrag (New York: Springer, 2010), 47.

22. Randall Curren, "The Cardinal Virtues of Academic Administration," in *The Ethical Challenges of Academic Administration,* ed. Elaine E. Englehardt, Michael S. Pritchard, Kerry D. Romesburg, and Brian E. Schrag (New York: Springer, 2010), 70.

23. Wilfried Decoo, *Crisis on Campus, Confronting Academic Misconduct* (Cambridge, MA: MIT Press, 2002).

24. Neil W. Hamilton, *Academic Ethics: Problems and Materials on Professional Conduct and Shared Governance* (Westport, CT: Praeger, 2002), 4.

25. John Kekes, "Academic Corruption," *The Monist* 79, no. 4 (1996): 564–576.

26. Michael Scriven, "Professorial Ethics," *Journal of Higher Education* 53, no. 3 (1982): 307.

27. Jacqueline Klein, "A Collegiate Dilemma: The Lack of Formal Training in Ethics for Professors," *Journal of College and Character* 6, no. 2 (2005): Article 4, page 1.

28. Candace De Russy, "Professional Ethics Begin on the College Campus," *Chronicle of Higher Education,* September 19, 2003, http://chronicle.com/article/Professional-Ethics-Begin-on/17511; with Michael Langbert, "The Corrosion of Ethics in Higher Education," *Inside Higher Ed*, July 5, 2005, http://www.insidehighered.com/views/2005/07/05/derussy.

29. Altbach, "Harsh Realities," 243.

30. Deborah C. Poff and Alex C. Michalos, "Editorial," *Journal of Academic Ethics* 1 (2003): 1.

31. Robert Liebler, "Action and Ethics Education," *Journal of Academic Ethics* 8, no. 2 (2010): 153–160.

32. Steven M. Cahn, *Saints and Scamps: Ethics in the Academy* (Lanham, MD: Rowman & Littlefield, 2011). For another collection of cases affecting faculty teaching and research, see Stephen L. Payne and Bruce H. Charnov, ed., *Ethical Dilemmas for Academic Professionals* (Springfield, IL: Charles C Thomas Publisher, 1987).

33. Steven M. Cahn, ed., *Morality, Responsibility, and the University: Studies in Academic Ethics* (Philadelphia: Temple University Press, 1992).

34. Steven M. Cahn, ed., *Moral Problems in Higher Education* (Philadelphia: Temple University Press, 2011).

4. A FIRST CASE FOR UNIVERSITY ETHICS: THE ADJUNCT FACULTY

1. Lisa Liberty Becker, "Class Warfare," *Boston Magazine* (May 2014), http://www.bostonmagazine.com/news/article/2014/04/29/adjunct-professors-boston/.

2. Derek Bok, *Higher Education in America* (Princeton: Princeton University Press, 2013), 187. He refers to *Chronicle of Higher Education* (November 9, 2012), A. 6; Jack H. Schuster and Martin J. Finkelstein, *The American Faculty: The Restructuring of Academic Work and Careers* (Baltimore: Johns Hopkins University Press, 2008), 194, 356.

3. Andrew Delbanco, *College: What It Was, Is and Should Be* (Princeton: Princeton University Press, 2012), 153.

4. See a similar acknowledgment about the matter in Peter D. G. Brown, "Confessions of a Tenured Professor," *Inside Higher Ed* (May 11, 2010), http://www.insidehighered.com/views/2010/05/11/brown.

5. Laurence R. Veysey, *The Emergence of the American University* (Chicago: University of Chicago Press, 1963), 418.

6. Bliss Perry, "The Life of a College Professor," *Scribner's* 22 (197) 513, cited in Veysey, *The Emergence of the American University*, 419.

7. Timothy Dwight to C. D. Kellogg, Nov. 25, 1908 (Yale MSS), in Veysey, *The Emergence of the American University*, 419.

8. Andrew Hacker and Claudia Dreifus, *Higher Education? How Colleges Are Wasting Our Money and Failing Our Kids: What We Can Do about It* (New York: Henry Holt and Company, 2010), 58.

9. M. Kevin Eagan and Audrey Jaeger, "Closing the Gate: Part-Time Faculty and Instruction in Gatekeeper Courses and First Year Persistence," John M. Baxton, ed., *The Role of the Classroom in College Student Performance* (San Francisco: Jossey-Bass, 2008), 39–54.

10. Iryna Y. Johnson, "Contingent Instructors and Student Outcomes: An Artifact or a Fact?" *Research in Higher Education* 52, no. 8 (2011): 761–785.

11. Bok, *Higher Education in America,* 187; see also his comments on 115.

12. David Figlio, Morton Shapiro, and Kevin Soter, "Are Tenure Track Professors Better Teachers?" *National Bureau of Economic Research Working Paper No. 19406* (September 2013), http://www.nber.org/papers/w19406.

13. Tamar Lewin, "Study Sees Benefit in Courses with Nontenured Instructors," *New York Times* (September 9, 2013), http://www.nytimes.com/2013/09/10/education/study-sees-benefit-in-courses-with-nontenured-instructors.html.

14. Bok, *Higher Education in America,* 186, quoting from Schuster and Finkelstein, *The American Faculty,* 89.

15. Bok, *Higher Education in America,* 187; Peter J. Bentley and Svein Kyvila, "Academic Work from a Comparative Perspective: A Survey of Faculty Work-Time across 13 Countries," *Higher Education* 63, no. 4 (2012): 529–547; Michael Finkelstein and William Cummings, "American Faculty and Their Institutions: The Global View," *Change: The Magazine of Higher Learning* 44, no. 3 (2012): 48–59.

16. Bok, *Higher Education in America,* 187. The study he refers to is Linda De Angelo, Sylvia Hurtado, et al. *The American College Teacher: National Norms for the 2007–2008 HERI Faculty Survey* (Los Angeles: Higher Education Research Institute, 2009), 1.

17. Bok, *Higher Education in America,* 187. The study he refers to is Lion F. Gardiner, *Redesigning Higher Education: Producing Dramatic Gains in Student Learning* (Hoboken: John Wiley and Sons, 1994), 2.

18. Bok, *Higher Education in America,* 334.

19. Julie Reuben, *The Making of the Modern University: Intellectual Transformation and the Marginalization of Morality* (Chicago: University of Chicago Press, 1996), 68.

20. Ibid., 207–208.

21. Ibid., 208–209.

22. Bok, *Higher Education in America,* 333.

23. A National Survey of Part-Time/Adjunct Faculty, *American Academic* 2 (March 2010), http://www.aft.org/pdfs/highered/aa_partimefaculty0310.pdf.

24. Ibid., 4.

25. Ibid., 5.

26. This basically means that whether a person completes a dissertation or gets published little affects the position or salary as a part-time adjunct faculty member.

27. "Dismantling the Professoriate," American Federation of Teachers, http://www.aft.org/newspubs/periodicals/oc/septoct12dismantling.cfm.

28. Carolyn Foster Segal, "Academic Hunger Games," *Inside Higher Ed* October 18, 2012, http://www.insidehighered.com/views/2012/10/18/new-academic-underclass-adjunct-committee-member-essay.

29. Steve Street, Maria Maisto, and Esther Merves, "Who is Professor 'Staff'? And How Can This Person Teach So Many Classes?" *Center for the Future of Higher Education Policy Report 2*, August 2012 http://www.insidehighered.com/sites/default/server_files/files/profstaff(2).pdf.

30. Sarah Kendzior, "Academia's Indentured Servants," *Al Jazeera*, April 11, 2013, http://www.aljazeera.com/indepth/opinion/2013/04/20134119156459616.html.

31. Janet Casey, "Taking the Leap," *Inside Higher Ed,* November 21, 2011, http://www.insidehighered.com/views/2011/11/21/essay-responsibilities-tenure-track-faculty-address-adjunct-issues.

32. Ibid.

33. Colleen Flaherty, "So Close Yet So Far," *Inside Higher Ed,* November 20, 2012, http://www.insidehighered.com/news/2012/11/20/college-cuts-adjuncts-hours-avoid-affordable-care-act-costs; Colleen Flaherty, "Who Deserves Affordable Care?" *Inside Higher Ed,* December 5, 2012, http://www.insidehighered.com/news/2012/12/05/higher-education-officials-look-washington-guidance-adjuncts-and-affordable-care-act; Colleen Flaherty, "Bucking the Trend," *Inside Higher Ed,* May 22, 2013, http://www.insidehighered.com/news/2013/05/22/college-offers-health-insurance-coverage-some-adjuncts-ahead-new-regulations; see also Colleen Flaherty and Doug Lederman, "Wellness Plans, Retirement and Adjunct Health Care: A Survey of Chief HR Officers," *Inside Higher Ed,* October 25, 2013, http://www.insidehighered.com/news/survey/wellness-plans-retirement-and-adjunct-health-care-survey-chief-hr-officers.

34. Scott Jaschik, "Getting Rid of an Adjunct," *Inside Higher Ed,* August 18, 2009, http://www.insidehighered.com/news/2009/08/18/njit.

35. Colleen Flaherty, "I Deserve to Work There," *Inside Higher Ed,* November 27, 2013, http://www.insidehighered.com/news/2013/11/27/adjunct-professor-challenges-mid-semester-dismissal-community-college.

36. Lisa Liberty Becker, "Class Warfare."

37. Harvest Moon, "Quitting an Adjunct Career," *Inside Higher Ed,* September 28, 2012, http://www.insidehighered.com/advice/2012/09/28/essay-ending-career-adjunct.

38. Alan Finder, "Decline of the Tenure Track Raises Concerns," *New York Times,* November 20, 2007, http://www.nytimes.com/2007/11/20/education/20adjunct.html.

39. Robbie Woliver, "Adjunct Professors: Low Pay and Hard Going," *New York Times*, May 7, 2000, http://www.nytimes.com/2000/05/07/nyregion/adjunct-professors-low-pay-and-hard-going.html.

40. Stacey Patton, "The Ph.D. Now Comes with Food Stamps," *The Chronicle of Higher Education*, May 6, 2012, http://chronicle.com/article/From-Graduate-School-to/131795/; Dean Dad, "Adjuncts on Food Stamps," *Inside Higher Ed*, May 8, 2012, http://www.insidehighered.com/blogs/confessions-community-college-dean/adjuncts-food-stamps.

41. Gary Rhoades, "Adjunct Faculty are the New Working Poor," *CNN*, September 25, 2013, http://www.cnn.com/2013/09/24/opinion/rhoades-adjunct-faculty/index.html.

42. *The Just-in-Time Professor: A Staff Report Summarizing eForum Responses on the Working Conditions of Contingent Faculty in Higher Education*, House Committee on Education and the Workforce Democratic Staff, January 2014, 34, http://democrats.edworkforce.house.gov/sites/democrats.edworkforce.house.gov/files/documents/1.24.14-AdjunctEforumReport.pdf.

43. Daniel Kovalik, "Death of an Adjunct," *Pittsburgh Gazette*, September 18, 2013, http://www.post-gazette.com/Op-Ed/2013/09/18/Death-of-an-adjunct/stories/201309180224.

44. L. V. Anderson, "Death of a Professor," *Slate*, November 17, 2013, http://www.slate.com/articles/news_and_politics/education/2013/11/death_of_duquesne_adjunct_margaret_mary_vojtko_what_really_happened_to_her.html.

45. Rhoades, "Adjunct Faculty Are the New Working Poor."

46. Mark Oppenheimer, "For Duquesne Professors, a Union Fight That Transcends Religion," *New York Times*, June 22, 2012, http://www.nytimes.com/2012/06/23/education/for-professors-at-duquesne-university-union-fight-transcends-religion.html.

47. Beth Griffin, "Adjunct Faculty Want to Form Union at Catholic University, Two Colleges," *Catholic News Service*, August 12, 2013, http://www.catholicnews.com/data/stories/cns/1303464.htm; Peter Schmidt, "Adjuncts Appeal to Higher Power in Debate Over Working Conditions at Religious Colleges," *The Chronicle of Higher Education*, December 9, 2013, http://chronicle.com/article/Debates-Over-Religious/143493/.

48. Catholic Scholars for Worker Justice, http://www.catholicscholarsforworkerjustice.org/.

49. The Adjunct Project. "About This Project," http://adjunct.chronicle.com/about/.

50. The Delphi Project on the Changing Faculty and Student Success, http://www.thechangingfaculty.org/.

51. Adrianna Kezar, Susan Albertine, and Dan Maxey, "A New Faculty Path," *Inside Higher Ed,* October 2, 2012, http://www.insidehighered.com/views/2012/10/02/essay-new-effort-rethink-faculty-roles-and-treatment-adjuncts. This essay is the manifesto launching the Delphi Project. See also Scott Jaschik, "Questions to Ask Adjunct Faculty," *Inside Higher Ed,* November 12, 2012, http://www.insidehighered.com/news/2012/11/12/new-guides-suggest-questions-ask-about-adjuncts.

52. Kezar et al., "A New Faculty Path."

53. Maria Maisto, "The Adjunct's Moment of Truth," *Inside Higher Ed,* September 10, 2009, http://www.insidehighered.com/views/2009/09/10/maisto.

54. New Faculty Majority. "Our Mission," http://newfacultymajority.info/equity/learn-about-the-issues/mission-a-identity/nfm-mission-statement.

55. Lee Besette, "The Time Is Now: Report from the New Faculty Majority Summit," *Inside Higher Ed,* January 30, 2012, http://www.insidehighered.com/blogs/time-now-report-new-faculty-majority-summit.

56. Maisto, "The Adjunct's Moment of Truth.

57. Josh Boldt, "NFM '12 Post Two: Stop Looking for the Treasure Map, and Start Laying Bricks," *Order of Education,* January 29, 2012, http://www.orderofeducation.com/nfm-12-post-two-stop-looking-for-the-treasure-map-and-start-laying-bricks/.

58. Audrey Williams June, "An Activist Adjunct Shoulders the Weight of a New Advocacy Group," *The Chronicle of Higher Education,* September 10, 2009, http://chronicle.com/article/An-Activist-Adjunct-Shoulders/48348.

59. "Democratic Lawmaker Wants Adjuncts to Share Their Stories," *Inside Higher Ed,* November 20, 2013, http://www.insidehighered.com/quicktakes/2013/11/20/democratic-lawmaker-wants-adjuncts-share-their-stories.

60. "University," *Encyclopedia Britannica* (Chicago: Encyclopedia Britannica, 2003), 27:748.

61. Deborah Foreman, "We Are Not Your Colleagues," *The Chronicle of Higher Education,* July 21, 2008, http://chronicle.com/article/We-re-Not-Your-Colleagues/45881.

62. Aristotle, *Ethics,* Book 8 (New York: Penguin Books, 1984) 1155a24–b8, 259.

63. Ibid., 1155a3–b8, 258–259.

64. Ibid., 1157a34–b20, 266.

65. Cathleen Kaveny, *Law's Virtues: Fostering Autonomy and Solidarity in American Society* (Washington, D.C.: Georgetown University Press, 2012); Stephen Pope, ed., *Hope and Solidarity: Jon Sobrino's Challenge to Christian Theology* (Maryknoll, NY: Orbis, 2008).

5. THE CULTURAL LANDSCAPE OF THE
UNIVERSITY WITHOUT ETHICS

1. Benjamin Ginsberg, *The Fall of the Faculty: The Rise of the All-Administrative University and Why It Matters* (New York: Oxford University Press, 2011), 164.

2. James F. Keenan, "Impasse and Solidarity in Theological Ethics," *Catholic Theological Society of America Proceedings* 64 (2009): 49.

3. M. Shawn Copeland, "Collegiality as a Moral and Ethical Practice," ed. James F. Keenan and Joseph Kotva, *Practice What You Preach* (Franklin, WI: Sheed and Ward, 1999), 315–332.

4. Martin Anderson, "The Isolation of the Academic Intellectuals Allows Their Natural Hubris to Flourish," *Chronicle of Higher Education*, October 21, 1992, http://chronicle.com/article/The-isolation-of-the-academic/74347/.

5. Robert Zemsky, "How to Build a Faculty Culture of Change," *Chronicle of Higher Education*, September 30, 2013, http://chronicle.com/article/How-to-Build-a-Faculty-Culture/141887/.

6. Samuel O. Thier, "Intellectual Isolation," *Chronicle of Higher Education*, May 27, 1992, http://chronicle.com/article/Intellectual-Isolation/79867/.

7. Robin Wilson, "The New Faculty Minority: Tenured Professors Fight to Retain Control as Their Numbers Shrink," *Chronicle of Higher Education*, March 18, 2013, http://chronicle.com/article/The-New-Faculty-Minority/137945/.

8. Grace Hollis, "Campaigners Continue Strike: Protestors Distribute Passage Indicating President Teresa Sullivan's Living Wage Support," *Cavalier Daily*, February 23, 2012, http://www.cavalierdaily.com/article/2012/02/campaigners-continue-strike/; Pablo Eisenberg, "Living Wages and College Campuses," *Huffington Post*, November 18, 2012, http://www.huffingtonpost.com/pablo-eisenberg/university-employee-wages_b_2154836.html; "Students Hunger Strike for Living Wage at UVA," *Living Wage at UVA*, http://www.livingwageatuva.org/2012/02/18/12-students-hunger-strike-until-uva-pays-a-living-wage/#sthash.bE88qnMX.dpuf.

9. Randy Hudson and Teresa A. Sullivan, *The Social Organization of Work* (Independence, KY: Wadsworth Company, 2007), 63.

10. "Salary Explorer," *Chronicle of Higher Education*, April 11, 2011, http://chronicle.com/article/2011-Salary-Explorer/126972.

11. For a different line of thought, see Matthew Reisz, "The Seven Deadly Sins of the Academy," *Times Higher Education*, September 17, 2009, http://www.timeshighereducation.co.uk/features/the-seven-deadly-sins-of-the-academy/408135.article.

12. Harvey E. Whitney Jr., "The Two Fiefdoms of Higher Education," *Swan's Commentary*, December 2, 2013, http://www.swans.com/library/art19/hewhit30.html.

13. Doug Mann, "The University as Feudal State: The Abysmal Failure of Interdisciplinarity in Higher Education," http://publish.uwo.ca/~dmann/feudal.htm.

14. Ken Howard, "A Palimpsest of Fiefdoms: Interdisciplinary Centers," *21stC*, http://www.columbia.edu/cu/21stC/issue-1.4/palimp.html.

15. Charles Hugh Smith, "The Ratchet Effect: Fiefdom Bloat and Resistance to Declining Incomes," *Of Two Minds.com*, August 23, 2010, http://www.oftwominds.com/blogaug10/ratchet-effect08-10.html.

16. Michael Day, "Family Fiefdoms Blamed for Tainting Italian Universities," *The Independent*, September 25, 2010, http://www.independent.co.uk/news/world/europe/family-fiefdoms-blamed-for-tainting-italian-universities-2089120.html.

17. See Derek Bok, "The Problem with Undergraduate Teaching," 186–191 in *Higher Education in America*, in which he explains how fundamentally ineffective the class lecture actually is.

18. Audrey Williams June, "For Chairs, the Seat's Gotten Hotter: With New Demands for Fund Raising and Assessment, Academe's Middle Managers Feel the Pressure," *Chronicle of Higher Education*, December 2, 2013, http://chronicle.com/article/Department-Chairs-Find/143309/.

19. Ginsberg, *The Fall of the Faculty*.

20. Jeffrey Williams, "The Great Stratification," *Chronicle of Higher Education*, December 2, 2013, http://chronicle.com/article/The-Great-Stratification/143285/.

21. Ginsberg, *The Fall of the Faculty*, 2.

22. Ibid., 3, cited from Henry Rosovsky, *The University: An Owner's Manual* (New York: W. W. Norton, 1990), 13.

23. Ibid., 16, cited from *Florida Memorial College*, 263 NLRB 1248 (1982), enforced, 820 F.2d 1182 (11th Cir. 1987); discussed in Donna Euben, "Some Legal Aspects of Collegial Governance," *Presentation Made to the 2003 AAUP Governance Conference*, Indianapolis, Indiana, October 11, 2003, 4.

24. Ginsberg, *The Fall of the Faculty*, 20–27.

25. Ibid., 4.

26. Ibid., 4. For other comments, see Dan Berrett, "'The Fall of the Faculty,'" *Inside Higher Ed*, July 14, 2011, http://www.insidehighered.com/news/2011/07/14/new_book_argues_bloated_administration_is_what_ails_higher_education; James Derounian, "University Administrators Should Enable, Not Disable Learning," *The Guardian*, July 31, 2012, http://www.theguardian.com/

higher-education-network/blog/2012/jul/31/the-role-of-university-
administrators.

27. Michael D. Cohen and James G. M. March, *Leadership and Ambiguity: The American College President* (New York: McGraw Hill, 1974). See also Robert Birnbaum, *How Colleges Work: The Cybernetics of Academic Organization and Leadership* (San Francisco: Jossey-Bass, 1988).

28. Michael D. Cohen, James G. March, and Johan P. Olsen, "A Garbage Can Model of Organizational Choice," *Administrative Science Quarterly* 17, no. 1 (1972): 1–25.

29. Alexandre Afonso, "How Academia Resembles a Drug Gang," *Alexandre Afonso: The Natural Order of Things,* November 21, 2013, http:// alexandreafonso.wordpress.com/2013/11/21/how-academia-resembles-a-drug-gang/.

30. Alexandre Afonso, "How Academia Resembles a Drug Gang," *The London School of Economics and Political Science,* http://blogs.lse.ac.uk/ usappblog/2013/12/21/how-academia-resembles-a-drug-gang/.

31. Scott Jaschik, "Academe as a Drug Gang," *Inside Higher Ed,* November 25, 2013, http://www.insidehighered.com/news/2013/11/25/blog-post-comparing-academe-drug-gang-provokes-much-discussion.

32. Steven D. Levitt and Sudhir A. Venkatesh, "An Economic Analysis of a Drug-selling Gang's Finances," *The Quarterly Journal of Economics* 115, no. 3 (2000): 755–789; Stephen J. Dubner and Steven D. Levitt, *Freakonomics: A Rogue Economist Explores the Hidden Side of Everything* (New York: Harper-Collins, 2006).

33. Afonso, "How Academia Resembles a Drug Gang."

34. Ibid.

35. Jordan Weissmann, "Why Haven't Humanities PhD Programs Collapsed?" *Atlantic Monthly,* September 16, 2013, http://www.theatlantic.com/ business/archive/2013/09/why-havent-humanities-phd-programs-collapsed/ 279733/.

36. Chris Blattman, "'How Academia Resembles a Drug Gang'" [critique], *International Development, Economics, Politics, and Policy,* November 27, 2013, http://chrisblattman.com/2013/11/27/how-academia-resembles-a-drug-gang/.

37. Pablo Eisenberg, "The 'Untouchables' of American Higher Education," *Huffington Post,* June 29, 2010, http://www.huffingtonpost.com/pablo-eisenberg/the-untouchables-of-ameri_b_629815.html.

38. Ibid.

39. Pablo Eisenberg, "The Caste System in Higher Education," *Huffington Post,* September 4, 2012, http://www.huffingtonpost.com/pablo-eisenberg/ caste-system-higher-education_b_1853917.html.

40. Ibid.

41. Martin Kitch, "The Deepening Caste System in Higher Education," *The Academe Blog,* July 8, 2013, http://academeblog.org/2013/07/08/the-deepening-caste-system-in-higher-education/. See also Leslie Madsen Brooks, "The Academic Caste System in an Age of Budget Cuts," *Blogher,* December 20, 2008, http://www.blogher.com/academic-caste-system-age-budget-cuts.

42. Marvin Kitch, "Corporatization and Administrative Bloat: 'Gilded Goodbyes,'" *Academe Blog,* November 30, 2013, http://academeblog.org/2013/11/30/corporatization-and-administrative-bloat-gilded-goodbyes/#more-5122.

43. Kitch, "The Deepening."

44. Robert L. Oprisko, Kirstie Lynn Dobbs, and Joseph DiGrazia, "Pushing Up Ivies: Institutional Prestige and the Academic Caste System," *Georgetown Public Policy Review,* August 21, 2013, http://gppreview.com/2013/08/21/pushing-up-ivies-institutional-prestige-and-the-academic-caste-system/. The recruiting of senior faculty has been a bit of a notorious game for a while; see Tim Cornwell, "Brilliant Objects of Desire," *The Times Higher Education,* June 1, 1998, http://www.timeshighereducation.co.uk/features/brilliant-objects-of-desire/107487.article.

45. Niall Ferguson, "College Becoming the New Caste System," *Newsweek,* August 27, 2012, http://www.newsweek.com/niall-ferguson-college-becoming-new-caste-system-64553.

46. Charles Murray, *Coming Apart: The State of White America, 1960–2010* (New York: Crown Forum/Random House, 2013).

47. See Martin Morse Wooster, "Unravelling America," *The Pope Center for Higher Education,* September 11, 2012, http://www.popecenter.org/commentaries/article.html?id=2736.

48. Ferguson, "College Becoming."

49. Rachel Cohen, "Higher Education's New Caste System," *The Washington Monthly,* September 5, 2013, http://www.washingtonmonthly.com/college_guide/blog/higher_educations_new_caste_sy.php#.

50. Jack Stripling, "President's Proposal Renews Debate Over How to Measure College Quality," *Chronicle for Higher Education,* September 5, 2013, http://chronicle.com/article/Presidents-Proposal-Renews/141391/.

51. Jon Gertner, "What is a Living Wage?" *New York Times,* January 15, 2006, http://www.nytimes.com/2006/01/15/magazine/15wage.html; C. Melissa Snarr, *All You That Labor: Religion and Ethics in the Living Wage Movement* (New York: NYU Press, 2011).

52. "Harvard Protest Moves into Second Week," *CBS News,* April 26, 2001, http://www.cbsnews.com/news/harvard-protest-moves-into-second-week/.

53. Susan Kinzie, "GU Protesters Savor Win—and a Meal: Nine-Day Hunger Strike Resulted in Better Compensation for Contract Workers," *Washing-*

ton Post, March 25, 2005, http://www.washingtonpost.com/wp-dyn/articles/A62829-2005Mar24.html.

54. "Staff and Students in US Rally to Back Low-paid Workers Striking to Win Higher Wages," *Times Higher Education,* May 12, 2006, http://www.timeshighereducation.co.uk/203059.article.

55. Rebecca Burns, "A 'Historic Moment' for Campus Solidarity: University of California Grad Students Will Join Service Workers on the Picket Lines in a Rare Sympathy Strike," *In These Times,* November 15, 2015, http://inthesetimes.com/article/15885/uc_grad_student_employees_declare_solidarity_with_service_workers/.

56. Pablo Eisenberg, "Campus Workers' Wages: A Disgrace to Academe," *Chronicle of Higher Education,* September 10, 2012, http://chronicle.com/article/A-Living-Wage-for-Campus/134232/.

57. ———, "Living Wages and College Campuses," *Huffington Post,* November 18, 2012, http://www.huffingtonpost.com/pablo-eisenberg/university-employee-wages_b_2154836.html.

58. Eisenberg, "Campus Workers' Wages."

59. Ibid.

60. Williams, "The Great Stratification."

61. Ibid.

6. CHEATING

1. Richard Pérez-Peña, "Students Accused of Cheating Return Awkwardly to a Changed Harvard," *New York Times,* September 16, 2013, www.nytimes.com/2013/09/17/education/students-accused-of-cheating-return-awkwardly-to-a-changed-harvard.html.

2. Donald McCabe and Linda Klebe Trevino, "Honesty and Honor Codes," *Academe* 88.1 (2002): 38. McCabe has dozens of essays, though the 2002 essay gets the most frequent attention. See Donald McCabe, Kenneth Butterfield, and Linda Trevino, *Cheating in College: Why Students Do It and What Educators Can Do about It* (Baltimore: Johns Hopkins University Press, 2012).

3. William Bowers, *Student Dishonesty and Its Control in College* (New York: Columbia University Press, 1964).

4. Jon Marcus, "Success at Any Cost? There May Be a High Price to Pay," *Times Higher Education,* September 27, 2012, http://www.timeshighereducation.co.uk/421248.article.

5. Richard Pérez-Peña, "Studies Find More Students Cheating, with High Achievers No Exception," *New York Times,* September 7, 2012, http://www.

nytimes.com/2012/09/08/education/studies-show-more-students-cheat-even-high-achievers.html.

6. Martin Finucane, "Harvard Freshmen, in Survey, Acknowledge Past Cheating," *Boston Globe,* September 6, 2013, http://www.bostonglobe.com/metro/2013/09/06/harvard-freshmen-survey-acknowledge-cheating-academic-careers/QVZMwxbGL3JBGDOar5Iz2K/story.html.

7. Pérez-Peña, "Studies Find More Students Cheating."

8. Alison Schneider, "Why Professors Don't Do More to Stop Students Who Cheat," *Chronicle of Higher Education,* January 22, 1999, http://chronicle.com/article/Why-Professors-Dont-Do-More/25673/.

9. Jon Kerkvliet and Charles Sigmund, "Can We Control Cheating in the Classroom?" *Journal of Economic Education* 30, no. 4 (1999): 331–343, http://EconPapers.repec.org/RePEc:taf:jeduce:v:30:y:1999:i:4:p:331-343.

10. Schneider, "Why Professors Don't Do More."

11. Then there is "Ed Dante," the pen name of Dave Tomar, who on November 12, 2010, appeared in the *Chronicle of Higher Education* as "The Shadow Scholar" (http://chronicle.com/article/The-Shadow-Scholar/125329/). See also "How I Helped Teachers Cheat," *New York Times,* November 9, 2013, http://www.nytimes.com/2013/11/10/opinion/sunday/how-i-helped-teachers-cheat.html. Tomar has since written a more extended account of his writing papers and even dissertations, for students willing to pay: *The Shadow Scholar: How I Made a Living Helping College Kids Cheat* (New York: Bloomsbury, 2012). The *Chronicle* did a fine review; see Dan Berrett, "An Academic Ghostwriter, the 'Shadow Scholar,' Comes Clean," *Chronicle of Higher Education,* August 21, 2012, http://chronicle.com/article/An-Academic-Ghostwriter-Comes/133904/.

12. Andrew Delbanco, *College: What It Was, Is and Should Be* (Princeton: Princeton University Press, 2012), 144.

13. "The Underlying Causes of the Epidemic of Cheating in College Classrooms," *Chronicle of Education,* February 26, 1999, http://chronicle.com/article/The-Underlying-Causes-of-the/31870.

14. McCabe and Trevino, "Honesty and Honor Codes," 38. McCabe defines a traditional code as "unproctored exams, a judicial process over which students have majority or complete control, and a written pledge requiring students to affirm they have completed their work honestly."

15. McCabe and Trevino, "Honesty and Honor Codes," 39–40.

16. Ibid., 38.

17. Jennifer Dirmeyer and Alexander C. Cartwright, "Honor Codes Work Where Honesty Has Already Taken Root," *Chronicle of Education,* September 24, 2012, http://chronicle.com/article/Honor-Codes-Work-Where-Honesty/134542/.

18. "Harvard Cheating Scandal Reveals Gaps in Costly Education," *Boston Globe,* September 6, 2012, http://www.bostonglobe.com/opinion/editorials/2012/09/06/harvard-cheating-scandal-reveals-gaps-costly-education/MPsyxJtBCm1PWWEf6ff1PP/story.html.

19. Mary Carmichael, "Harvard Students Bridle Over Test Cheating Investigation," *Boston Globe,* September 1, 2012, http://www.bostonglobe.com/metro/2012/08/31/harvard-cheating-scandal-raises-concerns-and-eyebrows/nN0YfkDMBsaQb8GtZAN48O/story.html.

20. Rebecca Harrington, "Song of the Cheaters," *New York Times,* September 14, 2012, http://www.nytimes.com/2012/09/15/opinion/the-long-legacy-of-cheating-at-harvard.html.

21. Jon Marcus, "Success at Any Cost? There May Be a High Price to Pay," *Times Higher Education,* September 27, 2012, http://www.timeshighereducation.co.uk/421248.article.

22. "Harvard College's Honor Code," *Harvard Magazine,* May 7, 2014, http://harvardmagazine.com/2014/05/harvard-college-adopts-honor-code.

23. Nicole Ruedy, Francesca Gino, Maurice Schweitzer, and Celia Moore, "The Cheater's High: The Unexpected Affective Benefits of Unethical Behavior," *Journal of Personality and Social Psychology* 105, no. 4 (2013): 531, http://www.apa.org/pubs/journals/releases/psp-a0034231.pdf.

24. Ibid., 544.

25. Ibid.

26. Jan Hoffman, "Cheating's Surprising Thrill," *New York Times,* October 7, 2013, http://well.blogs.nytimes.com/2013/10/07/in-bad-news-cheating-feels-good/.

27. The fudge factor comes from Dan Ariely in his *The Honest Truth About Dishonesty: How We Lie to Everyone—Especially Ourselves* (New York: Harper, 2013), 31–54.

28. James M. Lang, *Cheating Lessons: Learning from Academic Dishonesty* (Cambridge, MA: Harvard University Press, 2013).

29. Ibid, 22.

30. Horowitz, *Campus Life,* 36; see also 278 where she discusses how hidden the culture is from the faculty.

31. Wilfried Decoo, *Crisis on Campus, Confronting Academic Misconduct* (Cambridge, MA: MIT Press, 2002). See also the insightful essay by Raymond Schroth, "The Plagiarism Plague: Declining Standards Make Getting Caught the Primary Offense," *America Magazine* 208, no. 16 (2012): 12–16.

32. Paul D. Eisenberg, "The Truth, the Whole Truth, and Nothing But the Truth," ed. Stephen Cahn, *Morality, Responsibility and the University* (Philadelphia: Temple University Press, 1992), 109–118.

33. George Sher, "The Letter Writer's Dilemma," ed. Stephen Cahn, *Moral Problems in Higher Education* (Philadelphia: Temple University Press, 2011), 211–218.

34. Rudolph H. Weingartner, "Ethics in Academic Personnel Processes: The Tenure Decision," ed. Stephen Cahn, *Morality, Responsibility and the University* (Philadelphia: Temple University Press, 1992), 76–92.

35. David Lewis, "Academic Appointments: Why Ignore the Advantage of Being Right?" ed. Stephen Cahn, *Morality, Responsibility and the University* (Philadelphia: Temple University Press, 1992), 231–242.

36. Bruce A Kimball, "The Paradox of Prejudicially Applying Valid Academic Standards: A Historical Case Study in the Ethics of Academic Administration," ed. Elaine E. Englehardt, Michael S. Pritchard, Kerry D. Romesburg, and Brian E. Schrag, *The Ethical Challenges of Academic Administration* (New York: Springer, 2010), 151–172.

37. David Kline, "On Telling Faculty the Truth," ed. Elaine E. Englehardt, Michael S. Pritchard, Kerry D. Romesburg, and Brian E. Schrag, *The Ethical Challenges of Academic Administration* (New York: Springer, 2010), 143–150.

7. UNDERGRADUATES ACTING BADLY

1. Derek Bok, *Universities and the Future of America* (Durham, NC: Duke University Press, 1990), 100. See the astute observations by David Hokema, *Campus Rules and Moral Community: In Place of Loco Parentis* (Lanham, MD: Rowman & Littlefield, 1994), 127–129. *Campus Rules* is a fine book, the only of its kind, but now, twenty years later, its recommendations are unable to address the deteriorated state of student life.

2. Michael Sperber, *Beer and Circus: How Big-Time College Sports Is Crippling Undergraduate Education* (New York: Holt, 2001). On university sports fans getting out of hand, see Graham Spanier, "The Dark Side of School Spirit," *Chronicle of Higher Education,* October 27, 2008, http://chronicle.com/blogs/brainstorm/the-dark-side-of-school-spirit/6406. See also a list of university basketball teams in "The Worst College Fans," *Chronicle of Higher Education,* April 1, 2005, http://chronicle.com/article/The-Worst-College-Fans/26382/.

3. The videos of *I'm Shmacked* are designed to help students who are scouting colleges to see which are more "attractive." See Jennifer Collins, "University of Smacked," *The New York Times,* September 21, 2012, http://www.nytimes.com/2012/09/23/fashion/campus-life-gains-more-exposure-on-the-web.html. Collins refers readers to one YouTube video, *I'm Shmacked The Movie—West Virginia University: St. Patrick's Day Feat. Huey Mack (2012)*

(http://www.youtube.com/watch?v=tP0Xod-L1Yw), which "highlights among other antics, students smashing car windows, in between beer bongs, as part of a St. Patrick's Day charity party." Their site, http://imshmacked.com/, features *I'm Shmacked : 2013 Fall Semester Tour Recap,* a mix of media coverage on their antics that serves as a promotion to help students pick the right college. Sometimes *I'm Shmacked* parties get out of hand as one did at the University of Delaware in 2013; see Tyler Kingkade "'I'm Shmacked' Goes to University of Delaware, Several Thousand Students Flood the Streets in Frenzy," *Huffington Post,* September 10, 2013, http://www.huffingtonpost.com/2013/09/10/im-schmacked-university-of-delaware_n_3901418.html; and Netzanz Zimmerman, "College Students Riot after 'I'm Shmacked' Party Turns into Project X," *Gawker,* September 10, 2013, http://gawker.com/college-students-riot-after-im-shmacked-party-turns-1287844186. The University of Delaware made *University Primetime News* "Top College Riots of 2013–14," http://uprimenews.com/school/vt/article/top-college-riots-of-2013-2014.

4. Julie Reuben, *The Making of the Modern University: Intellectual Transformation and the Marginalization of Morality* (Chicago: University of Chicago Press, 1996).

5. Donna Freitas, *Sex and the Soul: Juggling Sexuality, Spirituality, Romance, and Religion on American College Campuses* (New York: Oxford University Press, 2008).

6. Margaret Farley, *Just Love: A Framework for Christian Sexual Ethics* (New York: Continuum, 2006).

7. Henry Davidson Sheldon, *Student Life and Customs* (New York: D. Appleton and Company, 1901), 81–94.

8. Ibid., 95: "The professors and tutors were not only instructors but also policemen and night watchmen."

9. Helen Lefkowitz Horowitz, *Campus Life: Undergraduate Cultures from the End of the Eighteenth Century to the Present* (Chicago: University of Chicago Press, 1987), 26. See also Sheldon, *Student Life,* 82: "Our first glimpses into the social life of the students discover a dreary round of fast days, early chapels, severe punishments and bad board."

10. Horowitz, *Campus Life,* 29.

11. Ibid., 27.

12. Ibid., p. 11. Horowitz's language of war does not seem excessive; see Sheldon, *Student Life,* 96: "The students considered their faculty natural enemies."

13. Horowitz, 13.

14. Ibid., 13.

15. Ibid., 35–37.

16. Ibid., 41.

17. "The Story of Cane Rush," *NYU Student Traditions Archive,* http://
www.cs.nyu.edu/courses/spring09/V22.0380-001/maw410/NYU_Student_
Traditions/canerushstory.html. In *Student Life,* Sheldon gives accounts of
rushing at Princeton, Yale, Amherst, and Harvard (102–107).

18. "College Athletics: History of Athletics in U.S. Colleges and Universities," *StateUniversity.com,* http://education.stateuniversity.com/pages/1846/
College-Athletics-HISTORY-ATHLETICS-IN-U-S-COLLEGES-
UNIVERSITIES.html.; http://www.scarletknights.com/football/history/first-
game.asp. Or, from another perspective, Sheldon, *Student Life:* "The football
game, annually played between the freshmen and sophomores, resembled a
rush much more than the modern game of that name" (102–103).

19. Horowitz, *Campus Life,* 35–40.

20. Ibid.

21. Ibid., 14.

22. Ibid.

23. Ibid., 193; see her entire chapter, "College Women and Coeds,"
193–220. See also Barbara Miller Solomon, *In the Company of Educated
Women: A History of Women and Higher Education in America* (New Haven,
CT: Yale University, 1985); Dorothy Dimbar Bromley and Florence Haxon
Britten, *Youth and Sex: A Study of 1300 College Students* (New Haven, CT:
Yale University, 1938). On co-education at Michigan, see Olive Anderson, *An
American Girl and Her Four Years in a Boys College* (New York: D. Appleton
and Company, 1878); Dorothy Gies McGuigan, *A Dangerous Experiment: 100
Years of Women at the University of Michigan* (Ann Arbor, MI: Center for
Continuing Education of Women, 1970). At Cornell, Charlotte Williams Con-
able, *Women at Cornell: The Myth of Equal Education* (Ithaca: Cornell Uni-
versity Press, 1977).

24. Horowitz, 42.

25. Ibid.

26. Ibid., 17.

27. Ibid., 67.

28. Ibid., 67–68.

29. Ibid., 68.

30. Ibid., 201.

31. Ibid., 94.

32. Ibid., 94.

33. Ibid., 95.

34. Caitlin Flanagan, "The Dark Power of Fraternities," *Atlantic Monthly,*
February 19, 2014, http://www.theatlantic.com/features/archive/2014/02/the-
dark-power-of-fraternities/357580/.

35. Ibid.

36. John Hechinger and David Glovin, "Fraternities Scuttle Proposals to Ban Freshman Rush after Drinking Deaths," *Bloomberg News,* October 15, 2013, http://www.bloomberg.com/news/2013-10-15/cal-poly-brings-back-freshman-pledging-after-lobbying.html. See also a host of other essays, including John Hechinger and David Glovin, "Deadliest Frat's Icy Torture of Pledges Evokes Tarantino Films," *Bloomberg,* December 30, 2013, http://www.bloomberg.com/news/articles/2013-12-30/deadliest-frat-s-icy-torture-of-pledges-evokes-tarantino-films and more recently John Hechinger and David Glovin, "Fraternity Chief Feared for Son as Hazings Spurred JP Morgan Snub," March 27, 2014, *Bloomberg,* http://www.bloomberg.com/news/articles/2014-03-27/fraternity-chief-feared-for-son-as-hazings-spurred-jpmorgan-snub. Hechinger and Glovin together with Caitlin Flanagan have given greater and greater attention to the issue of fraternities. See also Lauren Miller, "Q&A with Bloomberg Reporters David Glovin and John Hechinger," Bloomberg Content Service, http://www.bloomberg.com/content-service/blog/2014-03-14/qa-with-bloomberg-reporters-david-glovin-and-john-hechinger/.

37. Flanagan, "The Dark Power."

38. Peter Schworm, "Police Seek Charges in Apparent Fraternity Hazing at BU," *Boston Globe,* April 10, 2012, http://www.bostonglobe.com/metro/2012/04/10/boston-university-students-involved-apparent-hazing-face-expulsion/HxPvOjvmSkdYkivE2PTD9M/story.html.

39. Winton Solberg, "Harmless Pranks or Brutal Practices? Hazing at the University of Illinois, 1868–1913," *Journal of Illinois State Historical Society* 91, no. 4 (1988): 233–259. This article later appeared as "Hazing in a U.S. University from 1868 to 1913," ed. Anthony Potts and Tom O'Donoghue, *Schools as Dangerous Places* (Youngstown, New York: Cambria Press, 2007), 309–337.

40. Ibid., 332.

41. Ibid., 333.

42. In *Student Life,* Sheldon tells us that hazing is found in the Revolutionary War period and was violent: "Hazing undoubtedly terrorized and made miserable the lives of the more timid freshmen." He adds, "the damage must have been considerable." See his reference, "to cases of fatal illness occasioned by hazing" (106).

43. Hank Nuwer, *Broken Pledges: The Deadly Rite of Hazing* (Atlanta: Longstreet Press, 1990).

44. Hank Nuwer, *Wrongs of Passage: Fraternities, Sororities, Hazing and Binge Drinking* (Bloomington: Indiana University Press, 2001).

45. Hank Nuwer, ed., *The Hazing Reader* (Bloomington: Indiana University Press, 2004).

46. Irving Janis, "Groupthink," ed. Hank Nuwer, *The Hazing Reader* (Bloomington: Indiana University Press), 24–25. Previously published as "Groupthink," *Psychology Today* 5, no. 6 (1971): 43–46, 74–76.

47. Nuwer, *The Hazing Reader,* 19.

48. Ibid.

49. James Arnold, "Hazing and Alcohol in a College Fraternity," ed. Hank Nuwer, *The Hazing Reader* (Bloomington: Indiana University Press), 51–105.

50. James Arnold, "Alcohol, Hazing, and Fraternities as Addictive Organizations," StopHazing.org, http://www.stophazing.org/supporting-documents/alcohol-hazing-and-fraternities-as-addictive-organizations-by-dr-james-arnold/.

51. Arnold, "Hazing and Alcohol, 105.

52. Hank Nuwer, *All Things Hazing Worldwide,* http://hazing.hanknuwer.com/.

53. Hank Nuwer, "Hank Nuwer's List of Deaths by Hazing," *All Things Hazing Worldwide,* http://www.hanknuwer.com/hazingdeaths.html.

54. Elizabeth Allan and Mary Madden, "Hazing in View: College Students at Risk: Initial Findings from the National Study of Student Hazing," March 11, 2008, http://www.stophazing.org/wp-content/uploads/2014/06/hazing_in_view_web1.pdf.

55. Ibid.

56. *Stop Hazing,* http://www.stophazing.org/.

57. Elizabeth Allan and Susan Van Deventer Iverson, "Initiating Change: Transforming a Hazing Culture," ed. Hank Nuwer, *The Hazing Reader* (Bloomington: Indiana University Press), 256.

58. Ibid., 262.

59. Elizabeth Allan, "Hazing and Gender: Analyzing the Obvious," ed. Hank Nuwer, *The Hazing Reader* (Bloomington: Indiana University Press), 289.

60. Ibid., 294.

61. Jacob Hawley, "Frats in Trouble for Sexist, Racist Parties," *Higheredmorning,* July 12, 2012, http://www.higheredmorning.com/sexist-racist-frat-party; see also Hannah Croft, "Cal Poly Gains National Attention for 'Colonial Bros and Nava-hos' Party," *Mustang News,* November 22, 2013, http://mustangnews.net/cal-poly-gains-national-attention-for-colonial-bros-and-nava-hos-party/ ; Kate Abbey-Lambetz, "'Hood Ratchet Thursday' Party at University of Michigan Fraternity Canceled by School," *Huffington Post,* November 1, 2013, http://www.huffingtonpost.com/2013/11/01/hood-ratchet-thursday-party-theta-xi-u-of-m_n_4190523.html; Tyler Kingkade, "Dartmouth Fraternity, Sorority Host 'Bloods and Crips' Party, Apologize," *Huffington Post,* August 14, 2013, http://www.huffingtonpost.com/2013/08/14/dartmouth-bloods-and-crips-party-fraternity_n_3755959.html; Kingkade helps us out with a veri-

table collection of memorably disturbing actions by fraternities, "Frats Behaving Badly: 14 Examples of Racist Parties, Terrible Pranks, Misogyny, and Just Being Bad," *Huffington Post,* September 4, 2013, http://www.huffingtonpost.com/2013/09/03/frats-behaving-badly_n_3830905.html.

62. Randal Archibold, "California Campus Sees Uneasy Race Relations," *New York Times,* February 26, 2010, http://www.nytimes.com/2010/02/27/education/27sandiego.html.

63. Katie Baker, "'Pedo Parties' and Racist Ragers: Why Are Frat Bros Fixated on Fucked Up Theme Parties," *Jezebel,* February 12, 2013, http://jezebel.com/5983488/pedo-parties-and-racist-ragers-why-are-frat-bros-fixated-on-sketchy-theme-parties.

64. Ibid.

65. Katie Baker, "Fraternity Thought It Would be Awesome to Cross a Fake Mexican Border During a 'Fiesta,'" *Jezebel,* September 27, 2012, http://jezebel.com/5946929/fraternity-thought-it-would-be-awesome-to-let-partygoers-cross-a-fake-mexican-border-during-a-fiesta.

66. Katie Baker, "Indiana Sorority Girls Attend Totally Cute Homeless-Themed Party," *Jezebel,* April 19, 2013, http://jezebel.com/indiana-sorority-throws-spirited-homeless-themed-party-476310795.

67. Katie Baker, "Check Out This Frat Party Pic and Join the Poverty Party," *Jezebel,* April 26, 2013, http://jezebel.com/check-out-this-frat-party-pic-from-1930-and-join-the-po-480166953.

68. "Racial-Themed Parties Draw Fury on Campuses Across the Country," *Chronicle of Higher Education,* January 31, 2007, http://chronicle.com/article/Racial-Themed-Parties-Draw/38153/.

69. "Racial Gap Widens at Johns Hopkins Following Fraternity's Party," *Chronicle of Higher Education,* November 1, 2006, http://chronicle.com/article/Racial-Gap-Widens-at-Johns/37793/.

70. Alyssa Botelho, "Dartmouth Roiled, Again, by Student Insensitivity," *Boston Globe,* August 18, 2013, http://www.bostonglobe.com/metro/2013/08/17/dartmouth-college-roiled-again-student-insensitivity/35s6LL6khGgIamZmus21oK/story.html.

71. Sunhay You, "Racist and Sexist Duke Fraternity Parties Offend Absolutely Everyone, Incite Protest," *Identities.mic,* February 6, 2013, http://mic.com/articles/25012/racist-and-sexist-duke-university-fraternity-parties-offend-absolutely-everyone-incite-protest.Duke University's lacrosse team scandal stands in the background of any report on these frat parties. On the scandal see, William Cohan, *The Price of Scandal: The Duke Lacrosse Scandal, the Power of the Elite, and the Corruption of Our Great Universities* (New York: Scribner, 2014). In her book review ("Nothing to Cheer About," *New York Times,* April 24, 2014, http://www.nytimes.com/2014/04/27/books/review/the-

price-of-silence-by-william-d-cohan.html), Caitlin Flanagan concluded: "Every parent planning to send a child to an 'elite' college dominated by an overly powerful athletic program should buy this book. For those with children thinking of Duke, it is required reading."

72. Gina Garcia, Marc Johnston, et al., "When Parties Become Racialized: Deconstructing Racially Themed Parties," *Journal of Student Affairs Research and Practice* 48, no. 1 (2011): 5.

73. Ibid., 6-8.

74. Ibid., 9.

75. Ibid., 13.

76. Ibid., 16. Joe R. Feagin, Hernan Vera, and Nikitah Imani, *The Agony of Education: Black Students at White Colleges and Universities* (New York, NY: Routledge, 1996).

77. Garcia, et al., "When Parties Become Racialized," 16–17.

78. Walter Kim, "Drinking to Fit In," *New York Times,* October 3, 1997, http://www.nytimes.com/1997/10/03/opinion/drinking-to-fit-in.html.

79. Ibid.

80. Maria Konnikova, "18 US Presidents Were in College Fraternities," *Atlantic Monthly,* February 21, 2014, http://www.theatlantic.com/education/archive/2014/02/18-us-presidents-were-in-college-fraternities/283997/. See also Alan DeSantis, *Inside Greek U: Fraternities, Sororities, and the Pursuit of Pleasure* (Lexington: University Press of Kentucky, 2007).

81. Kevin Roose, "One-Percent Jokes and Plutocrats in Drag: What I Saw When I Crashed a Wall Street Secret Society," *New York Magazine,* February 18, 2014, http://nymag.com/daily/intelligencer/2014/02/i-crashed-a-wall-street-secret-society.html.

82. Jack Stripling and Benjamin Mueller, "College Trustees in Wall Street Club Clash with Campus Culture," *Chronicle of Higher Education,* March 31, 2014, http://chronicle.com/article/College-Trustees-in-Wall/145621/.

83. Flanagan makes this point and argues, "For fraternities to survive, they needed to do four separate but related things: take the task of acquiring insurance out of the hands of the local chapters and place it in the hands of the vast national organizations; develop procedures and policies that would transfer as much of their liability as possible to outside parties; find new and creative means of protecting their massive assets from juries; and—perhaps most important of all—find a way of indemnifying the national and local organizations from the dangerous and illegal behavior of some of their undergraduate members." She adds, "The way fraternities accomplished all of this is the underlying story in the lawsuits they face, and it is something that few members—and, I would wager, even fewer parents of members—grasp completely, comprising a

set of realities you should absolutely understand in detail if your son ever decides to join a fraternity."

84. Flanagan, "The Dark Side."

85. David J. Leonard and Richard C. King, "Animal House on Steroids," *Chronicle of Higher Education,* April 16, 2013, http://chronicle.com/blogs/conversation/2013/04/16/animal-house-on-steroids/.

86. Elizabeth A. Armstrong and Laura T. Hamilton, *Paying for the Party: How College Maintains Inequality* (Cambridge, MA: Harvard University Press, 2012). See also the work of University of Toronto sociologist Ann L. Mullen, *Degrees of Inequality: Culture, Class, and Gender in American Higher Education* (Baltimore: Johns Hopkins University Press, 2010).

87. Laura Hamilton and Elizabeth Armstrong, "Social Life and Social Inequality," *Chronicle of Higher Education,* July 2, 2012, http://chronicle.com/article/Social-LifeSocial/132631/.

88. As quoted by Sam Dillon in "Share of College Spending for Recreation Is Rising," *New York Times,* July 9, 2010, http://www.nytimes.com/2010/07/10/education/10education.html.

89. Nedra Pickler, "Obama Targets Sexual Assault Epidemic," *Associated Press,* January 22, 2014, http://bigstory.ap.org/article/obama-targets-college-sexual-assault-epidemic.

90. White House Council on Women and Girls Report, *Rape and Sexual Assault: A Renewed Call to Action,* The White House (January 22, 2014): 13. http://www.whitehouse.gov/sites/default/files/docs/sexual_assault_report_1-21-14.pdf.

91. Christopher P. Krebs, Christine H. Lindquist, and Tara D. Warner, *The Campus Sexual Assault (CSA) Study* (Washington, DC: National Institute of Justice, 2007). The Campus Sexual Assault Study was conducted by RTI International and funded by the National Institute of Justice. Data were collected using a web-based survey from undergraduate students (5,466 women and 1,375 men) at two large, public universities. See also C. Krebs, C. Lindquist, et. al., "College Women's Experiences with Physically Forced, Alcohol or Other Drug Enabled, and Drug Facilitated Sexual Assault Before and Since Entering College," *Journal of American College Health* 57, no. 6 (2009): 639–647. For the one-in-five assessment, see Centers for Disease Control and Prevention, "Sexual Violence: Facts at a Glance" (2012), http://www.cdc.gov/violenceprevention/pdf/sv-datasheet-a.pdf. Because of underreporting, the percentage is likely much higher. Bonnie S. Fisher, Francis T. Cullen, and Michael G. Turner, *The Sexual Victimization of College Women* (Washington, DC: U.S. Department of Justice, 2000), https://www.ncjrs.gov/pdffiles1/nij/182369.pdf.

92. D. Kilpatrick, H. Resnick, et al., *Drug Facilitated, Incapacitated, and Forcible Rape: A National Study* (NCJ 219181) (Charleston, SC: Medical University of South Carolina, National Crime Victims Research & Treatment Center, 2007).

93. Ibid.

94. T. Zawacki, A. Abbey, et al., "Perpetrators of Alcohol Involved Sexual Assaults: How Do They Differ from Other Sexual Assault Perpetrators and Non-perpetrators?" *Aggressive Behavior* 29, no. 4 (2003): 366–380.

95. Krebs et al., *The Campus Sexual Assault Study.*

96. Ibid.

97. D. Lisak and P. Miller, "Repeat Rape and Multiple Offending among Undetected Rapists," *Violence and Victims* 17, no. 1 (2002): 73–84.

98. Kilpatrick, et al., *Drug Facilitated.*

99. D. Eisenberg, E. Golberstein, and J. Hunt, "Mental Health and Academic Success in College," *B E Journal of Economic Analysis & Policy* 9, no. 1 (2009): 1–35; A. Arria, L. Garnier-Dykstra, et al., "Drug Use Patterns and Continuous Enrollment in College: Results from a Longitudinal Study," *Journal of Studies on Alcohol and Drugs* 74, no. 1 (2013): 71–83.

100. Kilpatrick, et al., *Drug Facilitated.*

101. The White House Council on Women and Girls, 5–6.

102. The White House Council on Women and Girls, 24–25.

103. U.S. Department of Education, "U.S. Department of Education Releases List of Higher Education Institutions with Open Title IX Sexual Violence Investigations," May 1, 2014, http://www.ed.gov/news/press-releases/us-department-education-releases-list-higher-education-institutions-open-title-i.

104. "White House Updates College Sex Assault Policy," *Circa,* December 30, 2014, http://cir.ca/news/obamas-college-sex-assault-task-force.

105. "School-by-School Enforcement Map," *Not Alone,* https://www.notalone.gov/data/ -school-by-school-enforcement-map.

106. U.S. Senate Subcommittee on Financial and Contracting Oversight, *Sexual Violence on Campus,* http://www.mccaskill.senate.gov/SurveyReportwithAppendix.pdf.

107. Jeff Mason, "White House Pushes Colleges to Crack Down on Sexual Assaults," *Reuters.com,* April 28, 2014, http://www.reuters.com/article/2014/04/29/us-usa-sexcrimes-idUSBREA3S01I20140429; Libby Sander, "The White House Raises the Bar for Colleges' Handling of Sexual Assault," *Chronicle of Higher Education,* April 29, 2014, http://chronicle.com/article/White-House-Raises-the-Bar-for/146255/.

108. Robin Wilson, "In Sex-Harassment Cases, No One is Happy with Colleges' Response," *Chronicle of Higher Education,* May 12, 2014, http://chronicle.com/article/In-Sex-Harassment-Cases-No/146491/.

109. Jennifer Steinhauer, "Behind Focus on College Assaults, a Steady Drumbeat by Students," *New York Times,* April 29, 2014, http://www.nytimes.com/2014/04/30/us/sexual-assault-on-university-campuses.html.

110. Jonah Newman and Libby Sander, "Promise Unfulfilled?" *Chronicle of Higher Education,* April 30, 2014, http://chronicle.com/article/Promise-Unfulfilled-/146299/.

111. Bok, *Universities,* 100–101.

8. GENDER

1. Kenneth Chang, "Bias Persists for Women of Science, a Study Finds," *New York Times,* September 24, 2012, http://www.nytimes.com/2012/09/25/science/bias-persists-against-women-of-science-a-study-says.htm.

2. Walt Bogdanich, "Reporting Rape, and Wishing She Hadn't: How One College Handled a Sexual Assault Complaint," *New York Times,* July 13, 2014, http://www.nytimes.com/2014/07/13/us/how-one-college-handled-a-sexual-assault-complaint.html.

3. "Education," *Take Back the Night,* http://takebackthenight.org/education/.

4. "About Take Back the Night," *Take Bake the Night,* http://takebackthenight.org/about-tbtn/. Their board members are at the University of Virginia, University of South Florida, Columbia University, Cornell University, Massachusetts Institute of Technology, University of Illinois at Chicago, James Madison University, University of Mary Washington, Merrimack College, Stevenson University, and North Illinois University.

5. Billie Wright Dzeich and Linda Weiner, *The Lecherous Professor: Sexual Harassment on Campus,* 2nd ed. (Chicago: University of Illinois Press, 1990).

6. Ibid., xxvii.

7. Courtney Letherman, "Key Feminist Scholar Recounts Facing Charges of Sex Harassment: Jane Gallop's Frank Book Attacks Policies That Limit Relationships between Professors and Their Student," *Chronicle of Higher Education,* March 7, 1997, http://chronicle.com/article/Key-Feminist-Scholar-Recounts/76078/.

8. Lyn Farley, *Sexual Shakedown: The Sexual Harassment of Women on the Job* (New York: McGraw Hill, 1978); Catherine MacKinnon, *Sexual Harassment of Working Women: A Case of Sex Discrimination* (New Haven: Yale University Press, 1979). Roughly concurrent with *Lecherous Professor,* Barbara Gutek, *Sex and the Workplace: The Impact of Sexual Behavior and Harassment on Men, Women, and Organizations* (San Francisco: Jossey-Bass, 1985).

9. Michele A. Paludi, ed., *Ivory Power: Sexual Harassment on Campus* (Albany: State University of New York Press, 1990); Michele A. Paludi, *Sexual Harassment on College Campuses: Abusing The Ivory Power* (Albany: State University of New York Press, 1996).

10. Bernice R. Sandler and Robert J. Shoop, eds., *Sexual Harassment on Campus: A Guide for Administrators, Faculty, and Students* (Boston: Allyn & Bacon, 1997); Virginia L. Stamler and Gerald L. Stone, *Faculty-Student Sexual Involvement: Issues and Interventions* (Thousand Oaks, CA: Sage, 1998); Allen Ottens and Kathy Hotelling, *Sexual Violence on Campus: Policies, Programs and Perspectives* (New York: Springer Publishing Company, 2000).

11. Martin Schwartz and Walter S. DeKeseredy, *Sexual Assault on the College Campus: The Role of Male Peer Support* (Thousand Oaks, CA: Sage, 1997).

12. Leslie Pickering Francis, *Sexual Harassment as an Ethical Issue in Academic Life* (Lanham, MD: Rowman & Littlefield, 2000).

13. Judith Glazer Raymo, "Sexual Harassment as an Ethical Issue in Academic Life," *Journal of Higher Education* 73, no. 5 (2002): 674.

14. Bonnie Fisher, Leah Daigle, and Francis Cullen, *Unsafe in the Ivory Tower: The Sexual Victimization of College Women* (Thousand Oaks, CA: Sage, 2010).

15. Dzeich and Weiner, *The Lecherous Professor,* xxvii.

16. George Will, "Colleges Become the Victims of Progressivism," *The Washington Post,* June 6, 2014, http://www.washingtonpost.com/opinions/george-will-college-become-the-victims-of-progressivism/2014/06/06/e90e73b4-eb50-11e3-9f5c-9075d5508f0a_story.html.

17. Hadas Gold, "George Will Slammed for Sexual Assault Column," *Politico,* June 10, 2014, http://www.politico.com/blogs/media/2014/06/george-will-slammed-for-sexual-assault-column-190088.html.

18. Katherine Mangan, "Tough Questions in Sexual-Harassment Cases: Suspension of U. of Houston Professor Raises Questions Echoed on Other Campuses," *Chronicle of Higher Education,* August 4, 1993, http://chronicle.com/article/Tough-Questions-in/73404/.

19. Billie Wright Dzeich, "The Bedeviling Issue of Sexual Harassment," *Chronicle of Higher Education,* http://chronicle.com/article/The-Bedeviling-Issue-of-Sexual/90245/.

20. Jess Bidgood, "At Wellesley, Debate over a Statue in Briefs," *New York Times,* February 6, 2014, http://www.nytimes.com/2014/02/07/arts/design/at-wellesley-debate-over-a-statue-in-briefs.html.

21. Now at the Davis, http://www.wellesley.edu/davismuseum/whats-on/current/node/40702.

22. "Move the 'Sleepwalker' Inside the Davis Museum," https://www.change.org/petitions/president-h-kim-bottomly-move-the-sleepwalker-inside-the-davis-museum.

23. Tom Finneran, "The Whiny Women of Wellesley," *GoLocal Worcester.com,* February 14, 2014, http://www.golocalworcester.com/politics/tom-finneran-the-whiny-women-of-wellesley/.

24. Lenore Skenazy, "Fear and Loathing at Wellesley: A Life-Like Statue of a Guy Sleepwalking in His Underwear Awakens a Protest by Campus Feminists," *Wall Street Journal,* February 11, 2014, http://online.wsj.com/news/articles/SB10001424052702304558804579376793890614128.

25. "Wall Street Journal Publishes Letter from President Bottomly," Wellesley College, February 20, 2014, http://www.wellesley.edu/news/2014/02/node/42411.

26. Bidgood, "At Wellesley."

27. Jaclyn Reiss, "Realistic Statue of Man in His Underwear at Wellesley College Sparks Controversy," *Boston Globe,* February 5, 2014, http://www.boston.com/yourcampus/news/wellesley/2014/02/realistic_statue_of_man_in_his_underwear_at_wellesley_college_sparks_controversy.html.

28. Roberta M. Hall and Bernice R. Sandler, *The Campus Climate: A Chilly One for Women?* (Washington, D.C.: Project on the Status and Education of Women, Association of American Colleges, 1982); Roberta M. Hall and Bernice R. Sandler, *Out of the Classroom: A Chilly Campus Climate for Women?* (Washington, D.C.: Project on the Status and Education of Women, Association of American Colleges, 1984); Bernice R. Sandler and Roberta M. Hall, *The Campus Climate Revisited: Chilly for Women Faculty, Administrators, and Graduate Students* (Washington, D.C.: Project on the Status and Education of Women, Association of American Colleges, 1986).

29. Jennifer Freyd and J. Q. Johnson, "References on Chilly Climate for Women Faculty in Academe," http://dynamic.uoregon.edu/jjf/chillyclimate.html#ReportsStudentEval.

30. Annemarie Vaccaro, "Still Chilly in 2010: Campus Climates for Women," *Association of American Colleges and Universities* 39, no. 2 (2010), http://www.aacu.org/ocww/volume39_2/feature.cfm?section=1; Hall and Sandler, *Out of the Classroom.*

31. Annemarie Vaccaro, "Third Wave Feminist Undergraduates: Avoiding Ivory Tower Bureaucracy by Fighting for Social Justice Off Campus," *Journal about Women in Higher Education* 2 (2009): 1–25.

32. Annemarie Vaccaro, "What Lies Beneath Seemingly Positive Campus Climate Results: Institutional Sexism, Symbolic Racism, and Male Hostility toward Equity Initiatives," *Journal of Equity and Excellence in Education* 43, no. 2 (2010): 205.

33. C. T. Liang and C. Alimo, "The Impact of White Heterosexual Students' Interactions on Attitudes toward Lesbian, Gay and Bisexual People: A Longitudinal Study," *Journal of College Student Development* 46, no. 3 (2005): 237–250; Xavier Zúniga, X. E. Williams, and J. Berger, "Action-Oriented Democratic Outcomes: The Impact of Student Involvement with Campus Diversity," *Journal of College Student Development* 46, no. 6 (2005): 660–678.

34. Vaccaro, "What Lies Beneath," 205–206.

35. Ibid., 213.

36. Mary F. Howard-Hamilton, Carla L. Morelon-Quainoo, Susan D. Johnson, Rachelle Winkle-Wagner, and Lilia Santiague, eds., *Standing on the Outside Looking In: Underrepresented Students' Experiences in Advanced Degree Programs* (Sterling, VA: Stylus, 2009).

37. Oiyan Poon and Shirley Hune, "Countering Master Narratives of the 'Perpetual Foreigner' and 'Model Minority,'" ed. Mary Howard-Hamilton, et al., *Standing on the Outside Looking In: Underrepresented Students' Experiences in Advanced Degree Programs* (Sterling, VA: Stylus, 2009), 82–102.

38. Juan Carlos González, "Latinas in Doctoral and Professional Programs: Similarities and Differences in Support Systems and Challenges," ed. Mary Howard-Hamilton, et al., *Standing on the Outside Looking In: Underrepresented Students' Experiences in Advanced Degree Programs* (Sterling, VA: Stylus, 2009), 103–123.

39. Venice Sulé, *Black Female Faculty and Professional Socialization: Constraints, Enablements and Enactments* (Ann Arbor, MI: Proquest, 2008). See also Christine Stanley, *Faculty of Color: Teaching in Predominantly White Colleges and Universities* (Bolton, MA: Anker, 2006); Kerry Ann Rockquemore and Tracey A. Laszloffy, *The Black Academic's Guide to Winning Tenure without Losing Your Soul* (Boulder, CO: Lynne Rienner, 2008).

40. Venice Sulé, "Oppositional Stances of Black Female Graduate Students," ed. Mary Howard-Hamilton, et al., *Standing on the Outside Looking In: Underrepresented Students' Experiences in Advanced Degree Programs* (Sterling, VA: Stylus, 2009), 147–168.

41. Diane Dean, Susan Bracken, and Jeanie Allen, eds., *Women in Academic Leadership: Professional Strategies and Personal Choices* (Sterling, VA: Stylus, 2009).

42. Claire Van Ummersen, "Foreword," eds. Diane Dean, Susan Bracken, and Jeanie Allen, *Women in Academic Leadership: Professional Strategies and Personal Choices* (Sterling, VA: Stylus, 2009), ix.

43. Ibid.

44. Ibid., x.

45. Caroline Sotello Viernes Turner and Janelle Kappes, "Preparing Women of Color for Leadership: Perspectives on the American Council on Educa-

tion Fellows Program," eds. Dean, Bracken, and Allen, *Women in Academic Leadership*, 149–170.

46. Yolanda Moses, "Advice from the Field: Guiding Women of Color to Academic Leadership," eds. Dean, Bracken, and Allen, *Women in Academic Leadership*, 181–207.

47. Vaccaro, "Still Chilly"; see Susan Rankin, Genevieve Weber, Warren Blumenfeld, and Somjen Frazer, *State of Higher Education for Lesbian, Gay, Bisexual, and Transgender People* (Charlotte, NC: Campus Pride, 2010).

48. Vaccaro, "Still Chilly"; see Wendy Geiger, Jake Harwood, and Mary Lee Hummert, "College Students' Multiple Stereotypes of Lesbians," *Journal of Homosexuality* 51, no. 3 (2006): 165–182.

49. Andrew Nichols and Stephen John Quaye, "Beyond Accommodation: Removing Barriers to Academic and Social Engagement for Students with Disabilities," Shaun R. Harper and Stephen John Quaye, ed., *Student Engagement in Higher Education: Theoretical Perspectives and Practical Approaches for Diverse Populations* (New York: Routledge, 2009), 39–60.

50. Rosemarie Garland-Thompson, "Integrating Disability, Transforming Feminist Theory," Lennard J. Davis, ed., *The Disability Studies Reader* (New York: Routledge, 2006), 257–274.

51. "Race, Ethnicity, and Gender of Students at More than 1,500 Institutions," *Chronicle of Higher Education*, November 2, 2012, B36.

52. Katherine Mangan, "Despite Efforts to Close Gender Gaps, Some Disciplines Remain Lopsided," *Chronicle of Higher Education*, B4.

53. Reports from the United Kingdom resemble those here. Luke Brunning, "Unfortunately Academic Sexism Is Alive and Well," *The Independent*, June 25, 2013, http://www.independent.co.uk/student/news/unfortunately-academic-sexism-is-alive-and-well-8667136.html; Naomi Alderman, "The Sexist Spires of Oxford University? Oxford University Has Had a Reputation for Sexist Behaviour and Attitudes, and While Things Have Certainly Changed, There's Still Room for Improvement," *The Guardian*, April 19, 2010, http://www.theguardian.com/education/2010/apr/20/oxford-university-women-sexism.

54. Mangan, "Despite Efforts," B4.

55. Katherine Mangan, "In the Humanities, Men Dominate the Fields of Philosophy and History," *Chronicle of Higher Education*, B5.

56. Marlene Zuk and Sheila O'Rourke, "Is Biology Just Another Pink-Collar Profession?" *Chronicle of Higher Education*, 20. See also the discussion by a variety of administrators of science, technology, engineering, and mathematics programs asking "Why STEM fields Still Don't Draw More Women," *Chronicle of Higher Education*, B24–27.

57. Marc Bousquet, "Lady Academe and Labor-Market Segmentation: The Narrative of Women's Success via Higher Educations Rests on a House of Cards," *Chronicle of Higher Education,* B19.

58. Marc Bousquet, *How the University Works: Higher Education and the Low Wage Nation* (New York: New York University Press, 2008).

59. Bousquet, "Lady Academe," B20.

60. Geoff Brumfiel, "Data show extent of sexism in physics," *Nature,* April 30, 2008, http://www.nature.com/news/2008/080423/full/452918a.html -cor1.

61. "Where Particles Collide, Sexism Is Rampant, Study Finds," *Chronicle of Higher Education,* April 24, 2008, http://chronicle.com/article/Where-Particles-Collide/40863/.

62. Heather Joslyn, "Women and Minorities Lag in Appointments to Top Fund-Raising Jobs," *Chronicle of Higher Education,* September 6, 2010, http://philanthropy.com/article/WomenMinorities-Lag-in/124249/.

63. The story is reported by Barres in an interview with him in *Nature:* http://www.nature.com/nature/podcast/v442/n7099/nature-2006-07-13.html.

64. Dan Berrett, "An Unwanted Consequence," *Inside Higher Ed,* March 25, 2011, http://www.insidehighered.com/news/2011/03/25/female_college_professors_still_find_bias_despite_gains.

65. *A Report on the Status of Women Faculty in the Schools of Science and Engineering at MIT, 2011,* MIT Press, http://web.mit.edu/newsoffice/images/documents/women-report-2011.pdf.

66. Chang, "Bias Persists."

67. Corinne Moss-Racusin, John Dovidio, Victoria Brescoli, Mark Graham, and Jo Handelsman, "Science Faculty's Subtle Gender Biases Favor Male Students," *Proceedings of the National Academy of the Sciences (PNAS)* 109, no. 41 (2012) 16474, http://www.pnas.org/content/109/41/16474.

68. Ibid.

69. Chang, "Bias Persists."

70. Moss-Racusin, et al., "Science Faculty's."

71. Ibid.

72. Chang, "Bias Persists."

73. Robin Wilson, "Scholarly Publishing's Gender Gap: Women Cluster in Certain Fields, According to a Study of Millions of Journal Articles, While Men Get More Credit," *Chronicle of Higher Education,* October 22, 2012, http://chronicle.com/article/The-Hard-Numbers-Behind/135236/. Wilson quoted Jennifer Jacquet, who noted, "The lab is like visiting a fraternity."

74. Ernesto Reuben, Paola Sapienza, and Luigi Zingales, "How Stereotypes Impair Women's Careers in Science," *Proceedings of the National Academy of the Sciences (PNAS)* 111, no. 12 (2014): 4403–4408.

75. Sharona E. Gordon, "Getting Nowhere Fast: The Lack of Gender Equity in the Physiology Community," *Journal of General Physiology* 144, no. 1 (2014): 1.

76. Ibid., 2.

77. Ibid., 3.

78. Erin Cech et al., "Professional Role Confidence and Gendered Persistence in Engineering," *American Sociological Review* 76, no. 5 (2011): 641–666, http://asr.sagepub.com/content/76/5/641.abstract.

79. Erica Perez, "Female Engineering Majors Struggle with Confidence Issues," *California Watch*, October 28, 2011, http://californiawatch.org/dailyreport/female-engineering-majors-struggle-confidence-issues-13307.

80. Erica Perez, "Cal Engineering School to Address Sexism," *California Watch*, November 11, 2011, http://californiawatch.org/dailyreport/cal-engineering-school-address-sexism-13525.

81. Kristen Renwick Monroe and William F. Chiu, "Gender Equality in the Academy: The Pipeline Problem," *PS: Political Science and Politics* 43, no. 2 (2010): 303.

82. Ibid., 305.

83. Ibid., 306.

84. Ibid.

85. Ibid., 304.

86. See other data that suggests it still might be more time: Allison K. Shaw and Daniel E. Stanton, "Leaks in the Pipeline: Separating Demographic Inertia from Ongoing Gender Differences in Academia," *Proceedings of the Royal Society, Biological Sciences* 279 (2012): 3736–3741.

87. NORC at the University of Chicago Conducts the Doctorate Recipients Survey in both the sciences and the humanities: http://www.norc.org/Research/Projects/Pages/survey-of-doctorate-recipients-.aspx.

88. Mary Ann Mason and Marc Goulden, "Do Babies Matter?" *Academe* 88, no. 6 (2002): 21–28.

89. Mary Ann Mason and Marc Goulden, "Do Babies Matter (Part II)? Closing the Baby Gap," *Academe* 90, no. 6 (2004): 11, http://www.uri.edu/advance/files/pdf/Do_Babies_Matter(II).pdf.

90. Ibid., 12.

91. Ibid., 16.

92. Ibid., 17.

93. Mary Ann Mason, Nicholas Wolfinger, and Marc Goulden, *Do Babies Matter? Gender and Family in the Ivory Tower* (New Brunswick, NJ: Rutgers University Press, 2013).

94. Colleen Flaherty, "The Mom Penalty," *Inside Higher Ed,* June 6, 2013, http://www.insidehighered.com/news/2013/06/06/new-book-gender-family-

and-academe-shows-how-kids-affect-careers-higher-education-ixzz38biXQMYB.

95. Nicholas Wolfinger, Mary Ann Mason, and Marc Goulden, "Alone in the Ivory Tower: How Birth Events Vary Among Fast-Track Professionals," *Population Association of America,* April 17, 2008, http://paa2008.princeton.edu/papers/81253.

96. Robin Wilson, "Bye, Bye Baby: Why Doctors and Lawyers Out-Reproduce Professors," *Chronicle of Higher Education,* April 17, 2008, http://chronicle.com/article/Bye-Bye-Baby-Why-Doctors-and/40827/; Scott Jaschik, "Does Academe Hinder Parenthood?" *Inside Higher Ed,* May 23, 2008, http://www.insidehighered.com/news/2008/05/23/nokids -sthash.NW4QH8F5.dpbs.

97. Report of the Steering Committee on Undergraduate Women's Leadership, *Princeton University Reports,* http://www.princeton.edu/reports/2011/leadership/. See also the campus study by Duke University's Women's Initiative 2002–2003, http://universitywomen.stanford.edu/reports/WomensInitiativeReport.pdf.

9. DIVERSITY AND RACE

1. Scott Jaschik, "Backwards on Racial Understanding," *Inside Higher Ed,* April 10, 2012, https://www.insidehighered.com/news/2012/04/10/study-suggests-students-grow-less-interested-promoting-racial-understanding.

2. Nick DeSantis, "Women Are Still Underrepresented as Medical-School Deans, Study Finds," *Chronicle of Higher Education,* June 28, 2012, http://chronicle.com/blogs/ticker/women-are-still-underrepresented-as-medical school-deans-study-finds/45007.

3. Nina Niu, et al., "The Impact of Cross-Cultural Interactions on Medical Students' Preparedness to Care for Diverse Patients," *Academic Medicine* 87, no. 11 (2012): 1530–1534, http://journals.lww.com/academicmedicine/Fulltext/2012/11000/The_Impact_of_Cross_Cultural_Interactions_on.36.aspx.

4. Marc Nivet, "Commentary: Diversity and Inclusion in the 21st Century: Bridging the Moral and Excellence Imperatives," *Academic Medicine* 87, no. 11 (2012): 1458–1460, http://journals.lww.com/academicmedicine/Fulltext/2012/11000/Commentary___Diversity_and_Inclusion_in_the_21st.10.aspx.

5. Ibid.

6. Daryl G. Smith, "The Diversity Imperative: Moving to the Next Generation," ed. Philip Altbach, et al., *American Higher Education in the Twenty-First Century* (Baltimore: Johns Hopkins, 2005): 465. See also Smith's *Diversity's Promise for Higher Education: Making it Work* (Baltimore: Johns Hopkins University Press, 2009).

7. Smith, "The Diversity Imperative," 471.

8. Ibid., 481.

9. "Women at the Top of Academe," *New York Times,* September 4, 2001, http://www.nytimes.com/2001/09/04/opinion/women-at-the-top-of-academe.html; similarly see Kit Lively, "Diversity Increases Among Presidents," *Chronicle of Higher Education,* September 15, 2000, http://chronicle.com/article/Diversity-Increases-Among/13046/.

10. Jack Stripling, "Simmons to Step Down as President of Brown U," *Chronicle of Higher Education,* September 15, 2011, http://chronicle.com/article/Simmons-to-Step-Down-as-Brown/129043/.

11. Tamar Lewin, "M.I.T. President Resigns; Was First Woman in the Job," *New York Times,* February 17, 2012, http://www.nytimes.com/2012/02/17/education/mit-president-resigns-was-first-woman-in-the-job.html.

12. Ariel Kaminer, "Princeton President Announces She Will Step Down," *New York Times,* September 22, 2012, http://www.nytimes.com/2012/09/23/education/shirley-tilghman-princeton-president-says-she-will-step-down.html.

13. American Council on Education, "Leading Demographic Portrait of College Presidents Reveals Ongoing Challenges in Diversity, Aging," March 12, 2012, http://www.acenet.edu/news-room/Pages/ACPS-Release-2012.aspx; Jack Stripling, "Survey Finds a Drop in Minority Presidents Leading Colleges," *Chronicle of Higher Education,* March 12, 2012, http://chronicle.com/article/Who-Are-College-Presidents-/131138/.

14. Jesse Rude, Gregory C. Wolniak, and Ernest T. Pascarella, "Racial Attitude Change during the College Years," for the 2012 Annual Meeting of the American Educational Research Association (AERA) in Vancouver, British Columbia, http://www.education.uiowa.edu/docs/default-source/crue-publications/Racial_Attitude_Change_during_the_College_Years_AERA_2012.pdf?sfvrsn=0.

15. Jaschik, "Backwards on Racial Understanding."

16. Ibid.

17. Rude et al., quoted in Jaschik, "Backwards on Racial Understanding."

18. Ernest T. Pascarella, Marcia Edison, Amaury Nora, Linda Serra Hagedorn, and Patrick T. Terenzini, "Influences on Students' Openness to Diversity and Challenge in the First Year of College," *Journal of Higher Education* 67, no. 2 (1996): 174–195.

19. Ibid., 184.

20. Pascarella et al., "Influences on Students' Openness." There's a fair amount of writing on blacks in fraternities and black fraternities. See Ricky Jones, *Black Haze: Violence, Sacrifice, and Manhood in Black Greek-Letter Fraternities* (Albany: State University of New York Press, 2004); Ricky Jones, "Examining Violence in Black Fraternity Pledging," ed. Hank Nuwer, *The*

Hazing Reader (Bloomington: Indiana University Press, 2004), 110–129; D. Jason DeSousa, Michael Gordon, and Walter Kimbrough, "Pledging and Hazing in African American Fraternities and Sororities," ed. Hank Nuwer, *The Hazing Reader* (Bloomington: Indiana University Press, 2004); Walter Kimbrough, "The Hazing Problem at Black Fraternities: Black Fraternities Face Different Challenges Than White Ones—But Both Groups Can Be Corrupted by Twisted Power Dynamics," *The Atlantic Monthly,* March 17, 2014, http://www.theatlantic.com/education/archive/2014/03/the-hazing-problem-at-black-fraternities/284452/.

21. Pascarella et al., "Influences on Students' Openness," 190–191.

22. Pascarella et al., "Influences on Students' Openness," 189.

23. Sylvia Hurtado, Jeffrey Milem, Alma Clayton-Pedersen, and Walter Allen, "Enacting Diverse Learning Environments: Improving the Climate for Racial/Ethnic Diversity in Higher Education," *ASHE-ERIC Higher Education Report* 26, no. 8 (1999), http://files.eric.ed.gov/fulltext/ED430514.pdf. They eventually published the study as a book with the same name with Jossey-Bass in Hoboken, 1999.

24. Ibid., 6–7.

25. United States Census Bureau, "U.S. Census Bureau Projections Show a Slower Growing, Older, More Diverse Nation a Half Century from Now," December 12, 2012, http://www.census.gov/newsroom/releases/archives/population/cb12-243.html.

26. Institute of International Education, "Open Doors 2011: International Student Enrollment Increased by 5 Percent in 2010/11," November 14, 2011, http://www.iie.org/en/Who-We-Are/News-and-Events/Press-Center/Press-Releases/2011/2011-11-14-Open-Doors-International-Students.

27. Jenny Lee and Charles Rice, "Welcome to America? International Student Perceptions of Discrimination," *Higher Education* 53 (2007): 381.

28. Ibid., 405.

29. Ibid., 406.

30. Elizabeth Redden, "I'm Not Racist, but. . ." *Inside Higher Education,* October 16, 2012, http://www.insidehighered.com/news/2012/10/16/tensions-simmer-between-american-and-international-students-sthash.BVIwYbCw.dpbs.

31. "Many International Students Have Few Close American Friends, Survey Says," National Communication Association, June 14, 2012, http://www.newswise.com/articles/many-international-students-have-few-close-american-friends-survey-says.

32. Elisabeth Gareis, "Intercultural Friendship: Effects of Home and Host Region," *Journal of International and Intercultural Communication* 5, no. 4 (2012): 324.

33. Philip G. Altbach, "The Volatility of International Student Flows," *Inside Higher Ed,* February 4, 2014, https://www.insidehighered.com/blogs/world-view/volatility-international-student-flows.

34. Zach Ritter, "Foreign Students and Tolerance-II," *Inside Higher Ed,* October 26, 2012, http://www.insidehighered.com/views/2012/10/26/essay-deadling-racist-ideas-international-students-sthash.ihFFlGla.LngCGBHZ.dpbs.

35. Derek Bok, "How to Teach," *Higher Education in America* (Princeton: Princeton University Press, 2013), 187.

36. See James Anderson, *The Education of Blacks in the South 1860–1935* (Chapel Hill: University of North Carolina, 1988).

37. William Watkins, *The White Architects of Black Education: Ideology and Power in America, 1865–1954* (New York: Teachers College Press, 2001).

38. Oberlin, "Early History," http://new.oberlin.edu/about/history.dot.

39. Oberlin, "Association of African Ancestry," http://new.oberlin.edu/office/alumni-affiliate-groups/association-of-african-ancestry.dot.

40. Stephen Provasnik, Linda L. Shafer, and Thomas D. Snyder, *Historically Black Colleges and Universities, 1976 to 2001,* National Center for Education Statistics, NCES 2004–062 (Washington, D.C.: U.S. Department of Education, 2004).

41. Hannah Purnell, "The History of Historically Black Colleges and Universities: A Tradition Rich in History," http://www.collegeview.com/articles/article/the-history-of-historically-black-colleges-and-universities. See also *White House Initiative on Historically Black Colleges and Universities,* http://www.ed.gov/edblogs/whhbcu/.

42. The debate began with the findings of the National Study of Black College Students that polled over four thousand students at eight historically Black and eight predominantly white universities. See Walter Allen's work, especially with E. G. Epps and N. Z. Haniff, eds., *College in Black and White: African American Students in Predominantly White and in Historically Black Public Universities* (Albany: State University Press, 1991) and his much quoted "The Color of Success: African-American College Student Outcomes at Predominantly White and Historically Black Public Colleges and Universities," *Harvard Educational Review* 62, no. 1 (1992): 26–45. See also Lemuel Watson and George Kuh, "The Influence of Dominant Race Environments on Student Involvement, Perceptions, and Educational Gains: A Look at Historically Black and Predominantly White Liberal Arts Institutions," *Journal of College Student Development* 37, no. 4 (1996): 415–424; Mikyong Minsun Kim, "Historically Black vs. White Institutions: Academic Development among Black Students," *The Review of Higher Education* 25, no. 4 (2002): 385–407.

43. For the language of white supremacy capturing better the environment of US culture than white privilege, see Edouardo Bonilla-Silva, *White Supremacy and Racism in the Post-Civil Rights Era* (Boulder: Lynne Rienner, 2001); Chip Smith, *The Cost of Privilege: Taking on the System of White Supremacy and Racism* (Rocky Mount, NC: Camino Press, 2007); Douglas Massey and Nancy Denton, *American Apartheid: Segregation and the Making of the Underclass* (Cambridge, MA: Harvard University Press, 1998); David Freund, *Colored Property: State Policy and White Racial Politics in Suburban America* (Chicago: University of Chicago Press, 2010); Michelle Alexander, *The New Jim Crow: Mass Incarceration in the Age of Colorblindness* (New York: New Press, 2012). See also Eric Foner, *Reconstruction* (New York: Harper, 2002); Edmund Morgan, *American Freedom, American Slavery* (New York: W. W. Norton, 2003). Special thanks here to Katie Grimes.

44. David Gillborn, "Rethinking White Supremacy: Who Counts in 'White World,'" *Ethnicities* 6, no. 3 (2006): 318.

45. M. Shawn Copeland, *Enfleshing Freedom: Body, Race and Being* (Minneapolis: Fortress Press, 2010), 2–4.

46. Bryan Massingale, *Racial Justice and the Catholic Church* (Maryknoll, NY: Orbis Books, 2010); see also his "The Systemic Erasure of the Black/Dark-Skinned Body in Catholic Ethics," ed. James F. Keenan, *Catholic Theological Ethics, Past, Present, and Future: The Trento Conference* (Maryknoll, NY: Orbis, 2011), 116–123. See also the argument that attention to racial difference as a social perspective might get us to a richer notion of the way we can form societies, Ki Joo Choi, "Should Race Matter? A Constructive Ethical Assessment of the Postracial Ideal," *Journal of the Society of Christian Ethics* 31, no. 1 (2011): 103–122.

47. "Slavery and Justice: A Report of the Brown University Steering Committee on Slavery and Justice," http://www.brown.edu/Research/Slavery_Justice/documents/SlaveryAndJustice.pdf.

48. See Ruth Simmons, "Facing Up to Our Ties to Slavery," *Boston Globe,* April 28, 2004. That statement, as well as the president's original charge to the committee, are available at http://www.brown.edu/slaveryjustice.

49. National Public Radio: "How Slavery Shaped Our Oldest and Most Elite Colleges" [Interview with Craig Steven Wilder], September 17, 2013, http://www.npr.org/blogs/codeswitch/2013/09/17/223420533/how-slavery-shaped-americas-oldest-and-most-elite-colleges.

50. Craig Steven Wilder, *Ebony & Ivy: Race, Slavery, and the Troubled History of America's Universities* (New York: Bloomsbury Press, 2013), 11.

51. For an informative read on how social justice could call American faculties to understand better the invitation to diversity, see Sara Ahmed's *On Being*

Included: Racism and Diversity in Institutional Life (Chapel Hill: Duke University, 2012).

52. Gloria Gadsen, "A Minority Report," *Chronicle of Higher Education,* October 24, 2008, http://chronicle.com/article/Minority-Report/4102/.

53. Gabriella Gutiérrez y Muhs, Yolanda Flores Niemann, et al., eds., *Presumed Incompetent: The Intersections for Race and Class for Women in Academia* (Salt Lake City: University of Utah Press, 2012).

54. "Administrative Diversity at the Ivies," *Chronicle of Higher Education,* June 9, 2013, http://chronicle.com/article/Administrative-Diversity-at/139701/.

55. Stacey Patton, "At the Ivies, It's Still White at the Top," *Chronicle of Higher Education,* June 9, 2013, http://chronicle.com/article/At-the-Ivies-Its-Still-White/139643/.

56. See Kerry Ann Rockquemore and Tracey Laszloffy, *The Black Academic's Guide to Winning Tenure Without Losing Your Soul* (Boulder: Lynne Rienner Publishers, 2008).

10. COMMODIFICATION

1. Mary Kupiec Cayton, "The Commodification of Wisdom," *Chronicle of Higher Education,* July 13, 2007, http://chronicle.com/article/The-Commodification-of-Wisdom/12006/.

2. Ibid.

3. Hans Radder, ed., *The Commodification of Academic Research: Science and the Modern University* (Pittsburgh: University of Pittsburgh Press, 2010).

4. Scott Jaschik, "Commodification of Academic Research," *Inside Higher Education,* October 25, 2010, http://www.insidehighered.com/news/2010/10/25/radder.

5. bzemsky bzemsky, "The Rise of Market Competition Part II," *Chronicle of Higher Education,* February 22, 2008, http://chronicle.com/blogs/brainstorm/the-rise-of-market-competition-part-ii/5723.

6. Richard Vedder, *Going Broke by Degree: Why College Costs Too Much* (Lanham, MD: AEI Press, 2004).

7. bzemsky, "The Rise of Market Competition."

8. Carlos J. Alonso, "Paradise Lost: The Academy Becomes a Commodity," *Chronicle of Higher Education,* December 12, 2010, http://chronicle.com/article/Paradise-Lost-the-Academy-as/125669/.

9. Ibid.

10. Margaret Radin, *Contested Commodities: The Trouble with Trade in Sex, Children, Body Parts, and Other Things* (Cambridge, MA: Harvard University Press, 1996).

11. Margaret Jane Radin and Madhavi Sunder, "The Subject and Object of Commodification," *UC Davis Law, Legal Studies Research Paper No. 16; Stanford Public Law Working Paper No. 97* (September 27, 2004), http://papers. ssrn.com/sol3/papers.cfm?abstract_id=582641.

12. Ibid., 6.

13. Ibid., 2.

14. Ibid., 2.

15. Michael Sandel, *What Money Can't Buy: The Moral Limits of Markets* (New York: Farrar, Straus and Giroux, 2012).

16. Debra Satz, *Why Some Things Should Not Be for Sale: The Moral Limits of the Market* (New York: Oxford University Press, 2012).

17. Ibid., 3.

18. Ibid.

19. Ibid., 4.

20. Ibid., 5.

21. George Keller, *Academic Strategy: The Management Revolution in American Higher Education* (Baltimore: Johns Hopkins University Press, 1983), 3.

22. Wilfred McClay, "George Keller: Intellectual Whirlwind," *Chronicle of Higher Education*, November 23, 2007, http://chronicle.com/article/George-Keller-Intellectual/26941/.

23. George Keller, *Transforming a College: The Story of a Little-Known College's Strategic Climb to National Distinction* (Baltimore: Johns Hopkins University Press, 2004; new edition, 2014).

24. "The Human Touch of George Keller," *Chronicle of Higher Education*, December 14, 2007, http://chronicle.com/article/The-Human-Touch-of-George/30443/.

25. James Doti, "An Economist's Tools of the Trade," *Chronicle of Higher Education*, December 9, 2008, http://chronicle.com/article/An-Economists-Tools-of-the/45896/.

26. John Petillo, "Getting Our Priorities Straight in Higher Education," *Huffington Post*, November 20, 2013, http://www.huffingtonpost.com/john-petillo/getting-our-priorities-straight_b_4298242.html.

27. Ibid.

28. Raynard Kington, "Can You Apply 'Pay for Performance' to Higher Education?" *Huffington Post*, February 4, 2014, http://www.huffingtonpost. com/raynard-kington/can-you-apply-pay-for-performance_b_4717504.html.

29. Charlayne Hunter-Gault, "Hard Times at Howard U," *New York Times*, February 4, 2014, http://www.nytimes.com/2014/02/09/education/edlife/a-historically-black-college-is-rocked-by-the-economy-infighting-and-a-changing-demographic.html.

30. See Jerome Karabel, *The Chosen: The Hidden History of Admission and Exclusion at Harvard, Yale, and Princeton* (New York: Mariner Books, 2006).

31. Katherine Mangan, "Business Enrollments Boom at For-Profit Colleges," *Chronicle of Higher Education,* October 1, 1999, http://chronicle.com/article/Business-Enrollments-Boom-at/6390/.

32. Goldie Blumenstyk, "Lessons from For-Profit Institutions about Cutting College Costs," *Chronicle of Higher of Education,* June 5, 2008, http://chronicle.com/article/For-Profit-Colleges-Share/867/.

33. Goldie Blumenstyk, "For-Profit Institutions Under More Scrutiny," *Chronicle of Higher Education,* January 7, 2005, http://chronicle.com/article/For-Profit-Institutions-Under/19657/.

34. Eric Wills, "For Profit Job Claims Said to Be Inflated," *Chronicle of Higher Education,* July 15, 2005, http://chronicle.com/article/For-Profit-Job-Claims-Said-to/9646/.

35. Eric Wills, "2 States Investigate For-Profit Colleges," *Chronicle of Higher Education,* August 12, 2005, http://chronicle.com/article/2-States-Investigate/25836/.

36. Senate Health, Education, Labor and Pensions Committee, *Benefiting Whom? For-Profit Education Companies and the Growth of Military Education Benefits,* December 8, 2010, http://www.harkin.senate.gov/documents/pdf/4d01011f6076e.pdf.

37. Peter Wood, "For-Profit Colleges on the Brink," *Chronicle of Higher Education,* January 7, 2011, http://chronicle.com/blogs/innovations/for-profit-colleges-on-the-brink-part-2/28284.

38. Goldie Blumenstyk, "For-Profit Colleges' Lawsuit Accuses GAO of Malpractice," *Chronicle of Higher Education,* February 2, 2011, http://chronicle.com/blogs/ticker/for-profit-colleges-lawsuit-accuses-gao-of-malpractice/30189.

39. Goldie Blumenstyk, "First Report from Research Center Created by U. of Phoenix Attacks Critics of For-Profit Education," *Chronicle of Higher Education,* September 2, 2010, http://chronicle.com/article/First-Report-From-U-of/124231/.

40. Kelly Field, "Undercover Probe Finds Lax Academic Standards at Some For-Profit Colleges," *Chronicle of Higher Education,* November 22, 2011, http://chronicle.com/article/Undercover-Probe-Finds-Lax/129881/.

41. Frank Donoghue, "Who Goes to For-Profit Colleges?" *Chronicle of Higher Education,* June 27, 2011, http://chronicle.com/blogs/innovations/who-goes-to-for-profit-colleges/29725.

42. Dan Berret, "Graduates of For-Profits Lag behind Their Peers in Earnings and Employment, Study Finds," *Chronicle of Higher Education,* February 22, 2012, http://chronicle.com/article/Graduates-of-For-Profits-Lag/130900/.

43. Dan Berrett, "Graduates of For-Profit and Community Colleges Fare about the Same in Earnings Study," *Chronicle of Higher Education*, August 27, 2012, http://chronicle.com/article/Graduates-of-For-Profits-and/133968/.

44. Michael Stratford, "Senate Report Paints a Damning Portrait of For-Profit Higher Education," *Chronicle of Higher Education*, July 30, 2012, http://chronicle.com/article/A-Damning-Portrait-of/133253/.

45. Senate Health, Education, Labor and Pensions Committee, *For Profit Higher Education: The Failure to Safeguard the Federal Investment and Ensure Student Success*, July 29, 2012, http://www.help.senate.gov/imo/media/for_profit_report/Contents.pdf.

46. Stratford, "Senate Report."

47. http://www.help.senate.gov/imo/media/doc/8%205%2014%20Corinthian%20Letter.pdf

48. Goldie Blumenstyk, "Meet the New For-Profit: The Low-Profit," *Chronicle of Higher Education*, October 14, 2012, http://chronicle.com/article/Meet-the-New-For-Profit-the/135054.

49. Rick Ayers, "Education as a Commodity," *Huffington Post*, August 24, 2009, http://www.huffingtonpost.com/rick-ayers-/education-as-a commodity_b_266670.html; on a related note, after following one hundred students for eight years at Hamilton College, these authors sound a lot like Ayers, Daniel Chambliss and Christopher Takacs, *How College Works* (Cambridge: Harvard University Press, 2014).

50. Peter Scott, "'Student experience' Is the New Buzzword, but What Does It Mean?" *The Guardian*, February 3, 2014, http://www.theguardian.com/education/2014/feb/04/university-education-not-just-about-student-experience.

51. William Deresiewicz, *Excellent Sheep: The Miseducation of the American Elite and the Way to a Meaningful Life* (New York: Free Press, 2014).

52. William Deresiewicz, "Don't Send Your Kid to the Ivy League: The Nation's Top Colleges Are Turning Our Kids into Zombies," *The New Republic*, July 22, 2014, http://www.newrepublic.com/article/118747/ivy-league-schools-are-overrated-send-your-kids-elsewhere.

53. Martin Mulford shows how the PhD itself has been commodified and deprofessionalized by an industry that sells them but does not hire a person who gets one: "The Commodification and the Deprofessionalization of the Ph.D," *The American Historical Association*, February 2009, http://www.historians.org/publications-and-directories/perspectives-on-history/february-2009/the-commodification-and-deprofessionalization.

54. Josh Boldt, "First Year Commodity: The Adjunct Professor Labor Crisis in Composition Departments," *TheOrderofEducation.Com*, October 19, 2012,

http://www.orderofeducation.com/first-year-commodity-the-adjunct-professor-labor-crisis-in-composition-departments/.

55. Ibid.

56. Scott Carlson, "Administrator Hiring Drove 28% Boom in Higher-Ed Work Force, Report Says," *Chronicle of Higher Education,* February 5, 2014, http://chronicle.com/article/Administrator-Hiring-Drove-28-/144519/.

57. Jacob H. Rooksby, "Colleges Need Free Speech More Than Trademarks," *Chronicle of Higher Education,* February 24, 2014, http://chronicle.com/article/Colleges-Need-Free-Speech-More/144907/.

58. Jennifer Howard, "Some Associations, Scholars Protest Bill That Would Curb Public Access to Research," *Chronicle of Higher Education,* January 25, 2012, http://chronicle.com/blogs/wiredcampus/some-associations-scholars-protest-bill-that-would-curb-public-access-to-research/35166.

59. Colleen Flaherty, "Saving the Library," *Inside Higher Ed,* February 6, 2014, https://www.insidehighered.com/news/2014/02/06/faculty-win-fight-preserve-berkeley-libraries.

11. A CONCLUSION: CLASS, ATHLETICS, AND OTHER UNIVERSITY MATTERS

1. Nancy Hogshead-Makar, "Tie Money to Values," *Chronicle of Higher Education,* December 11, 2011, http://chronicle.com/article/NCAA-Nancy-Hogshead-Makar/130074/.

2. Among the most famous cases are the Robertson Foundation and Princeton University, "A Bitter End," *Chronicle of Philanthropy,* January 9, 2009; "Robertson vs. Princeton vs. Donor's Intent," *Chronicle of Philanthropy,* January 29, 2009, http://philanthropy.com/article/Robertson-vs-Princeton-vs/56664/; Steve Wieberg, "Pickens Understands UConn's Donor's Anger," *USA Today,* January 28, 2011, http://usatoday30.usatoday.com/sports/college/2011-01-27-pickens-burton-university-donors_N.htm.

3. "UCLA Professor Stirs Debate over $10 Million Law-School Gift," *Philanthropy Today,* August 23, 2011, http://philanthropy.com/blogs/philanthropytoday/ucla-professor-stirs-debate-over-10-million-law-school-gift/38891; "Columbia U Professor Sues over Use of Endowment Funds," *Philanthropy Today,* March 20, 2013, http://philanthropy.com/blogs/philanthropytoday/columbia-u-professor-sues-over-use-of-endowment-funds/64699.

4. "Dartmouth Investments with Trustees' Firms Stir Contention," *Philanthropy Today,* January 8, 2013, http://philanthropy.com/blogs/

philanthropytoday/dartmouth-investments-with-trustees-firms-stir-contention/60553.

5. "CASE Offers Perspectives on Ethical Decision-Making in Fundraising," http://www.case.org/Samples_Research_and_Tools/Ethics_Resources_and_Issues/Perspectives_on_Ethical_Decision-Making_in_Fundraising.html; see also the extensive bibliography on related legal questions concerning donors, "Institutional Advancement: Tainted Gifts, Reneging Donors, and Donor Control," *Lex Collegii* 28, no. 3 (2005): http://www.collegelegal.com/taint(spc-offer).pdf.

6. "President Obama Pushes More Economic Diversity in Higher Ed," *Education News,* January 19, 2014, www.educationnews.org/higher-education/president-obama-pushes-more-economic-diversity-in-higher-ed.

7. "Higher Education," The White House, http://www.whitehouse.gov/issues/education/higher-education.

8. Paul Basken, "White House Tries a New Tactic on Student Debt: Email Alerts," *Chronicle of Higher Education,* August 21, 2014, http://chronicle.com/article/White-House-Tries-a-New-Tactic/148441/.

9. "Number Of Americans Who Value College Education on the Rise," *Education News,* December 20, 2013; see more at http://www.educationnews.org/higher-education/more-american-believe-college-education-is-very-important.

10. Richard Pérez-Peña, "Despite Promises, Little Progress in Drawing Poor to Elite Colleges," *New York Times,* August 25, 2014,) http://www.nytimes.com/2014/08/26/education/despite-promises-little-progress-in-drawing-poor-to-elite-colleges.html.

11. Quoted in Pérez-Peña.

12. Quoted in Pérez-Peña.

13. Anthony P. Carnevale and Jeff Strohl, "Separate and Unequal: How Higher Education Reinforces the Intergenerational Reproduction of White Racial Privilege," *Georgetown University Public Policy Institute* (July 2013), https://georgetown.app.box.com/s/vjfxgz8tlxgwd10c5xn2.

14. Lynn Zinser, "Widening U.N.C. Scandal Prompts Independent Review," *New York Times,* August 17, 2012, http://thequad.blogs.nytimes.com/2012/08/17/widening-u-n-c-scandal-prompts-independent-review/; Brad Wolverton, "Alleged Academic Fraud at U. of North Carolina Tests NCAA's Reach," *Chronicle of Education,* September 7, 2012, http://chronicle.com/article/Alleged-Academic-Fraud-at-U/134270/.

15. "Notre Dame Investigating Four Players," *New York Times,* August 15, 2014, http://www.nytimes.com/2014/08/16/sports/ncaafootball/notre-dame-investigating-four-players.html; "The Gold and Blue Loses a Bit of Its Luster,"

New York Times, August 20, 2014, http://www.nytimes.com/2014/08/20/sports/ncaafootball/notre-dame-is-rocked-by-charges-of-academic-cheating.html.

16. Taylor Branch, *The Cartel: Inside the Rise and Imminent Fall of the NCAA* (Byliner, 2011); Taylor Branch, "The Shame of College Sports," *Atlantic Monthly,* October 2011, http://www.theatlantic.com/magazine/archive/2011/10/the-shame-of-college-sports/308643/.

17. Brad Wolverton, "Female Participation in College Sports Reaches All-Time High," *Chronicle of Higher Education,* January 22, 2012, http://chronicle.com/article/Female-Participation-in/130431/.

18. "Women in Intercollegiate Sport: A Longitudinal, National Study, 1977–2012," Smith College's Project on Women and Social Change and Brooklyn College of the City University of New York, http://acostacarpenter.org/AcostaCarpenter2012.pdf.

19. Brad Wolverton, "A Student Centered NCAA," *Chronicle of Higher Education,* October 14, 2012, http://chronicle.com/article/A-Student-Centered-NCAA/135062.

20. Brad Wolverton, "How Should Big-Time College Sports Change," *Chronicle of Higher Education,* February 10, 2014, http://chronicle.com/article/How-Should-Big-Time-College/144637/.

21. "What the Hell Has Happened to College Sports and What Should We Do About it," *Chronicle of Higher Education,* 2011, http://chronicle.com/article/What-Happened-to-College-Sports/130071.

22. Hogshead-Makar, "Tie Money to Values."

23. Frank Deford, "Bust the Amateur Myth," *Chronicle of Higher Education,* December 11, 2011, http://chronicle.com/article/NCAA-Frank-Deford/130058/.

24. Nathaniel Popper, "Committing to Play for a College, Then Starting 9th Grade," *New York Times,* January 26, 2014, http://www.nytimes.com/2014/01/27/sports/committing-to-play-for-a-college-then-starting-9th-grade.html.

INDEX

Abelard, Peter, 64
"Academic Corruption" (Kekes), 32
academic ethics, 18, 33, 68, 202;
    accountability in, 182; adjunct faculty
    in, 37–38; university ethics from,
    33–35, 206
*Academic Ethics: Problems and Materials
    on Professional Conduct and Shared
    Governance* (Hamilton, N.), 32
Academic Medicine, 149
academic publishing, 59
*Academic Strategy: The Management
    Revolution in American Higher
    Education* (Keller), 186
accountability: in academic ethics, 182;
    Alonso on culture of, 181; in
    commodification debate, 180–182;
    ethical, 4; in fiefdoms, 64; in ministry
    profession, 13, 15–16; in university
    ethics, 18
"Accrediting Agency Raises Questions
    about Chapel Hill's Compliance"
    (Young), 3
adjunct faculty, 7, 33, 66, 147, 173; in
    academic ethics, 37–38; AFT surveys
    of, 44–45, 46; Bok on, 38–39, 41; Boldt
    on commodification of, 199; caste
    system metaphor, 71–77; civil liberties
    of, 48; concerns of, 45; cost-cutting
    procedures affecting, 47–48; Delbanco
    on, 39; drug gang metaphor for, 69–71;

Eisenberg on CEO salaries and, 72;
    ethical proposal for, 53–55; Hacker
    and Dreifus on, 41; ignoring of, 39–40;
    lack of resources for, 46; as market
    issue, 47; NFM on, 52–53; as
    outsiders, 38–39; responses to
    conditions of, 50–53; rise of, 56;
    situation of, 46–49; solidarity among
    tenure-line and, 54–56; stories about,
    49–50; versus tenure in teaching,
    40–42; three preliminaries of, 39;
    university ethics in, 202–203;
    unsustainable construction of, 48;
    Wilson on, 60–61
Adjunct Project, 50, 51, 199
"The Adjunct's Moment of Truth"
    (Maisto), 52, 53
administrator, 73; cheating indifference
    of, 84; as feudal lord in fiefdom, 67–68
Affordable Care Act, 48
Afonso, Alexandre, 69; on academic job
    market as drug gang, 70; on internal
    wage structure of drug gang, 69–70
African Americans, 150, 204; educational
    access of, 164–165; faculty and
    administration regarding, 163; ghosts
    of slavery about, 166–167; negative
    stereotypes of, 162; on promoting
    racial understanding, 152; white
    supremacy over, 165–166

AFT. *See* American Federation of
    Teachers
Air Force Academy, 82
Albertine, Susan, 51
Alfred University, 106
Allan, Elizabeth, 110, 111, 112; on
    objectification of women in hazing,
    111–112; study of hazing by, 109–110
Allen, Jeanie, 135
Allen, Walter, 155
"Alone in the Ivory Tower: How Birth
    Events Vary Among Fast-Track
    Professionals" (Mason, Goulden and
    Wolfinger), 146
Alonso, Carlos: on commodification, 181;
    on culture of accountability, 181
Alpha Tau Omega, 113
Altbach, Philip G., 21, 32, 160–161
America Competes Act, 6
American Association of Universities, 43
American Association of University
    Professors, 32, 42, 77
*The American College and University: A
    History* (Rudolph), 24
American Council on Education, 152
American Enterprise Institute, 74
American Federation of Teachers (AFT):
    adjunct faculty surveys of, 44–45, 46;
    concerns in report by, 45; summary
    insights of, 44–45
American Missionary Association, 165
American Public University, 194
American Revolution, 100
Amherst College, 102, 109
Anderson, L. V., 50
Anderson, Martin, 59
Animal House, 102
"Animal House on Steroids" (Leonard
    and King), 120
Ariely, Dan, 92
Aristotle, 14, 147; on common good, 66;
    on friendship, 54
Armstrong, Elizabeth A., 120
Arnold, James, 108–109
Asians, 153; racial misunderstandings of,
    162; university difficulties of, 159–160,
    161–162
Associated Press, 121

Association of American Medical
    Colleges, 149
Association of American Universities, 200
athletics, 2, 208–210, 210–211, 211,
    212–213; academic abuses in, 5–6;
    health of, 211; parasitic structure of,
    211; reforms of, 211–212; scandals in,
    211
The Atlantic Monthly, 70, 119
"At the Ivies, It's Still White at the Top"
    (Patton), 170
Ayers, Rick, 196, 199

Baker, Katie, 113–114
Barres, Ben, 139–140, 140
Bastedo, Michael N., 209
Becker, Lisa Liberty, 37, 39–40, 48
*Beer and Circus: How Big-Time College
    Sports Is Crippling Undergraduate
    Education* (Sperber), 97
Beloved (Morrison), 166
*Benefiting Whom? For-Profit Education
    Companies and the Growth of Military
    Education Benefits* (GAO), 191–192
Berea College, 164
Berg, Haley, 212–213
Berrett, Dan, 4; on Barres, 139–140; on
    for-profit colleges, 192
Bérubé, Michael, 200
*Beyond the Ivory Tower: Social
    Responsibilities of the Modern
    University* (Bok), 23
Bishop, Amy, 28
"Black Female Faculty and Professional
    Socialization" (Sulé), 135
Blattman, Mark, 71
Bloomberg News, 105
Blumenstyk, Goldie, 191, 194–195
Bok, Derek, 23, 28, 163; on adjunct
    faculty, 38–39, 41; on moral
    development, 97, 124; on research,
    42–43, 44; on teaching, 42
*A Bold Plan for Reforming Our Colleges
    and Universities* (Taylor), 29
Boldt, Josh, 53, 199
Boston Globe, 1–2, 87–88
Boston University, 99, 105, 211
Bottomly, H. Kim, 132

Bousquet, Marc, 138, 139; on tenured faculty women, 138; on women in business administration, 138
Bowers, William, 82, 86
Bracken, Susan, 135
Brainstorm blog, 179
Branch, Taylor, 211, 213
Brandt-Sarif, Trevor, 81
Broken Pledges: The Deadly Rite of Hazing (Nuwer), 106
Brown University, 151, 167–168, 216
Brown University Steering Committee on Slavery and Justice report, 167, 214
Bush, George W., 6
business ethics, 4
business schools. *See* for-profit universities
"Bust the Amateur Myth" (Duford), 212
bzemsky bzemsky, 179–180, 181

Cahn, Steven, 22, 33–34, 35, 37–38, 128, 182, 206
The Campus Climate: A Chilly One for Women? (Hall and Sandler), 133
The Campus Climate Revisited: Chilly for Women Faculty, Administrators, and Graduate Student (Hall and Sandler), 133
Campus Life: Undergraduate Cultures from the End of the Eighteenth Century to the Present (Horowitz), 25, 92, 100, 116
campus rebels, 104, 105, 111, 126
Campus Rules and Moral Community: In Place of Loco Parentis (Hokema), 237n1
Campus Sexual Assault Study, 244n91
Career Education Corporation, 191
Carlson, Scott, 199
Carnegie Foundation, 43
Carnegie Mellon University, 77
Carnevale, Anthony P., 209, 210
Casey, Janet, 47, 55
caste system metaphor, 2–3, 71, 72–73, 74–77; Eisenberg on, 71–72; Fergusson on, 74; *Georgetown Public Policy Review* on, 74
Catholic Scholars for Worker Justice, 50

Catholic Theological Society of America, 57
Catholic University of America, 123
Catholic University of Ireland, 22
The Cavalier Daily, 86
CAW. *See* Coalition on the Academic Workforce
Cayton, Mary Kupiec, 173, 176, 179, 182, 185, 198; on government interventions, 176; on outsourcing of staff, 176; on saleable education, 177; on standardization, 175–176
Center for the Study of Higher and Postsecondary Education, University of Michigan, 209
The Challenge and Promise of a Catholic University (Hesburgh), 23
Champion, Robert, 2
Chang, Kenneth, 140, 141
Chapman University, 188
"The Cheater's High: The Unexpected Affective Benefits of Unethical Behavior" (Ruedy), 90
CheatHouse.com, 84
cheating, 95, 203; administrator indifference to, 84; faculty opinions on, 83–85; Harvard scandal on, 82, 87–88, 118; honor codes and university culture, 86–87; insights about, 81; McCabe and Trevino on, 81–82; *New York Times* on, 82–83, 88, 91; peer pressure in, 82, 91, 91–92; Pérez-Peña on, 82–83, 83; as pervasive, 82–83; plagiarism, 84–85, 93–94; Ruedy on, 90, 91; Schneider on, 83–84; thrill of, 90–92; unclear instructions on, 89
Cheating Lessons: Learning from Academic Dishonesty (Lang), 92
Cheyney University of Pennsylvania, 165
Chiu, William, 143, 144
Chronicle of Higher Education, 6, 63, 72, 76, 77, 146, 220n16; "A Minority Report" in, 169; on caste system in India, 2–3; commodification letter in, 85; on departments, 65; on diversity, 170; Dzeich interviewed by, 127; "Faculty Reps Botch Sports-Oversight Role" in, 5; on federal initiatives, 208–209; on for-profit universities,

191, 193–194; *Gender Issue* of, 137; honor code article in, 87; on racially themed parties, 114; research on Kappa Beta Phi, 119; as scandal sheet, 3–4; Schneider essay on cheating in, 83–84; on sports, 212; "Women and Minorities Lag in Appointments to Top Fund- Raising Jobs" essay in, 139; "Women Are Still Underrepresented as Medical School Deans, Study Finds" article in, 149

"Class Warfare" (Becker), 48

Clayton-Pedersen, Alma, 155

Clemson University, 89, 114

climate, campus, 214; chilly regarding women, 133–137; of international students, 158; women of color experience of, 135–136

CNN, 49

Coalition on the Academic Workforce (CAW), 46

cognitive elites, 74–75

Cohen, Michael, 68

"College Becoming the New Caste System" (Fergusson), 74

"Colleges Become the Victims of Progressivism" (Will), 129–130

"Colleges' Prestige Doesn't Guarantee a Top Flight Learning Experience" (Berrett), 4

College: What It Was, Is and Should Be (Delbanco), 29–30

"Collegiality as a Moral and Ethical Practice" (Copeland), 58

"A Collegiate Dilemma: The Lack of Formal Training in Ethics for Professors" (Klein), 32

Columbia University, 71, 168

Coming Apart (Murray), 74

commodification, 85, 87–88, 89–90, 93, 205–206; accountability debate in, 180–182; adjunct faculty as, 173; Alonso on, 181; Boldt on, 199; bzemsky blogger on, 179–180; Cayton on, 175–176; ethics in, 182–185; faculty concerns in, 185; for-profit universities in, 191–195; international student recruitment as, 173; introductions to, 175–180; letter on,

85; limits to, 181, 183; mission of higher education on, 186–190; Radder on, 178; Radin and Sunder on humanity and, 183–184; sale of education in, 198; university as corporate business, 173–175; in university culture, 195–200; university history of, 174–175; Vedder on, 180

The Commodification of Academic Research: Science and the Modern University (Radder), 177

"The Commodification of Wisdom" (Cayton), 175–176

"Conquistadors and Aztec Hoes" theme, 112–113

Contested Commodities: The Trouble with Trade in Sex, Children, Body Parts, and Other Things (Radin), 183

contingent teachers, 72. *See also* adjunct faculty

Copeland, M. Shawn, 58, 166–167

Corinthian College, 194

Cornell University, 5, 103, 104, 109

"The Corruption of Ethics in Higher Education" (Heyneman), 2

Council for the Advancement and Support of Education, 207

Council of Graduate Schools, 70

Crisis on Campus: Confronting Academic Misconduct (Decoo), 31–32

critical race theory (CRT), 115, 166

Curren, Randall, 31

Dalits, 3

Dartmouth College, 5, 114, 123, 168

"Data Show Extent of Sexism in Physics" article, 138

Davis Museum, 130–131

Day, Michael, 64

Dean, Diane, 135

Decoo, Wilfried, 31–32, 93–94

"The Deepening Caste System in Higher Education" (Kitch), 72–73

Delbanco, Andrew, 29–30, 94; on adjunct faculty, 39; on plagiarism, 84–85

Delphi Project, 50, 52, 56, 214, 229n51; on adjuncts, 66; five guidelines of, 51–52

"The Delphi Project on Changing Faculty and Student Success" (Kezar, Albertine and Maxey), 51
Delta Cost Project, 120
Delta Upsilon fraternity, 112
Democratic Staff Report of the House Committee on Education and the Workforce, 49
Department of Education, 137, 189, 194
Department of Education Office for Civil Rights, 123
Deresiewicz, William, 198; on educational values, 198; on inequality, 197–198; on Ivy League schools, 197; on sales pitch about status, 198
De Russy, Candace, 32
"Despite Efforts to Close Gender Gaps, Some Disciplines Remain Lopsided" (Mangan), 137
"Developing Human Capacity: The Rationale for Leadership Diversity" (Smith, D.), 151
development, 206, 206–207
DeVry, 194
diversity: among faculty, 169–172; future face of, 156–163; in leadership, 151–152; in learning environment, 155–156; mixing students together assumption in, 153; multicultural course requirements as, 153, 157, 163; negative influence of fraternities and sororities on, 154; Nivet on inclusion and, 149–150; Pascarella institutional policies in, 154–155; in student population, 151; universities on matters of, 152–156; U. S. Census Bureau report on, 156–157; Vaccaro on, 134
Diversity's Promise for Higher Education: Making it Work (Smith, D.), 150
"Do Babies Matter?" (Mason and Goulden), 144
Do Babies Matter? Gender and Family in the Ivory Tower (Mason, Goulden and Wolfinger), 145
Donoghue, Frank, 192
Doti, James, 188
Douglass, Frederick, 165
Dreifus, Claudia, 29, 41

"Drinking to Fit In" (Kim), 118
drug gang metaphor, 69, 70–71; academic job market as, 70; internal wage structure of, 69–70
DuBois, W. E. B., 165
Duford, Frank, 212
Duke University, 114, 211, 242n71–243n72
Duquesne University, 49, 50, 199
Dwight, Timothy, 41
Dzeich, Billie Wright, 127–128, 130

Ebony & Ivy: Race, Slavery, and the Troubled History of America's Universities (Wilder), 168
Eisenberg, Pablo: on adjuncts and CEO salaries, 72; on budgets and public officials, 77; caste system metaphor by, 71–72; on class divide, 76; on solidarity between students and workers, 75–76, 76–77, 77; on university staff, 75–76
Eisenberg, Paul D., 94
Eliot, Charles, 23
elite colleges, 209, 210
Elon University, North Carolina, 187
The Emergence of the American University (Veysey), 23, 25
Emory University, 123
"Enacting Diverse Learning Environments: Improving the Climate for Racial/Ethnic Diversity in Higher Education" study (Hurtado), 155–156
Encyclopedia Britannica, 53
Enfleshing Freedom: Body, Race and Being (Copeland), 166
ethical accountability, 13
The Ethical Challenges of Academic Administration, 30–31
ethical responsibility, 4
ethics, 201–202, 219n2; as academic discipline, 1, 4; in church ministry, 12–17; in commodification, 182–185; in development, 206, 206–207; lack of, 1, 4, 6–7; in medical profession, 9, 10–12, 16; need for, 7
Excellent Sheep: The Miseducation of the American Elite and the Way to a Meaningful Life (Deresiewicz), 197

faculty, 51; adjunct versus tenure in, 40–42; African Americans knowledge by, 163; Bousquet on, 138; Casey on, 47; caste system in, 71–77; cheating opinions of, 83–85; commodification concerns of, 185; community builders in, 216–217; diversity among, 169–172; drug gang metaphor for, 69–71; ethical proposal for, 53–55; gender topic involvement of, 204; Ginsberg on control of, 68; hazing literature by, 106–112; ignoring of adjuncts by, 39–40; isolationist culture of, 57–62; issue of tenure, 207–208; knowledge of other domains, 63; knowledge of party scene, 98–99; need for student engagement by, 99; old boy networks in, 171–172; plagiarism issues of, 94–95; racially themed parties resources for, 115; research emphasis of, 42–44; sexual assault consciousness raising of, 126, 127–130, 147; as singularly accountable agent, 62; solidarity among adjunct and, 54–56; - student dating, 127–128; students' lives knowledge of, 203; university culture support of, 93; Wilson on, 60–61. *See also* adjunct faculty
Faculty Athletics Representatives Association, 5
"Faculty Reps Botch Sports-Oversight Role" (Chronicle of Higher Education), 5
The Fall of the Faculty: The Rise of the All Administrative University and Why it Matters (Ginsberg), 67
Farley, Margaret, 99
Faust, Drew Gilpin, 89
"Fear and Loathing at Wellesley" (Skenazy), 131–132
Fergusson, Niall: on caste system, 74; on cognitive elites, 74–75
Fermilab, 139
fiefdoms: accountability in, 64; departments as part of, 64–65; feudal lord administrators in, 67–68; relationality in, 65–66; in student affairs, 65; term use of, 64; as trademark, 64; university as, 64–68

Field, Kelly, 192
Finder, Alan, 48–49
Finneran, Tom, 131
"First Year Commodity: The Adjunct Professor Labor Crisis in Composition Departments" (Boldt), 199
Fischman, Lisa, 132
Fishman, Teddi, 89–90
Fisk University, 189
Flaherty, Colleen, 145
Flanagan, Caitlin, 105, 119; on fraternities, 116, 243n83–244n84; on university ethical backbone, 116–117
Florida A&M University, 2
Foreman, Deborah, 54
"For-Profit Colleges and Universities: America's Least Costly and Most Efficient System of Higher Education" (University of Phoenix), 192
For-Profit Higher Education: The Failure to Safeguard the Federal Investment and Ensure Student Success (Harkin), 193
for-profit universities (business schools), 191–195
Francis, Leslie Pickering, 128
Franklin College, Indiana, 106
Franklin Seminary, Kentucky, 109
fraternities, 97; birth of, 102–103; corporate world relationships with, 119; diversity negative influence of, 154; Flanagan on, 105, 243n83–244n84; hazing articles on, 105–106; insurance policies on, 119; predatory capacities of, 118; racially themed parties at, 112–115; universities legacy of, 116–121
"Frats in Trouble for Sexist, Racist Parties" (Hawley), 112
Frederick, Wayne A. J., 190
Freedmen's Bureau, 165
Freitas, Donna, 99
Freyd, Jennifer, 133

Gadsen, Gloria, 169
GAO. *See* Government Accounting Office
"A Garbage Can Model of Organizational Choice" (Cohen and March), 68
Garcia, Gina, 114–115

Gareis, Elisabeth, 160
gender: campus rebels on, 126; Mason
    and Goulden on, 144–146; studies and
    reports on inequity of, 137–142; topic
    involvement of faculty, 204
Georgetown Public Policy Institute, 71
Georgetown Public Policy Review, 74
Georgetown University, 75, 77
Georgetown University's Center on
    Education and the Workforce, 209
"Getting Nowhere Fast: The Lack of
    Gender Equity in the Physiology
    Community" (Gordon), 141
"Gilded Goodbyes" (Kitch), 73
Gillborn, David, 166
Ginsberg, Benjamin, 57; on faculty
    control, 68; on rise of administrators,
    67–68
Glovin, David, 105
*Going Broke by Degree: Why College
    Costs Too Much* (Vedder), 180
Golding, William, 102
Go Local Worcester, 131
Gordon, Sharona E., 141–142
Goulden, Marc, 144–146
Government Accounting Office (GAO),
    191–192
"Graduates of For-Profits Lag Behind
    Their Peers in Earnings and
    Employment" (Berrett), 192
Grafton, Anthony, 30
"Great Stratification" (Williams), 77–78
greekthink, 107–108
Grinnell College, 188
"Groupthink" (Janis), 107
Guttman, Amy, 151, 170

Habitat for Humanity, 55
Hacker, Andrew, 29, 41
Hall, Roberta, 133–134
Hamden-Sydney College, 87
Hamilton, Laura T., 120
Hamilton, Neil, 32
Handelsman, Jo, 141
"Hard Times at Howard U" (Hunter-
    Gault), 189
Harkin, Tom, 191, 193, 194
"Harmless Pranks or Brutal Practices?
    Hazing at the University of Illinois,

1868–1913" (Solberg), 106
Harrington, Charles F., 49
Harrington, Rebecca, 88
Harvard Crimson, 83, 88, 89
Harvard University, 1–2, 23, 41, 67, 75,
    90; cheating scandal at, 82, 87–88, 118;
    honor code resistance in, 88; Markus
    on integrity of, 89; Title IX
    investigations at, 123
Hawley, Jacob, 112
hazing, 97; Allan study of, 109–110;
    Arnold on, 108; articles on, 105–106;
    faculty literature on, 106–112;
    Flanagan on, 105; greekthink in,
    107–108; groupthink in, 107;
    homophobia in, 111–112; Nuwer on,
    106–108, 109; objectification of
    women in, 111–112; as part of
    university culture, 105–112; Sheldon
    on, 106; Solberg on, 106; student
    deaths related to, 109; student issues
    about, 110–111
"Hazing and Alcohol in a College
    Fraternity" (Arnold), 108
"Hazing and Gender: Analyzing the
    Obvious" (Allan), 111
"Hazing in View: College Students at
    Risk: Initial Findings from the
    National Study of Student Hazing"
    (Allan), 109–110
The Hazing Reader (Nuwer), 107
HBCUs. See historically Black colleges
    and universities
Hechinger, John, 105
Hesburgh, Theodore M., 23
Heyneman, Stephen, 1, 2
Higher Ed Morning, 112
*Higher Education? How Colleges Are
    Wasting Our Money and Failing Our
    Kids: What We Can Do About It*
    (Hacker and Dreifus), 29
Higher Education in America (Bok), 23
"Higher Education's New Caste System"
    forum, 75
Hispanic, 118, 153, 156, 204
historically Black colleges and universities
    (HBCUs), 189
history: college social structure, 100–105;
    of race at university, 164–168;

university commodification, 174–175; of university culture, 99–105; university literature, 24–28

A History of American Higher Education (Thelin), 25

Hockfield, Susan, 152

Hoffman, Jan, 91

Hofstra University, 49

Hogshead-Makar, Nancy, 201, 212

Hokema, David, 237n1

honor codes, 86, 87, 95, 205; McCabe on, 86–87, 235n14; resistance of, 88

Hopkins, Nancy, 125

Horowitz, Helen Lefkowitz, 25, 92–93, 98, 108, 116; on campus rebels, 104, 105, 111, 126; on "college men", 101–102, 118; on history of college social structure, 100–105; on outsiders, 103–104

House Education and the Workforce Committee, 53

"How Academia Resembles a Drug Gang" (Afonso), 69

Howard-Hamilton, Mary, 135

Howard University, 189, 189–190

"How Hard Would It Be for Avian Flu to Spread?" article, 2

"How Should Big-Time College Sports Change" (Wolverton), 211–212

"How Stereotypes Impair Women's Careers in Science" study, 141

How the University Works: Higher Education and the Low Wage Nation (Bousquet), 138

The Huffington Post, 76

humanities, 1, 7, 60, 99, 144

Hune, Shirley, 135

Hunter-Gault, Charlayne, 189; on enrollment in HBCUs, 187; on financial issues, 189–190

Hurtado, Sylvia, 155, 156

Idea of a University (Newman), 22

"I'm not Racist, but" (Redden), 159–160

"The Impact of Cross-Cultural Interactions on Medical Students' Preparedness to Care for Diverse Patients" study, 149

"Impasse and Theological Ethics" presentation, 57–58

I'm Shmacked, 98, 120, 237n3–238n4

The Independent, 64

Indiana University–Purdue University Indianapolis, 5, 113

"Influences on Students' Openness to Diversity and Challenge in the First Year of College" study (Pascarella), 154

"Initiating Change: Transforming a Hazing Culture" (Allan and Iverson), 110

Inside Higher Education, 51, 52, 69, 145, 146, 152, 177–179

Institute for Higher Education Policy, 192

Institute for International Education, 158

International Center for Academic Integrity, Clemson University, 89

international students, 205; Altbach on recruitment of, 160–161; campus climate of, 158; Chinese student enrollment, 158; difficulties of, 159–160; recruitment of, 158–159, 173

"In the Humanities, Men Dominate the Fields of Philosophy and History" (Mangan), 137

"Is Biology Just Another Pink-Collar Profession?"(Zuk and O'Rourke), 137–138

isolationist culture, 57–62, 60

Issues in Academic Ethics (Cahn), 34, 128, 206

Iverson, Susan Van Deventer, 110, 111, 112

Ivory Power: Sexual Harassment on Campus (Paludi), 128

James, William, 23–24, 88–89, 91

Janis, Irving, 107

Jaschik, Scott, 69, 149, 152–153, 177

Jezebel, 113

Johns Hopkins University, 114

Johnson, J. Q., 133

Johnston, Marc, 114–115

Jonsen, Albert R., 221n7

Journal of Academic Ethics, 3, 33

Journal of General Physiology, 141

Journal of Personality and Social Psychology, 90
Just Love (Farley), 99

Kansas State University, 86
Kaplan, 194
Kappa Alpha Society, 116
Kappa Beta Phi, 119
Kekes, John, 32
Keller, George, 195; on comparative advantage and strategic planning, 186–187; organizational model of, 186–188
Kendzior, Sarah, 46, 47
Kent State, 110
Kerkvliet, Jon, 84
Kezar, Adrianna, 51
Kim, Walter, 118
Kimball, Bruce, 95
King, Richard C., 120, 120–121
King's College London, 69
Kington, Raynard, 188–189
Kitch, Martin, 72; on academy imitation of corporate model, 73; on overpaid university administrators, 73; on publicly funded university, 73
Klein, Jacqueline, 32
Kline, David, 95
Knight Commission on Intercollegiate Athletics, 5
Konnikova, Maria, 119
Kotva, Joseph, 58
Kovalik, Daniel, 49–50
Krueger, Scott, 118

"Lady Academe and Labor-Market Segmentation: The Narrative of Women's Success via Higher Education Rests on a House of Cards" (Bousquet), 138
Lambert, Leo, 187–188
Lang, James M., 92, 93
Larrabee, Catherine, 112
La Sapienza University, 64
The Lecherous Professor: Sexual Harassment on Campus (Dzeich and Weiner), 127, 128
Lee, Jenny, 159
legal ethics, 1, 4

Leonard, David J., 120, 120–121
"Lessons from For-Profit Institutions about Cutting College Costs" (Blumenstyk), 191
Levy, Anita, 41–42
Lewis, David, 94
Lincoln University, Pennsylvania, 165
London School of Economics, 69
Lord of the Flies (Golding), 102
Lynch, Barbara, 49
Lynn University, Florida, 188

Maisto, Maria, 48, 52, 53
The Making of the Modern University: Intellectual Transformation and the Marginalization of Morality (Reuben), 25
Mangan, Katherine, 137
March, James, 68
Marcus, Jon, 82, 89; on Harvard integrity, 89; on Yale, 89
Maricopa Community Colleges, 89
Mason, Mary Ann, 144–146
Massachusetts Institute of Technology (MIT), 139–140, 152, 168
Massingale, Bryan, 167
Matelli, Tony, 130, 131, 132
Maxey, Dan, 51
McCabe, Donald, 81–82, 83, 86–87, 235n14
McCaskill, Claire, 123, 125
McClay, William, 186, 195; on 80's education, 186; on Keller strategies, 187
medical ethics, 1, 4, 9, 10, 11, 16; collective wisdom in, 10, 11; confidences question in, 10; information questions in, 10; patient consent in, 11; physicians and ethicists in dialogue about, 10–11, 12. *See also* nursing ethics
Meeks, Wayne, 9, 14, 172
Milem, Jeffrey, 155
ministry profession: accountability in, 13, 15–16; Christian ethics courses in, 15; corporate responsibility in, 16–17; ethics role in, 12–17; sex abuse crisis of, 12–13, 27
"A Minority Report" (Gadsen), 169

MIT. *See* Massachusetts Institute of
    Technology
Mitzenmacher, Michael, 88
Modern Language Association (MLA),
    200
The Monist, 32
Monroe, Kristen Renwick, 143, 144
Moon, Harvest, 48
*Morality, Responsibility, and the
    University: Studies in Academic Ethics*
    (Cahn), 34, 37
Moral Problems in Higher Education
    (Cahn), 34, 37
"More Low-Income Students Begin at
    For-Profits" (Donoghue), 192
Moreno, Jonathan, 28
Morrill Land-Grant Act of 1862, 165
Morrill Land-Grant Act of 1890, 165
Morrison, Toni, 166
Moses, Yolanda, 136
Moss-Racusin, Corinne, 141
Mount Holyoke College, 86
Mulford, Martin, 261n53–261n54
Murray, Charles, 74

National American University, 194
National Consumer Law Center, 191
National Institute of Justice, 244n91
National Labor Relations Board, 67
National Public Radio, 168
National Science Foundation (NSF), 6
National Study of Black College Students,
    256n42
Nature, 138
New American Foundation, 75
New Faculty Majority (NFM), 48, 51, 52,
    56, 72, 214; on adjunct faculty, 52–53;
    mission statement of, 52
Newman, John Henry, 22
New Republic, 197
New York Review of Books, 29
New York Times, 2, 28, 29, 48, 49, 113,
    209; on Berg, 212–213; on cheating,
    82–83, 88, 91; rape reporting article in,
    125, 130; on "Sleepwalker", 131; social
    pressure article in, 118; on women in
    university leadership, 151; Yale
    research study in, 140
NFM. *See* New Faculty Majority

Nichols, Andrew, 136
Nicomachean Ethics (Aristotle), 147
1984 (Orwell), 107
Nivet, Marc: on diversity and inclusion,
    149–150; on fundamental inequities,
    150
Northwestern University, 41
Notalone.gov, 123
Notre Dame University, 23
NSF. *See* National Science Foundation
nursing ethics, 1, 4; primary loyalty in, 11,
    16; responsibilities in, 11
Nuwer, Hank, 106–108, 109, 112

Obama, Barack, 75, 188; affordable
    college education plan of, 208; pay-for-
    performance model initiative of, 188
O'Bannon ruling, 212
Oberlin College, 103, 164
Oberlin's Alumni Association of African
    Ancestry, 164
Ohio University, 120
"On the Dark Side: Lessons Learned as
    Interim Dean" (Werner), 31
O'Rourke, Sheila, 137–138
Orwell, George, 107
*Our Underachieving Colleges: A Candid
    Look at How Much Students Learn
    and Why They Should Be Learning
    More* (Bok), 23
*Out of the Classroom: A Chilly Campus
    Climate for Women?* (Hall and
    Sandler), 133
outsiders, 38–39, 103–104

Paludi, Michele, 128
Pascarella, Ernest T., 153, 154, 154–155
Patton, Stacey, 170
*Paying for the Party: How College
    Maintains Inequality* (Armstrong and
    Hamilton, L.), 120
"Pedo Parties' and Racist Ragers: Why are
    Frat Bros Fixated on Fucked up
    Theme Parties" (Baker), 113
Penn State (Pennsylvania State
    University), 2, 181
Perez, Erica, 142
Pérez-Peña, Richard, 82–83, 83; on elite
    colleges, 209; on low-income students,

209–210; on rankings, 210
Perry, Bliss, 41
Petillo, John, 188
"The Ph.D. Octopus" (James), 24
pipeline, 142–146
Pittsburgh Gazette, 49
plagiarism, 84–85, 93–95
Polytechnic University, 49
Poon, Oiyan, 135
Popper, Nathaniel, 212–213
Presumed Incompetent: The Intersections for Race and Class for Women in Academia, 169–170
Princeton University, 118, 123, 147, 151, 152, 168
"Professional Role Confidence and Gendered Persistence in Engineering" study, 142
Project on the Status and Education of Women of the Association of American Colleges, 133

Quaye, Stephen John, 136

racially themed parties, 97, 112; Baker on, 113–114; *Chronicle of Higher Education on*, 114; faculty resources for, 115; at fraternities, 112–115; Garcia and Johnston on, 114–115; student thoughts on, 113, 114. *See also* school party scene
"Racial Themed Parties Draw Fury on Campuses across the Country" (Chronicle of Higher Education), 114
Radder, Hans, 177, 179, 182, 185, 199; on commodification in science department, 178; ethical standards call of, 179; on function of research, 178–179; *Inside Higher Education* interview of, 177–179
Radin, Margaret, 183–184
Ramis, Harold, 102
rape (sexual violence), 97; faculty consciousness raising about, 126, 127–130, 147; reporting of, 125–126; Sleepwalker statue controversy regarding, 130–133; Title IX investigations of, 123–124; in university culture, 121–124; use of

power in, 121; White House Council on Women and Girls report on, 121–122, 122–123, 125, 129, 214
Rape and Sexual Assault: A Renewed Call to Action report (White House Council on Women and Girls), 121–122, 122–123, 125, 129, 214
Raymo, Judith Glazer, 128
Redden, Elizabeth, 159–160
"References on Chilly Climate for Women Faculty in Academe" (Freyd and Johnson), 133
"Reporting Rape, and Wishing She Hadn't: How One College Handled a Sexual Assault Complaint" article, 125
Report of the Steering Committee on Undergraduate Women's Leadership (Tilghman), 147
A Report on the Status of Women Faculty in the Schools of Science and Engineering at MIT, 140
research, 2, 119, 140; Bok on, 42–43, 44; faculty emphasis on, 42–44; NSF plan in, 6; Radder on function of, 178–179; Reuben on, 43–44
Research Works Act, 200
Reuben, Julie, 25–26, 27, 29, 43–44, 62, 98
Rhoades, Gary, 50
Rice, Charles, 159
Ritter, Zach, 162
Rockefeller Foundation, 43
Rodin, Judith, 151
Rolling Stone, 3
Roman Catholic Church, 12
Rooksby, Jacob H., 199–200
Rosovsky, Henry, 67
Ross, Kevin, 188
Rowman & Littlefield, 34
RTI International, 244n91
Rude, Jesse, 153
Rudolph, Frederick, 24, 25
"Rudolph Rediscovered" (Thelin), 25
Ruedy, Nicole, 90, 91

Sacred Heart University, Connecticut, 188
Saints and Scamps: Ethics in the Academy (Cahn), 33–34, 37

Sandel, Michael, 184

Sandler, Bernice, 133–134

Satz, Debra, 184, 185

Schneider, Alison, 83–84, 85

school party scene, 98; faculty knowledge of, 98–99; *I'm Shmacked* involvement in, 98, 120, 237n3–238n4; Leonard and King on, 120, 120–121; need for student engagement about, 99; racially themed in, 112–115; student affairs in, 98

"Science Faculty's Subtle Gender Biases Favor Male Students" (Moss-Racusin), 140–141

Scriven, Michael, 32

SEIU. *See* Service Employees International Union

Senate Health, Education, Labor and Pensions Committee, 191, 193

"Senate Report Paints a Damning Portrait of For- Profit Higher Education" (Stratford), 193

Senate Subcommittee on Financial and Contracting Oversight, 123

"Separate and Unequal: How Higher Education Reinforces the Intergenerational Reproduction of White Racial Privilege" (Carnevale and Strohl), 210

Service Employees International Union (SEIU), 48

Sex and the Soul: Juggling Sexuality, Spirituality, Romance, and Religion on American College Campuses (Freitas), 99

Sexual Harassment as an Ethical Issue in Academic Life (Francis), 128

Sexual Harassment on College Campuses: Abusing the Ivory Power (Paludi), 128

sexual violence. *See* rape

The Shame of College Sports (Branch), 211

Sheldon, Henry Davidson, 106, 240n42

Sher, George, 94

Simmons, Ruth J., 151, 167, 171, 216

Skenazy, Leonore, 131–132, 132

Slate, 50

"Sleepwalker", 130–133

Smith, Charles Hugh, 64

Smith, Daryl G., 150–151

Smith College, 86, 151

The Social Organization of Work (Sullivan), 61

Solberg, Winton, 106

solidarity, 54–56, 58; Eisenberg on, 75–76, 76–77, 77; university lack of, 59

"Song of the Cheaters" (Harrington, R.), 88

sororities, 104, 116, 118, 154. *See also* fraternities

Southern Methodist University, 123

special snowflake syndrome, 71

Sperber, Michael, 97

Standing on the Outside Looking In (Howard-Hamilton), 135

Stanford University, 75, 183

Stenzel, Chuck, 106, 109

StopHazing.org, 110

"Stop Looking for the Treasure Map, and Start Laying Bricks" (Boldt), 53

Stratford, Michael, 193, 194; on for-profit college expenditures, 193; on retention in for-profit colleges, 193

Strohl, Jeff, 210

"A Student Centered NCAA" (Wolverton), 211

Student Life and Customs (Sheldon), 106, 240n42

students: deaths related to hazing of, 109; diversity in population of, 151; -faculty dating, 127–128; faculty engagement need for, 99; faculty knowledge of lives of, 203; issues about hazing, 110–111; mixing together assumption in diversity, 153; Pérez-Peña on low-income, 209–210; racially themed parties thoughts of, 113, 114; solidarity between workers and, 75–76, 76–77, 77

"Studies Find More Students Cheating, With High Achievers No Exception" (Pérez-Peña), 82–83

Stuyvesant High School, 82

"The Subject and Object of Commodification" (Sunder and Radin), 183

Sulé, Venice, 135

Sullivan, Theresa, 61

Sunder, Madhavi, 183–184

Take Back the Night Foundation, 126
Taylor, Mark C., 29
Thelin, John, 25
Thier, Samuel O., 60
Thomason, Andy, 3
"Tie Money to Values" (Hogshead-Makar), 212
Tilghman, Shirley M., 147, 151, 152, 171
Times Higher Education, 89
Title IX, 123–124, 129, 211
Tomar, Dave, 235n11
"To What Extent Should the University Investigator Be Relieved from Teaching?" conference session, 43
trademark registrations, 199–200
Trevino, Linda Klebe, 81–82
"The Truth, the Whole Truth and Nothing but the Truth" (Eisenberg, Paul), 94

UCLA. *See* University of California, Los Angeles
UNC. *See* University of North Carolina
unethical practices: at American universities, 2; at universities worldwide, 2–3
Union College, 116
United Negro College Fund, 189, 190
United Steelworkers Union, 49
Universities in the Marketplace: The Commercialization of Higher Education (Bok), 23
university: academic publishing in, 59; bureaucracy of, 66; caste system in, 71–77; commodification and mission of, 186–190; contrast partnership or teamwork with, 58–59; as corporate business, 173–175; on diversity matters, 152–156; drug gang metaphor in, 69–71; ethical standards resistance of, 117; ethical structure needs of, 78–79; as fiefdoms, 64–68; for-profit, 191–195; future face of diversity in, 156–163; history of race at, 164–168, 204; isolationist culture of, 57–62; Kitch on publicly funded, 73; lack of solidarity in, 59; market strategies

influencing, 190; mission of, as first priority, 197; office hours in, 61–62; as organized anarchies, 68; as president of, 213–217; published ideas and personal practices, 61; racism in, 169–172, 204; social landscape of, 62–63; structure and geography of, 63; studies and reports on gender inequity in, 137–142; three foundational insights about, 57; writing style in, 59
university culture, 81, 84, 203; academic integrity in, 86, 87, 92–95; American Revolution in, 100; birth of fraternities in, 102–103; without code, 87–90; commodification in, 195–200; dormitories and drinking as, 207; faculty support of, 93; fraternity legacy in, 116–121; fundamental inequities in, 150–152; hazing as part of, 105–112; history of, 99–105; honor codes as, 86–87; outsiders in, 103–104; racially themed parties in, 112–115; rape in, 121–124; women in, 103–104
university ethics, 207; academic ethics to, 33–35, 206; accountability in, 18; adjunct faculty in, 202–203; class and athletics in, 208–213; corporate identity and structure of, 26–27; Flanagan on, 116–117; lack of books on, 18; obstacles to forming, 17–18; other topics for, 206–208; presumption of, 28
University Ethics Committee (fictitious): climate culture consideration of, 214; ethical flourishment location on campus, 214; ethical violations reporting of, 214; formation of, 213; programs and practices by, 216; promote ethics culture, 215–216; quarterly reports by, 215; reports read by, 214; social and structural issues found by, 214
university literature, 106–112; ethical critique on academic life in, 30–33; four categories of, 21–22; genesis and history of, 24–28; philosophical foundations of, 22–24; public intellectuals critiques on, 28–30
University of Alabama, 2, 28

University of Arizona, 82
University of California, Los Angeles (UCLA), 162
University of California, San Diego, 113
University of California–Berkeley, 71, 144, 200
University of California–Berkeley College of Engineering, 142
University of California–Davis, 2
University of Central Florida, 89
University of Chicago, 112, 123
University of Colorado, 3–4
University of Georgia, 189
University of London, 166
University of Louisiana, 2
University of Maine, 110
University of Miami, 75, 77
University of Michigan, 102, 103, 104, 209
University of Nebraska, Lincoln, 159
University of North Carolina (UNC), 3
University of North Carolina, Pembroke, 49
University of Pennsylvania, 28, 151, 168, 170
University of Phoenix, 192
University of Southern California, 5
University of Texas, 113
University of Virginia (UVA), 3, 61, 86, 117, 123
University of Wisconsin, 2
university staff, 75–76, 76, 176
Unsafe in the Ivory Tower: The Sexual Victimization of College Women, 128
U. S. Census Bureau, 156–157
US News and World Report Rankings, 176, 210
UVA. See University of Virginia
"UVA Temporarily Suspends Fraternities in Response to Rape Allegations" (Young), 3

Vaccaro, Anne Marie, 134, 135, 151, 152; on college women with disabilities, 136–137; on diversity, 134; on lesbian and bisexual women, 136
Vanderbilt University, 86
Van Ummersen, Claire, 135–136
Vedder, Richard K., 120, 180

Veysey, Laurence R., 23, 25, 27, 29, 40–41
Virginia Tech, 6
Voice of the Faithful, 16–17
Vojtko, Margaret Mary, 49–50

wage structure, 69–70
Wall Street Journal, 131, 132
Wang, Annie, 132
Washington, Booker T., 165
Washington and Lee University, 86
Washington Monthly, 75
Washington State University, 120
Weiner, Linda, 127, 128, 129
Weingartner, Rudolph H., 94
Weissmann, Jordan, 70
"Welcome to America? International Student Perceptions of Discrimination" (Lee and Rice), 159
Wellesley College, 86, 130–133
"We're Not Your Colleagues" (Foreman), 54
Werner, Donna, 31
What Money Can't Buy: The Moral Limits of Markets (Sandel), 184
"What the Hell Has Happened to College Sports and What Should We Do about It?" forum, 212
"When Parties Become Racialized: Deconstructing Racially Themed Parties" (Garcia and Johnston), 114–115
White House Council on Women and Girls, 121
"Why Professors Don't Do More to Stop Students Who Cheat?" (Schneider), 83–84
Why Some Things Are Not for Sale: The Moral Limits of the Market (Satz), 184
Wilberforce College, Ohio, 165
Wilder, Craig Steven, 168
Will, George, 129–130
Williams, Jeffrey, 77–78
Williams College, 41, 102
Wills, Eric, 191
Wilson, Robin, 60–61, 146
Wolfinger, Nicholas, 145, 146
Wolniak, Gregory C., 153
Wolverton, Brad, 211–212

women, 146–148, 150; Bousquet on tenured faculty, 138; in business administration, 138; chilly climate regarding, 133–137; with disabilities, 136–137; objectification of , in hazing, 111–112; -of color climate experience, 135–136; pipeline explanation for discrimination against, 142–146; studies and reports on gender inequity of, 137–142; in university culture, 103–104; in university leadership, 151; Vaccaro on lesbian and bisexual, 136; White House Council on Women and Girls report, 121–122, 122–123, 125, 129, 214
"Women and Minorities Lag in Appointments to Top Fund- Raising Jobs" (*Chronicle of Higher Education*), 139
Women in Academic Leadership: Professional Strategies and Personal Choices (Dean, Bracken and Allen, J.), 135
Wrongs of Passage: Fraternities, Sororities, Hazing and Binge Drinking (Nuwer), 106

Yale Daily News, 89
Yale University, 14, 41, 89, 99, 103, 140, 168
Young, Jeffrey R., 3

Zemsky, Robert, 59–60
Zuk, Marlene, 137–138

ABOUT THE AUTHOR

James F. Keenan, SJ, holds the Canisius Chair at Boston College and is director of the Jesuit Institute. He is the author or editor of sixteen books, including *Moral Wisdom: Lessons and Texts from the Catholic Tradition* and *Ethics of the Word: Voices in the Catholic Church Today*.